Be the Architect of Leadership Excellence: Program Your Mind for Unstoppable Success

MASTERING THE ART OF SUSTAINABLE DEVELOPMENT

Dr. Sudip Sinha

ISBN 979-8-89610-355-4

Everyone wants to be successful in life, but can they all achieve it? Every team player wants to win the championship, but is it always possible? Success is about performance at the moment, but that's only the tip of the iceberg. Behind the scenes, there are strategies, hard work, sacrifices, and, most importantly, belief, emotions, and self-talk.

Communicative leadership focuses on what you say to yourself. If you consistently tell yourself, "I am powerful, I am blessed, I am skilful, I am thankful, and I have the strength to achieve my goals," your body, mind, and spirit will align to help you succeed. Your brain's neuroplasticity will help you focus on your goals, boost your actions, and attract success. By regularly practicing and mastering your tasks, you will develop the habits of a champion.

Communicative leadership combines modern management tools and techniques to help you stay mindful, use resources efficiently, communicate effectively, and grow steadily for long-term success.

The question is: What do consistently successful people do differently to achieve positive outcomes in whatever they do? Do they follow a different thinking pattern, have a unique outlook, or communicate in a special way? Is their decision-making process different from that of ordinary people? What is the "X factor" that makes them extraordinary, while others struggle for success in their personal and professional lives?

How do successful people feel when they face setbacks and difficult situations? How do they overcome stressful moments and turn key challenges into opportunities, which becomes their winning edge?

This book will help you understand the guiding principles of consistent success through proven methods. The tools discussed in this book, when practiced regularly, will lead to gradual transformation over time. Success is not achieved overnight; it's not a magic pill. But with regular practice, along with discipline, dedication, devotion, and determination, you can reach your desired destiny and achieve your dreams.

The definition of success is different for each person. Your idea of success may not be the same as your friend's. It's your responsibility to use the tools in your own way to begin your journey toward sustainable growth. You are the one responsible for making improvements in your life. While your guide, parent, mentor, or teacher can influence you, only you can do the work needed to build your "muscles."

Breaking out of your comfort zone, overcoming procrastination, and adopting a "do it now" mindset can lead to remarkable breakthroughs in your life. So, what's stopping you from starting? Why are you hesitating? Let's begin now!

The **architecture of mind programming** refers to the structure and methodology through which individuals intentionally guide, influence, and reprogram their mental processes to improve thought patterns, emotions, behaviours, and ultimately, their life outcomes. Mind programming involves a deliberate process of shaping neural pathways to foster positive thinking, emotional regulation, and effective actions. Below is a breakdown of the key components of the architecture of mind programming:

1. **Input Layer: Information and Sensory Data**

    - **Sensory Input**: Our mind processes external information through sensory channels like sight, sound, touch, taste, and smell. This is the first step where external stimuli impact the mind and influence thought patterns.

    - **Environment**: The environment plays a crucial role in shaping our thoughts and beliefs. Positive or negative environments influence the data entering the mind.

    - **Information Sources**: The books we read, the people we interact with, the media we consume, and the experiences we encounter provide raw input for programming our subconscious.

    Example: A student continuously exposed to success stories of entrepreneurs through books, mentors, and positive environments will start believing in possibilities for personal success.

2. **Processing Layer: Conscious and Subconscious Mind**

    - **Conscious Mind**: The conscious mind is the rational, analytical part of the brain that interprets immediate information. It sets short-term goals, solves problems, and controls logical thinking.

    - **Subconscious Mind**: The subconscious mind, however, is the deeper, emotional part that stores beliefs, habits, and memories. It controls automatic reactions and behaviours based on programming established over time.

    - **Belief System**: The belief system is programmed largely through repetitive experiences, thoughts, and emotions. Positive beliefs lead to positive actions, while limiting beliefs cause mental blocks and negative behaviours.

Example: A corporate leader regularly practicing mindfulness may consciously develop a sense of calm and control in stressful situations, while their subconscious mind helps reinforce this emotional stability over time.

3. **Programming Layer: Techniques and Strategies**

The core techniques of mind programming fall into this layer. These strategies are designed to overwrite negative patterns, reinforce positive behaviour, and rewire the mind for success.

- **Affirmations**: Repeated positive statements that consciously influence the subconscious. For example, affirmations like "I am capable of achieving my goals" can rewire self-doubt into self-confidence.

- **Visualization**: Mentally rehearsing desired outcomes or behaviours creates neural pathways similar to the actual experience. Athletes, for example, use visualization to see themselves succeeding in competition, which enhances performance.

- **Meditation and Mindfulness**: Meditation helps quiet the mind, reduce stress, and create space for conscious, intentional thought patterns. It strengthens focus and emotional regulation.

- **Hypnotherapy**: This technique uses guided relaxation and focused attention to influence the subconscious mind, often to eliminate negative habits or introduce positive change.

- **Neuro-Linguistic Programming (NLP)**: NLP focuses on the connection between neurological processes, language, and behaviour patterns. It aims to "reprogram" the mind to respond more positively to situations.

- **Cognitive Behavioural Therapy (CBT)**: CBT teaches individuals to recognize distorted thinking and to replace negative thought patterns with more constructive ones.

- **Gratitude Practice**: Cultivating gratitude rewires the brain to focus on positive aspects of life, which improves emotional well-being and satisfaction.

Example: An entrepreneur facing financial setbacks uses daily affirmations, visualization of success, and mindfulness techniques to maintain a resilient mindset, helping them persist and ultimately succeed.

4. **Memory and Learning Layer: Neural Pathways and Conditioning**

   - **Neuroplasticity**: The brain's ability to form and reorganize synaptic connections, especially in response to learning or experience, plays a central role in mind programming. Repeated thoughts and behaviours strengthen neural pathways, making them habitual.

   - **Repetition and Conditioning**: The subconscious mind learns through repetition. Consistently practicing positive thoughts, behaviours, and emotions reinforces new neural pathways.

   - **Emotional Anchoring**: Emotional intensity attached to specific experiences can anchor memories in the subconscious. For example, success tied to feelings of gratitude or excitement will anchor that experience as positive in the mind.

   Example: A researcher uses repetition to shift from negative thinking (fear of failure) to positive reinforcement (embracing challenges), which strengthens new, empowering neural connections.

5. **Output Layer: Behavioural Responses and Outcomes**

   - **Behavioural Change**: The ultimate goal of mind programming is to translate new thought patterns into real-world actions. Positive programming results in constructive behaviours, such as resilience, problem-solving, and proactive decision-making.

- **Emotional Intelligence**: Mind programming strengthens emotional regulation, leading to more balanced emotional responses and better social interactions.

- **Success and Well-Being**: The culmination of a reprogrammed mind is seen in the external world through improved relationships, greater success, better health, and an overall sense of well-being.

Example: A project manager who practices mindfulness and positive visualization leads a team effectively through a crisis by maintaining emotional stability and decision-making clarity, resulting in project success.

Summary of the Architecture:

1. **Input Layer**: Sensory data, environment, and information shape initial thought patterns.

2. **Processing Layer**: Conscious and subconscious minds interpret and store beliefs, driving actions.

3. **Programming Layer**: Techniques like affirmations, visualization, meditation, and NLP rewrite mental patterns.

4. **Memory and Learning Layer**: Repetition and neuroplasticity reinforce new behaviours and habits.

5. **Output Layer**: Behavioural responses manifest in success, emotional control, and improved outcomes.

By understanding this architecture, individuals can intentionally reprogram their minds for greater emotional control, confidence, and success in all aspects of life. Through consistent practice of these techniques, anyone can reshape their mental habits and create a lasting, positive impact on their personal and professional journeys.

Take one A4 size blank paper, 2 pencils of different outside colors, 2 erasers in different colors and 2 sharpeners in different colors. Find a comfortable place and put the objects on top of A4 size paper. Drink half a glass of water. Sit quiet. Take a few slow deep breaths and try to focus on the A4 size paper, erasers, sharpeners and pencils. Do you have any observations? Think of focusing on them and try to identify 5 observations that you have now. Keep your other thoughts away for now and keep on focusing on the objects and trying to observe 5 unique things?

Pencil: If you put your focus on the pencil then you will find that whatever you write can be erased so even if you make a mistake, you have a chance to rectify it. When the pencil is not pointed enough you need to sharpen it to write it again smoothly. If the pencil falls and breaks into two pieces then you and sharp again 4 sides so instead of writing only in one side, you have more opportunities to keep on writing for long. It is problem-solving mindset development focusing on the solution rather than blaming on the problem. It is a great collaboration opportunity between pencil eraser, sharper together to have harmony in your writing journey. If sharper or eraser don't do their work properly, can you write seamlessly? Simple answer is "No". When the pencil is sharpened, with the wooden object coming out you can decorate creative art to create wow! Pencil helps us learn from mistakes and create good imprint marking on the piece of paper. With the pencil you can write what is important for you, it is an inside out process. Even if the pencils has got multiple colors, the key purpose is the same keep on writing and design your blueprint of success.

Is your observation and though similar to the above? How many points are matching?

Eraser: Eraser provide us the conscious awareness that it is OK to do mistake, it can be erased. But multiple mistakes can not be erased easily. There will be imprint of older failures if we don't learn from it and take action from them. Earer helps to clear up older traces and gives us opportunities to write again by undoing things and redoing afresh. So nothing to be blamed on darkness can be cleanup, we need to keep patience until it is clear to write or draw again.

Sharpener: The key objective of the Sharpener is to sharpen the pencil. Even it is hurting and painful process, pencil has to go through it to rejuvenate again for writing efficiently. It gives the pointed needles for harmonized learning experience.

Is your observation and though similar to the above? How many points are matching?

Now, You can have a question what is the meaning of this activity and what is the purpose? With mindful observation, you can discover unnoticed object which can have greater inside meaning which gives us the catalyst and pointers for making our life meaningful and purposeful. This is part of programming your mind by observation and thoughtful assessment which can help your winning habit formation which is the key of your life transformation journey.

Now, focus on the A4 size blank page that you have. Continue observing the page. What thought are coming to your mind? Is it something to draw? Is it something to write or it is something to convert that a paper ball to play cricket?

If you keep on observing the A4 size blank paper, you can do many thing with it. You can create your vision board, what is your goal, what you want to become in next 5 years time, why you want to become that you can write down. You can write down your strategy and planning how you can achieve your desired goal. You can write your yearly, monthly, weekly and daily planning as your every minute is important. You can design your success blueprint on the blank page to start.

But the question is, why is every minute important?

Lets take two very common examples.

You have seen the package drinking water, when you procure a bottle of package drinking water from your local shop you pay X amount of money. The same water bottle for package drinking water when you purchase from airport hotel you pay 10X amount of money and you have no choice but to pay. Life will give you always choice, to be in local shop or Airport hotel. You need to uplift yourself. In order to uplift yourself you need right mindset, right skill and right attitude. Your mind is the best gift but by default it is the negativity dashboard. Until you nourish regularly, to develop your winning mindset and for which mind programming is the essential key element which is necessary to include in your daily practice.

Similarly if you have a pen in your chest pocket of your shift, the people will only see the lead of the pain – the top portion which is just the tip of the iceberg. The lead of the pen is to care the ink such that it should not be dried out. But the hard work of writing is done by the lower portion of the pen and the ink itself. In the same way, you will observe when a building is made lots of engineers put their hard work but in the inauguration of the building the CEO of the building gets opportunity to cut the ribbon. You always have a choice to blame your current position or sharpen our mindset to uplift yourself to create your future bright vivid bold with full of achievements and compelling. For that mind programming is a must do habit that you will learn in each of your chapters. Put your learning into your daily practice and see the magical changes over the period of time by developing rich mindset as true winner.

Remember you are responsible for creating your own destiny, when you take decision, you become slave of your choice. You are the architect of your mindset development, take ownership, accountability, responsibility of your life as you are the true mechanic of fixing your own issue and making your life sustainable, creating, aspiring and growing.

Contents

Chapter 1

Mind Your Mind

The Almighty has given us all the greatest gift—a supercomputer, our mind. However, we only use a small percentage of its potential, often leading to an ordinary life. Instead of tapping into its full power, we tend to blame others and lower our self-esteem. The mind can be your greatest ally, as all great ideas begin there and are turned into reality through strategic actions.

A trained and controlled mind can work miracles. But an untrained, uncontrolled mind is like a "monkey mind"—often confused, unfocused, overwhelmed, and unable to accomplish important tasks. An uncontrolled mind is your greatest enemy.

Imagine a chariot with five horses, a passenger, and a driver. If the driver falls asleep, the horses will pull in different directions, and the chariot won't reach its destination on time. But if the driver takes control of the horses with discipline, the journey will be fast, safe, and pleasant for the passenger.

In this analogy, the five horses represent the mind, and the driver represents our intellect, which is meant to guide and govern the mind. Every success begins in the mind, so taking proper care of it is crucial—something we often overlook or fail to realize.

Your mind has two parts: the conscious mind and the subconscious mind. The conscious mind is logical—it questions and validates things based on reality. The subconscious mind, on the other hand, is the feeling and habit mind. The problem many people face is that there's often a lack of sync between the conscious and subconscious mind, which prevents them from achieving their desired results.

For example, you might read a self-help book and feel highly motivated for a week. But after 30 days, that motivation usually fades. What happened? When you read the book, your conscious mind gets excited, but you don't deeply connect with what it would feel like to achieve your goals. You may not fully understand why you need to reach that state, fail to write down a strategy, or don't take focused action. As a result, your state of being never truly changes.

In this book, we will learn how to strengthen the subconscious mind to create better harmony between the conscious and subconscious, leading to more consistent and successful results. (For better understanding, you can think of the term 'unconscious mind' as 'subconscious mind.')

Situation	Conscious Mind Involvement	Subconscious Mind Involvement
Goal Setting	Actively sets specific, measurable, and actionable goals. Thinks logically and plans steps to achieve them.	Stores long-term goals, beliefs, and desires. Motivates you even when you're not actively thinking about them.
Decision Making	Weighs pros and cons, analyses risks, and makes rational decisions.	Influences decisions through deep-seated beliefs, past experiences, and emotional conditioning.
Learning New Skills	Focuses on acquiring information, consciously practicing and memorizing steps.	Reinforces learned skills through repetition, gradually automating actions and muscle memory.
Problem Solving	Actively evaluates different strategies and solutions to overcome challenges.	Provides creative insights, intuitive solutions, and "gut feelings" based on past knowledge stored in the subconscious.

Situation	Conscious Mind Involvement	Subconscious Mind Involvement
Performing Under Pressure	Analyses the immediate situation, responds quickly, and consciously tries to stay calm.	Reacts based on deeply programmed responses—past practice, automatic reflexes, and emotional resilience.
Time Management	Prioritizes tasks, creates schedules, and consciously allocates time to specific activities.	Influences efficiency through habitual behaviours and ingrained time-management habits developed over time.
Handling Criticism	Actively interprets feedback, rationally analyses its validity, and decides how to respond.	Reacts emotionally based on past conditioning—whether positively (adaptation) or negatively (defensiveness).
Building Relationships	Focuses on conscious communication, empathy, and active listening.	Shapes interactions based on internalized social cues, past relationship experiences, and deep-rooted emotional patterns.
Creativity and Innovation	Uses logic to connect ideas, plan experiments, and think critically about potential outcomes.	Draws on the subconscious mind to access intuition, inspiration, and creative flow from stored knowledge, experiences, and imagination.
Habit Formation	Consciously decides to develop new habits or break old ones. Focuses on repeating actions consistently.	Automates repeated behaviors through repetition, forming habits that eventually become subconscious actions.
Public Speaking or Presentations	Prepares content consciously, memorizes key points, and monitors delivery during the presentation.	Relies on subconscious memory, body language, and emotional control to handle nerves and stay confident during delivery.

Situation	Conscious Mind Involvement	Subconscious Mind Involvement
Overcoming Challenges	Consciously seeks solutions and creates action plans to tackle obstacles.	Subconsciously draws on past experiences and resilience, providing emotional strength and perseverance.
Physical Exercise or Sports	Plans workout routines and consciously monitors form and technique during practice or competition.	Activates muscle memory, reflexes, and flow states during performance, allowing for effortless movement in high-pressure moments.
Emotional Regulation	Consciously identifies feelings and applies strategies like deep breathing to stay calm.	Subconscious emotional patterns influence how you react automatically to stressful or triggering situations.
Work-Life Balance	Consciously allocates time between work and personal life, creating schedules and boundaries.	Subconsciously drives tendencies towards overwork or relaxation, depending on ingrained beliefs and emotional connections to work/life.

This table highlights how both the conscious and subconscious minds collaborate in various high-performance situations, enabling you to balance logic, creativity, and instinct for optimal success.

Activity

Think of the biggest challenge that you have currently and that you overcome in 2 years' time. Write down brief about the challenge.

____

____

____

____

____

____

Now, write down 5 things you are grateful and blessed about. Why do you think you have some special capabilities using which you can overcome the challenge. Write down your previous most successful event that you enjoyed a lot. Recall, remember, think and write down in brief.

____

____

____

____

____

____

____

Now write down 3 solution options you can try to solve your current problem which will help you to overcome. Put priority which will you try 1st, 2nd and 3rd based on priority. Will you do parallel run to solve the problem? Who will help you in this journey? What kind of help, support you need. Write down in brief.

____

____

____

____

____

____

When you do this exercise, your bigger challenge is no more a challenge, options come as opportunities to explore to overcome the difficult hurdles. Try this for any situation in your life journey.

A **boosted, trained, and ignited mind** operates very differently from an **ordinary, untrained, fearful, and stressed mind,** particularly in how it attracts and responds to success. The key differences between these two mental states lie in how they handle challenges, opportunities, emotions, and mindset. Let's explore these contrasts in terms of thinking, behaviour, and outcomes, and how a trained mind works more effectively toward achieving success.

1. **Optimism vs. Fear**

   - **Boosted Mindset:** A trained mind approaches life with **optimism** and a belief in possibilities. It recognizes that failures are learning opportunities and remains motivated even when things don't go as planned. This mindset actively looks for ways to solve problems and push through adversity.

   - **Untrained Mindset:** An untrained mind is often governed by **fear**, stress, and self-doubt. It focuses on worst-case scenarios, worries about failures, and avoids risks. This fear-driven approach leads to **paralysis** in decision-making and prevents the person from seizing opportunities.

   Example:

   Sarah, a project leader with a trained and ignited mind, faces a setback in a key project. Instead of panicking, she calmly assesses the situation, identifies the problem, and develops a new strategy to move forward. Her optimism drives her team to stay motivated and work toward a solution. On the other hand, another project leader with a fearful mindset might freeze when the same setback occurs, doubting their ability to recover and consequently delaying corrective actions.

2. **Proactivity vs. Reactivity**

   - **Boosted Mindset:** A trained mind is **proactive** and takes charge of situations. It plans ahead, anticipates challenges, and creates strategies to mitigate risks. This mind takes ownership of circumstances and is constantly looking for ways to improve.

- **Untrained Mindset:** An untrained mind is **reactive**, waiting for things to happen before responding. It is driven by external events rather than internal control, often reacting with stress or panic when faced with challenges.

Example:

John, a business owner with a proactive mindset, anticipates market shifts and prepares by diversifying his services. When the economic downturn hits, his business continues to thrive because he had planned ahead. Meanwhile, his competitor, who didn't foresee the change and remained reactive, struggles to adapt, making hasty decisions under pressure.

3. **Focus on Solutions vs. Problems**

   - **Boosted Mindset:** A trained mind is **solution-oriented**. It views challenges as puzzles to be solved rather than insurmountable problems. When faced with difficulties, it channels energy into finding creative solutions rather than dwelling on the issue.

   - **Untrained Mindset:** An untrained mind gets trapped in **problem-focused thinking**, where it spends too much time worrying about the problem and the potential negative outcomes. This drains energy and makes it harder to see a way out.

Example:

An entrepreneur with a boosted mindset encounters an unexpected delay in their supply chain. Instead of fixating on the problem, they immediately brainstorm alternatives, such as finding new suppliers or optimizing other areas of the business to minimize the impact. The solution-oriented approach keeps them moving forward. A person with a problem-focused mindset, on the other hand, might spend weeks worrying about the delay without taking action, resulting in lost business and frustration.

4. **Growth Mindset vs. Fixed Mindset**

   - **Boosted Mindset:** A trained mind embraces a **growth mindset**, believing that abilities and intelligence can be developed through effort, learning, and experience. It welcomes challenges and sees failure as a stepping stone to success.

   - **Untrained Mindset:** An untrained mind operates with a **fixed mindset**, believing that abilities are static, and that failure is a reflection of inherent limitations. It avoids challenges for fear of failure.

   Example:

   Jane, a software developer with a growth mindset, views a difficult coding problem as an opportunity to learn and improve her skills. She tackles the challenge head-on, even if it takes time and effort. Conversely, her colleague, who has a fixed mindset, avoids taking on complex tasks, believing that if she fails, it means she is not skilled enough. Over time, Jane becomes more proficient and sought after for her skills, while her colleague stagnates in her career.

5. **Emotional Resilience vs. Emotional Reactivity**

   - **Boosted Mindset:** A trained mind has developed **emotional resilience**, meaning it can maintain calm and composure in the face of stress or setbacks. It controls emotional responses, staying level-headed and focused on the end goal.

   - **Untrained Mindset:** An untrained mind is more **emotionally reactive**, allowing stress and anxiety to take over. It can become easily overwhelmed by challenges, leading to rash decisions and burnout.

   Example:

   During a high-pressure product launch, a CEO with emotional resilience remains calm under pressure, offering guidance and support to the team. This helps everyone stay focused and solve last-minute issues without panic. A CEO who lacks emotional control, on the other hand, might lash out at employees or become paralyzed by stress, contributing to a chaotic work environment that increases the chances of failure.

6. **Action-Oriented vs. Hesitation**

   - **Boosted Mindset:** A trained and ignited mind is **action-oriented**, meaning it takes calculated risks and decisive steps toward goals. It doesn't wait for the perfect moment but acts with intention, learning and adapting along the way.

   - **Untrained Mindset:** An untrained mind is prone to **hesitation and indecision**. It second-guesses itself, overanalyses, and avoids taking action due to fear of making mistakes or failing.

Example:

An investor with a trained mindset seizes an opportunity to invest in an emerging tech startup, understanding the potential risks but believing in the long-term value. This proactive approach leads to significant gains. In contrast, another investor might hesitate for fear of losing money, missing out on the opportunity altogether.

7. **Long-Term Vision vs. Short-Term Survival**

- **Boosted Mindset:** A trained mind is focused on **long-term vision**. It makes decisions that align with future goals and avoids being swayed by short-term setbacks or immediate gratification. Patience and perseverance are key.

- **Untrained Mindset:** An untrained mind is stuck in **short-term survival mode**, reacting to immediate problems without a clear vision for the future. This leads to shortsighted decisions that may fix immediate issues but hurt long-term growth.

Example:

An athlete with a long-term vision focuses on building endurance and perfecting their technique, even if it takes time and doesn't yield immediate results. Over time, this training pays off with exceptional performance in a major competition. An athlete who only focuses on quick wins may push themselves too hard, risking injury or burnout, and missing the chance for future success.

8. **Confidence vs. Self-Doubt**

- **Boosted Mindset:** A trained mind is fuelled by **confidence**, built from consistent learning, preparation, and past experiences. This confidence attracts success, as the individual takes bold steps toward their goals.

- **Untrained Mindset:** An untrained mind is filled with **self-doubt**, constantly questioning its abilities. This leads to missed opportunities and fear-driven decisions, which hinder progress.

Example:

A job seeker with a trained, confident mindset applies for leadership roles even when they don't meet every qualification. They know they can learn and grow into the role. Conversely, another job seeker might not apply due to self-doubt, believing they aren't good enough, and thus misses a valuable opportunity.

9. **Continuous Learning vs. Stagnation**

- **Boosted Mindset:** A trained mind has a passion for **continuous learning**, constantly seeking to improve through acquiring new skills, knowledge, and experiences. It adapts quickly to change and stays ahead in competitive environments.

- **Untrained Mindset:** An untrained mind is prone to **stagnation** and resists change. It is content with the status quo and reluctant to invest in self-improvement, making it less adaptable and vulnerable to being left behind.

Example:

An entrepreneur who continuously learns about market trends, new technologies, and leadership practices is able to innovate and stay ahead of competitors. In contrast, an entrepreneur who resists change and doesn't invest in learning may fall behind, unable to keep up with industry shifts.

Conclusion:

A **boosted, trained, and ignited mind** thrives on optimism, proactivity, resilience, confidence, and a growth mindset. It takes decisive action, focuses on solutions, and invests in continuous learning. This type of mind attracts success by remaining calm in the face of challenges, seeing opportunity in adversity, and making well-informed, bold decisions. In contrast, an **untrained, fearful, and stressed mind** operates from a place of hesitation, self-doubt, and reactivity, which often leads to missed opportunities and underperformance. Cultivating a trained mindset is key to achieving both personal and professional success.

Chapter 2
State of Mind

Let's say there is huge traffic, and you are stuck 1 hour and getting late for an interview for your next job. What will be your mental state? What will you do on that moment? It is high road and there is no possibility to take U turn. You are in your hired cab. What will be your strategy and cope up mechanism?

____

____

____

____

____

____

You are travelling on the same road and travelling by hired car. Again, you are on huge traffic. This day is your very special day, your birthday and today you will receive your best performance award in the annual function of your organization. You are getting late there. What will be your emotional state? What will be your strategy for this?

____

____

____

____

____

____

Is there any fundamental difference between two mental states of the above situation? Is your strategic action helps to make your mental state lighter?

____

____

____

____

____

____

The state of mind can be divided into two categories: the **resourceful state** and the **unresourceful state**.

In a **resourceful state**, we feel happy, energetic, peaceful, and mindful. Our enzymes and hormones are in harmony, which primes us to take action effectively. For instance, if you are a well-trained goalkeeper who has practiced enough and reviewed previous successful saves, you will be proactive and ready to perform. In this state, your probability of success increases. This is what we refer to as the "resourceful state."

On the contrary, in an **unresourceful state**, fear and self-doubt dominate. If you focus on past failures—like missing five goals in your last match—your body will enter "fight-or-flight" mode, driven by negative hormones, and your system will be in disorder. In this state, your likelihood of success diminishes. This is what we call the "unresourceful state."

The key is to cultivate a **resourceful internal emotional state**, regardless of external circumstances, to perform at your best and achieve positive outcomes. Taking a few slow, deep breaths and exhaling slowly can calm the vagus nerve, helping you become more mindful, agile, flexible, and alert.

Aspect	Resourceful State	Unresourceful State
Emotional State	Happy, energetic, peaceful, mindful, and confident	Fearful, anxious, stressed, self-doubting, and frustrated
Physical Response	Hormones and enzymes harmonized; body feels energized	Fight-or-flight response; body feels tense and overwhelmed
Mental Clarity	Focused, clear, and solution-oriented	Distracted, negative, and focused on past failures
Preparedness	Well-prepared and proactive	Unprepared, reactive, and hesitant
Decision-Making	Quick, confident, and rational decisions	Impulsive, fearful, and irrational decisions
Outcome Likelihood	High probability of success	Lower probability of success
Example	A well-trained goalkeeper visualizes past successful saves and feels ready to defend the goal confidently.	A goalkeeper fixates on missed goals from the last match and doubts their ability to save the next one.

This table provides a clear comparison between the two states, emphasizing how each one affects emotions, physical response, mental clarity, and overall performance.

Write down one instance when inspite of unfavorable situation, you kept your state of mind resourceful to overcome the situation well.

____

____

____

____

____

____

Programming your mind to control your emotional state—especially shifting from negative emotions like anger to a more positive, mindful state—involves intentional mental habits and practices that create a shift in perception, awareness, and emotional response. Key techniques for transforming your emotional state into a positive one include mindfulness, self-awareness, and cognitive restructuring. These practices foster emotional intelligence and promote a calm approach to life's challenges.

Here's a step-by-step process with examples to help you cultivate a more positive mindset and reduce anger:

1. **Develop Self-Awareness Through Mindfulness**

   - **Mindfulness** involves being fully present in the moment without judgment. By practicing mindfulness, you become aware of your thoughts and emotions as they arise, without reacting impulsively.

   - Regularly practicing mindfulness meditation or mindful breathing helps in recognizing the triggers that lead to anger or negative emotions. Once you become aware of these triggers, you can create a pause before reacting, giving yourself the opportunity to choose a more constructive response.

   Example:

   Alex, a corporate manager, used to get frustrated quickly during stressful meetings. He started practicing mindfulness meditation for 10 minutes each morning. Over time, he noticed that instead of immediately reacting with anger when a project went wrong, he could pause, take a few deep breaths, and approach the situation more calmly. This allowed him to respond with clarity and patience, improving both his emotional control and relationships with his colleagues.

2. **Reframe Negative Thoughts**

   - Our emotional responses are often a result of how we interpret events, not the events themselves. **Cognitive reframing** involves identifying negative, distorted thinking and reinterpreting situations in a more balanced, positive way.

- When you catch yourself thinking in a negative or anger-inducing way, consciously challenge these thoughts. Ask yourself, "Is there another way to see this?" By changing your perspective, you can reduce the intensity of negative emotions.

Example:

Sarah, a teacher, used to get angry when students disrupted her class. She would think, "They don't respect me." After learning about cognitive reframing, she began to see the disruptions differently, interpreting them as a sign that her students needed more engaging lessons or were dealing with personal issues. This shift in mindset allowed her to respond with empathy and understanding, rather than frustration.

3. **Practice Emotional Detachment**

- Emotional detachment doesn't mean ignoring your emotions but recognizing that you don't need to act on every emotion that arises. It's the ability to observe your emotions from a distance without being controlled by them.

- When anger arises, instead of identifying with the emotion ("I am angry"), practice saying, "I am noticing anger." This subtle shift creates distance between you and the emotion, helping you realize that emotions are temporary and do not define your response.

Example:

Tom, an entrepreneur, had a habit of reacting angrily to customer complaints. After learning emotional detachment techniques, when a complaint came in, he would acknowledge his frustration without letting it control him. He'd think, "I feel frustrated, but this is just a momentary reaction." This awareness gave him the space to respond calmly and focus on resolving the issue, which improved customer satisfaction.

4. **Regulate Your Breathing**

   - **Breath control** is one of the most effective ways to manage anger and stress. When we become angry or stressed, our breathing becomes shallow and rapid, triggering a fight-or-flight response. By consciously slowing your breathing, you signal to your body that you are not in danger, which calms your nervous system and reduces anger.

   - Practice deep breathing techniques, such as inhaling for a count of four, holding for a count of four, and exhaling for a count of four (known as box breathing), to reduce the intensity of emotional responses.

Example:

Lisa, a parent, would often lose her temper when her children misbehaved. She started practicing deep breathing whenever she felt her anger rising. By focusing on her breath, she was able to calm her mind and respond to her children's behaviour with patience instead of yelling, leading to a more harmonious household.

5. **Focus on Empathy**

   - **Empathy** allows you to see situations from another person's perspective, which can soften your emotional response. By understanding the motivations, emotions, or struggles of others, you can transform anger into compassion and connection.

   - When you feel anger toward someone, take a moment to imagine what that person might be feeling or experiencing. This doesn't excuse bad behaviour, but it helps you respond more thoughtfully and less emotionally.

Example:

Jake, a project manager, used to get angry when his team missed deadlines. After working on building empathy, he began asking his team members about their challenges and difficulties instead of getting upset. He realized that many were struggling with workload issues, so instead of reacting with anger, he focused on finding solutions and supporting his team, which improved both morale and productivity.

6. **Set Positive Intentions**

- Setting **positive intentions** at the beginning of the day or before engaging in potentially stressful situations can help anchor you in a calm and focused mindset. By stating your intention to remain calm, patient, and open, you prime your mind to act in accordance with these values.

- This technique not only helps prevent anger but also promotes a positive, solution-oriented attitude in all aspects of life.

Example:

Every morning before heading to work, Mark, a sales executive, would set the intention: "Today, I will remain calm and patient, no matter what challenges arise." By doing this consistently, he noticed that even during stressful client meetings, he could maintain his composure and think clearly, which helped him close more deals and build stronger client relationships.

7. **Practice Gratitude**

- Cultivating **gratitude** is a powerful way to shift your mindset away from negative emotions like anger and frustration. When you focus on what you are grateful for, you redirect your attention from what's wrong to what's going well, which creates a more positive emotional state.

- Keeping a daily gratitude journal, where you write down three things you are thankful for, can retrain your brain to focus on the positives, reducing the likelihood of anger and increasing your overall sense of well-being.

Example:

Emily, a student, used to get angry and stressed about her workload and exams. She started writing in a gratitude journal every night, listing things she was thankful for, such as supportive friends and opportunities to learn. Over time, she noticed that she felt less stressed about her studies and more motivated, which improved both her mood and academic performance.

8. **Engage in Physical Activity**

- Physical exercise helps release built-up stress and tension, reducing anger and negative emotions. It also boosts mood by releasing endorphins, the body's natural feel-good chemicals. Regular exercise can act as a natural stress-reliever and improve emotional control.

- Engaging in activities like yoga, running, or even walking can significantly improve your mood and help manage negative emotions.

Example:

Kevin, a lawyer, struggled with managing anger during tough cases. He took up running and noticed that after his runs, he felt more calm and level-headed. Running allowed him to clear his mind, making it easier for him to tackle difficult situations at work with a more composed and focused attitude.

9. **Visualize Positive Outcomes**

- Visualization is a powerful mental tool. **Visualizing** how you want to react in a stressful or anger-inducing situation can help train your brain to respond in a calmer, more constructive way when the real situation arises. By mentally rehearsing calm and thoughtful responses, you program your mind to behave in that way when challenges occur.

- Picture yourself handling difficult situations with ease, confidence, and positivity, which builds emotional resilience.

Example:

Before attending a difficult meeting with a client, David, a product manager, would visualize himself staying calm, listening carefully, and responding thoughtfully, even if the client became upset. This mental rehearsal helped him stay grounded during the meeting, avoid defensiveness, and reach a resolution, which earned the client's respect.

Chapter 3

Your Identity and Belief is the Starting Point

Remember, there may be thunderstorms and cloudy skies, but the reality is that bad weather never lasts long. The sun will rise again! It's all about mindset. Once the rain stops on a dark night, winners look at the sky and enjoy seeing the stars again. They go out with umbrellas and protective gear, ready for the challenge. Meanwhile, those with an ordinary mindset focus on the water in front of their door, refuse to go out, and blame the weather. Mindset matters in every situation. It's all about your strategy—how you cope with challenges, turn difficulties into opportunities, and improve the situation.

Sometimes, you might feel bogged down, just barely surviving. If your focus is only on survival, your creativity and ability to upgrade yourself are generally blocked, making it difficult to consistently climb the ladder of success.

You need to pause. You need to give time to yourself to clam down. Take 15 minutes every day. Practice sitting in a quiet place. Drink water to make your body hydrated. Stay away from electronic devices and other disturbances. Take few deep breaths, 1 – 2 – 3 – 4. Slow deep breaths. Hold for 1 – 2 – 3 – 4 – 5. Breath out slowly, 1 – 2 – 3 – 4 – 5 – 6. Just focus on your breathing, feel how nicely fresh oxygen is coming to your nose, getting into your lungs, fresh oxygen is going to your bold, brain and whole body. Your belly is coming out then chest. And when you exhale, slowly, all garages are going out and your body and mind is getting refreshed. Continue this deep breathing exercise for 2 – 5 minutes. And once done come back to the original state and remember last 3 digit of your mobile number. Rub your palm and feel the energy by touching your forehead, face, throat, chest, stomach, knee, foot.

Now think who you are. What will be written in your business card after 5 years? How people or whole world you know? What will be your specialization? What contribution will you bring to the world to make difference? How will you solve problem which is giving people much pain? How will your contribution enhance the quality of life? Think what is your purpose of life? What is the reason you being here? Is your work well aligned with your current actions / job / assignment? Or there is any conflict? If your purpose of life and contribution is well aligned, then you are on right track boosting your identity upright and you will become a role model which other can follow.

____

____

____

____

____

Can I do it, it is impossible to achieve. Even if someone has achieved, it is not possible for me to achieve. I am fearful. How can I do this – I don't have strength and capabilities. What will happen if I fail – what people will think for my failure. These are self-limiting belief that are the show stoper of your success.

An ordinary mindset focuses on problems, often perceiving them as much larger than their capabilities. In contrast, individuals with a rich mindset and an extraordinary attitude believe in their abilities, draw from a universal energy source, and trust in their capacity to overcome challenges. Self-limiting beliefs can be transformed into a positive and stronger belief system by practicing new methods, gaining experience, harmonizing knowledge, and moving forward.

Once a positive belief is established, confidence levels increase, and certainty replaces uncertainty. This clarity brings immense visibility, opening up possibilities to adapt and discover different ways of implementation.

Situation	Ordinary Mindset Behaviour	Extraordinary Mindset Behaviour	Belief
Facing Challenges	Avoids challenges; sees them as obstacles	Embraces challenges as opportunities for growth	"Every challenge is a chance to learn and grow."
Dealing with Failure	Dwells on failures; feels defeated and hopeless	Analyses failures; uses them as stepping stones to success	"Failure is a part of the journey to success."
Adapting to Change	Resists change; feels uncomfortable and uncertain	Welcomes change; sees it as a natural part of progress	"Change leads to new opportunities."
Setting Goals	Sets small, easily achievable goals; fears big aspirations	Sets ambitious goals; believes in their ability to achieve them	"I can achieve anything I set my mind to."
Responding to Feedback	Takes criticism personally; feels defensive	Accepts feedback as a tool for improvement	"Feedback helps me grow and improve."
Viewing Success	Sees success as limited and scarce; compares with others	Believes in abundant success; celebrates the success of others	"Success is abundant, and there's enough for everyone."
Handling Stress	Becomes overwhelmed and anxious; struggles to cope	Manages stress through positive strategies and problem-solving	"I can handle stress and find solutions."

Situation	Ordinary Mindset Behaviour	Extraordinary Mindset Behaviour	Belief
Taking Risks	Avoids taking risks; prefers to stay in the comfort zone	Takes calculated risks; understands the value of stepping out of comfort	"Taking risks is essential for growth."
Building Relationships	Limits connections; focuses only on immediate circles	Seeks diverse relationships; values collaboration and networking	"Relationships are key to personal and professional growth."
Overall Perspective	Generally negative; sees the glass as half empty	Generally positive; sees the glass as half full	"Positivity attracts more positivity."

This table outlines how ordinary and extraordinary mindsets differ in their behaviours, beliefs, and responses to various situations.

Write down 3 self-limiting belief that you had last year but this year they are no more and you have overcome the fear by your matured strategic actions.

____

____

____

____

____

Changing a negative belief requires a structured approach that involves self-awareness, challenging the belief, replacing it with a positive belief, and reinforcing the new belief through consistent actions. Below is a process for changing negative beliefs, explained with an example.

Steps to Change a Negative Belief

1. **Identify the Negative Belief**

   - The first step is to become aware of the limiting belief that is holding you back. These beliefs often stem from past experiences, societal conditioning, or self-doubt. A negative belief may manifest as self-criticism or automatic negative thoughts in specific situations.

   - To identify the belief, ask yourself: "What do I believe that is preventing me from achieving my goal?" Look for recurring thoughts or self-talk that limits your actions.

   Example:

   Jane is a software engineer who believes, "I'm not good at public speaking." She avoids speaking up in meetings or giving presentations because she thinks she will fail or embarrass herself. This belief stems from a bad experience during a high school presentation where she froze up in front of her classmates.

2. **Challenge the Negative Belief**

   - Once you've identified the negative belief, start questioning its validity. Is this belief absolutely true, or is it based on fear and a narrow interpretation of past experiences? Look for evidence that contradicts the belief.

   - Ask questions like:

     - "Is there proof that this belief is accurate?"

     - "What evidence do I have that goes against this belief?"

     - "Have I ever succeeded in a similar situation?"

     - "How would I behave if I didn't hold this belief?"

   Example:

   Jane begins to challenge her belief by asking herself, "Is it true that I'm not good at public speaking?" She realizes that she has successfully explained technical concepts to her team on multiple occasions in informal settings. Although she doesn't do it often, she has successfully communicated her ideas before, which contradicts the belief that she's incapable of public speaking.

3. **Replace the Negative Belief with a Positive Belief**

   - After challenging the validity of the negative belief, replace it with a more empowering and positive belief. The new belief should be more aligned with your goals and reflect a more balanced view of yourself.

   - The key is to craft a belief that is realistic, actionable, and motivates you to take constructive action.

   - Example questions to ask:

     ○ "What is a more balanced belief I can adopt?"

     ○ "What belief would serve me better in achieving my goals?"

Example:

Jane replaces her negative belief with a more empowering one: "I can improve my public speaking skills through practice." She acknowledges that while she may not be perfect now, she can get better by taking steps to practice and improve. This new belief motivates her to take action rather than avoid situations where she needs to speak publicly.

4. **Take Action to Reinforce the New Belief**

   - To solidify the new belief, it's essential to take consistent, small actions that reinforce it. Action creates evidence for the new belief and weakens the grip of the old one. Start with manageable challenges and gradually build confidence.

   - Actions should align with the new belief, creating positive experiences that reinforce the belief over time.

Example:

To reinforce her new belief, Jane starts by practicing public speaking in low-pressure environments. She signs up for small team presentations and rehearses her talks beforehand. She also joins a public speaking group to further improve her skills. Each time she successfully delivers a presentation, her confidence grows, reinforcing her new belief that she can become a good public speaker with practice.

5. **Reaffirm the New Belief through Affirmations and Visualization**

- Regularly using affirmations and visualization helps reinforce the new belief at a subconscious level. Affirmations are positive statements that you repeat to yourself, while visualization involves mentally rehearsing your desired outcome.

- This mental reinforcement creates strong neural pathways that support the new belief, making it a permanent part of your mindset.

  Example:

  Jane uses daily affirmations like "I am becoming a confident speaker" and visualizes herself speaking calmly and effectively in front of an audience. She imagines the applause and positive feedback she will receive. This mental reinforcement helps reduce her anxiety and strengthens her new belief.

6. **Monitor Progress and Adjust as Needed**

- Changing a belief is an ongoing process. It's important to track your progress, recognize improvements, and continue challenging any lingering doubts or negative thoughts.

- If you experience setbacks, remind yourself that change takes time and keep reinforcing the positive belief.

Example:

Jane tracks her progress by noting each successful presentation and the positive feedback she receives. Whenever she feels nervous, she reminds herself of the times she succeeded and continues practicing her new belief. Gradually, her fear of public speaking diminishes, and she starts to enjoy sharing her ideas with others.

Summary of Process:

1. **Identify** the negative belief that is limiting you.

2. **Challenge** its validity by questioning the evidence for and against it.

3. **Replace** the negative belief with a positive, empowering belief.

4. **Take Action** to reinforce the new belief with small, manageable steps.

5. **Reaffirm** the belief through affirmations and visualization.

6. **Monitor Progress** and keep reinforcing the new belief over time.

Chapter 4

Vision, Goals, Opportunities

When you have clarity about who you are and what your greater purpose is on this earth, it becomes easier to define your vision. What exactly do you want to become? Where do you want to go? What do you want to achieve? How do you want to be recognized by the world for your unique capabilities?

Your vision will transform your future into something special, meaningful, and fulfilling, and it must align with your mission, smaller achievable goals, milestones, and objectives. Once you are aligned with these elements, wherever you go and whatever you do, you will consistently see opportunities and strive to create value to make a difference. Gradually, you will become result-oriented and continually optimize your time, energy, and resources to achieve favourable outcomes that align with your greater purpose in life.

Aspect	Life with Goals	Life without Goals
Motivation	Inspires and motivates action	Often leads to procrastination and lack of motivation
Focus	Helps maintain focus on important tasks	Easily distracted; may struggle to prioritize
Decision-Making	Informed and purposeful decisions aligned with goals	Indecisive; decisions often made reactively

Aspect	Life with Goals	Life without Goals
Achievement	Progress is measurable; celebrates milestones	Limited progress; difficult to track accomplishments
Resilience	Enhances resilience; setbacks are viewed as learning opportunities	Vulnerable to setbacks; may feel defeated
Time Management	Encourages effective use of time	Time may be wasted; less structure in daily activities
Personal Growth	Promotes continuous self-improvement	Limited personal development; stagnant
Sense of Fulfilment	Greater sense of fulfilment and satisfaction	May feel unfulfilled or dissatisfied
Adaptability	Encourages adaptability and flexibility in pursuit of goals	Less adaptable; may resist change

This table highlights the key differences in how individuals experience life when they have clear goals versus when they lack them.

Let's consider an example.

1. **Vision**

   A **vision** is a broad, long-term **aspirational statement** that outlines what you (or an organization) ultimately want to achieve. It's the big-picture view of the future.

   - **Characteristics**:

     ○ Future-oriented

     ○ Inspirational

     ○ Defines the end result or desired future state

- **Example**:
- **Personal Vision:**
- "To become a leading expert in sustainable energy solutions, helping the world transition to renewable energy sources by 2050."

Company Vision:

Tesla's Vision: "To create the most compelling car company of the 21st century by driving the world's transition to electric vehicles."

2. **Mission**

A **mission** is a **purpose-driven statement** that defines **what you do**, **who you serve**, and **how you serve them**. It is more action-oriented and focuses on the present, outlining what is being done to reach the vision.

- **Characteristics**:
  - Focuses on the present
  - Action-oriented
  - Purposeful
- **Example**:
- **Personal Mission:**
- "To develop innovative solar energy technologies that reduce carbon emissions and provide affordable energy to underserved communities."

Company Mission:

Google's Mission: "To organize the world's information and make it universally accessible and useful."

3. **Goal**

A **goal** is a **specific, long-term outcome** that supports the mission and helps you move closer to achieving the vision.

Goals are broader than objectives but still specific enough to be measurable over time.

- **Characteristics**:
  - Long-term
  - Broad outcomes aligned with the mission
  - Usually qualitative, though they can also have measurable aspects
- **Example**:
- **Personal Goal**:
- "To reduce carbon emissions by 10% in my community through solar energy projects within the next 5 years."

Company Goal:

"To increase electric vehicle sales by 20% over the next 3 years."

4. **Objective**

An **objective** is a **short-term, specific, and measurable action** that helps you achieve a goal. Objectives are usually **quantifiable**, have a clear **time frame**, and are **action-oriented**.

- **Characteristics**:
  - Specific and measurable
  - Time-bound
  - Clear action steps
- **Example**:
- **Personal Objective:**
- "To install solar panels in 100 homes by the end of the next 12 months."

Company Objective:

"To launch a new electric car model by Q2 of next year and sell 10,000 units in the first year."

5. **Milestone**

A **milestone** is a **key point or checkpoint** in a project or plan. Milestones are **measurable indicators of progress** toward an objective. They are often **smaller achievements** within a larger goal or project.

- **Characteristics**:
    - Specific progress markers
    - Often tied to deadlines
    - Help track progress towards an objective or goal
- **Example**:
- **Personal Milestone:**
- "By month 3, have completed the installation of solar panels in 25 homes."

Company Milestone:

"Complete the prototype of the new electric vehicle by the end of Q1."

Putting It All Together: Example of a Solar Energy Company

Let's say you are starting a solar energy company. Here's how these concepts work together:

1. **Vision:**

2. *"To make clean energy accessible and affordable to every household in the country, significantly reducing reliance on fossil fuels by 2040."*

3. **Mission**:

4. *"To develop and provide cost-effective solar energy solutions for residential and commercial use, helping to reduce carbon footprints and energy costs."*

5. **Goal**:

6. *"To install solar energy systems in 10,000 homes by 2028, reducing overall energy costs by 15% in targeted areas."*

7. **Objective**:

8. *"To complete installations in 500 homes by the end of this year."*

9. **Milestone**:

10. "Complete 100 installations by the end of Q2 this year."

Example: Fitness Trainer

1. **Vision**:

2. *"To inspire people to lead healthier lives by becoming one of the most recognized fitness trainers in the world by 2030."*

3. **Mission**:

4. *"To provide personalized training and nutrition programs that help individuals achieve their health and fitness goals."*

5. **Goal**:

6. *"To have 1,000 clients successfully complete personalized fitness programs by the end of the next 3 years."*

7. **Objective**:

8. *"To onboard 100 new clients in the next 6 months."*

9. **Milestone**:

10. *"Sign up 50 clients by the end of the first quarter."*

Summary of Differences:

- **Vision**: Long-term aspiration (where you want to be in the future).

- **Mission**: Current purpose (what you're doing now to achieve the vision).

- **Goals**: Long-term outcomes that contribute to achieving the mission.

- **Objectives**: Short-term, measurable steps toward the goals.

- **Milestones**: Key checkpoints that measure progress toward an objective.

Each one builds on the other to form a structured plan for success!

Write down your vision and mission statement:

____

____

____

____

____

Lets say you boarded a Bus. The conductor came to you for you to buy ticket. If you can not specify where you should go, how can he give you the ticket. In your personal and professional life, goal is very important to move forward.

Write down your goal:

____

____

____

____

____

Your goal should be SMARTIES.

- Is that Simple and Specific?
- Is that measurable? How much progress you are making over the period of time?
- Is that achievable?
- Is that realistic?
- Is that timeline oriented?
- Is that Inspiring?
- Is that Emotionally connected and ecologically, correct?
- Is that long term consistent success and sustainability oriented?

Please re write your goal aligned with the above best practices:

____

____

____

____

____

____

Once your goal is clear, break it down into smaller, achievable milestones. Check if each step is ecologically correct. Identify the resources that will be working on this, as well as the support that will be required. Determine how funding will be secured and establish a timeline for accomplishing each task. Create a monthly, weekly, and daily job schedule for implementation.

During execution, consistency and focus are essential. Regular evaluation is critical to ensure you are on the right path. Adjust your journey as needed to achieve the milestones, which will ultimately help in completing your larger goal. Always set appropriate expectations with your group, customers, and manager, and include a buffer to mitigate the risk of missing deadlines.

Write 3 instances where you missed your goal recently. What are the key learning and how can you improve in the future to avoid such failure.

____

____

____

____

____

____

Chapter 5
Passion and Focus

It is said that things grow where your focus goes. When you focus on your goals and tasks, they will attract you like a magnet. You may find yourself getting out of bed before the alarm clock rings. Your focus will provide clarity on the tasks to be performed, and your passionate contribution will open up options to overcome obstacles and maintain your momentum. You will experience failures, as it is impossible to hold all the knowledge during your journey. However, your positive spirit and high level of focus are key to helping you bounce back.

When faced with deep failure, let your inner voice inspire you by saying, "Get up one more time." Mindset comes first, followed by the skill to stand firm and fight back with mature actions to get back on track.

In the current post-pandemic phase, we are overwhelmed by information overload, and numerous energy drainers can easily distract us. We need to rethink what is important for us. Stay away from negative emotions and energy drainers, and concentrate on the factors that will accelerate your growth today for a better future.

Story: The Journey of Asha – A Tale of Passion, Focus, and Triumph

Asha was a young woman living in a small town in India. She had always been passionate about **becoming an engineer**. From a young age, she would dismantle household gadgets just to understand how they worked. Her fascination with machines grew into a full-blown dream of designing innovative technology that could help improve people's lives, especially in underdeveloped areas.

But her journey wasn't going to be easy.

The Obstacles

Asha's family was not well off. Her parents were supportive but could barely afford her school fees, let alone the cost of an engineering degree. On top of this, the societal pressure in her town was immense; many believed that girls should focus on getting married rather than pursuing higher education.

As the obstacles mounted, many suggested she should reconsider her path. But Asha's **passion for engineering** burned brightly. She knew that if she stayed focused and took the right actions, she could overcome anything.

Focused Action Begins

Despite the challenges, Asha never lost sight of her dream. She began by setting small, focused goals to work towards her ambition.

1. **Study with Intensity:**

2. Asha realized she didn't have access to expensive tuition classes or private tutors, so she made full use of **online resources** and **local libraries**. She dedicated herself to self-study, often waking up at 4 a.m. to work through physics and math problems. She broke down her study material into small, manageable chunks and studied with laser focus every day.

3. **Scholarship Hunt:**

4. Asha knew her family couldn't afford her education, so she made it a goal to apply for every scholarship she could find. She spent countless nights researching scholarship programs, perfecting her essays, and preparing her applications. After many rejections, she finally earned a scholarship that covered most of her college fees.

5. **Overcoming Social Pressure**:

6. In a society where pursuing engineering as a woman was still seen as unusual, Asha faced constant judgment from people around her. But she stayed **focused on her passion** and used the criticism as fuel to push herself harder.

The Turning Point

During her second year in engineering school, Asha's village faced a severe drought. People were struggling with the lack of water, and traditional irrigation methods weren't helping. The situation was dire, and Asha saw an opportunity to put her engineering skills to good use.

Inspired by her community's need, she designed a **low-cost water filtration and irrigation system** that could recycle wastewater for agricultural use. She worked tirelessly on the project, using every bit of knowledge she had learned and seeking advice from her professors. The focus on applying her passion to a real-world problem became her obsession.

She also reached out to local government officials to pitch her solution. After multiple failed meetings, one officer saw potential in her idea and agreed to fund a pilot project.

Success Through Passion and Focus

With her project funded, Asha assembled a small team of fellow students and worked day and night to build the system. The pilot was a success, helping farmers in her village save water and improve crop yields. News of her project spread, and soon, her design was being implemented in neighbouring villages as well.

Her focused action and unwavering passion led her to **not only complete her engineering degree with honours** but also to **develop a solution that brought real impact to her community.** She went on to receive national recognition, and offers from prestigious companies poured in.

The Victory

Asha's journey from a small-town girl facing financial and societal challenges to an award-winning engineer is a testament to the power of **passion and focused action**. She never wavered in her pursuit of her dream, setting clear goals and taking consistent action, even when the odds were stacked against her.

Asha's story shows that when you align your passion with focused action, you can overcome seemingly impossible obstacles and achieve remarkable success.

Lessons from Asha's Story:

1. **Passion drives perseverance**: Asha's love for engineering helped her keep going, even when external circumstances were tough.

2. **Focused action leads to results**: Instead of feeling overwhelmed by challenges, she broke her goals down and stayed disciplined in pursuing them.

3. **Turn obstacles into opportunities**: The drought in her village became the turning point for her career, as it gave her the chance to apply her skills and showcase her abilities.

By staying focused on her passion and taking determined actions, Asha turned her challenges into stepping stones for success.

Passion is a powerful motivator, but when not balanced, it can lead to burnout, unrealistic expectations, or poor decision-making. Here's what to avoid, along with an example:

1. **Avoid Burnout by Overworking:**

Example:

Sarah, a young entrepreneur, was incredibly passionate about launching her tech startup. She worked 16-hour days for months, believing that sheer effort would lead to success. However, her non-stop work led to burnout, affecting her decision-making and creativity. Eventually, she struggled to maintain focus, and her startup began to suffer.

What to avoid:

While passion often drives hard work, it's important to take breaks, maintain a work-life balance, and ensure that you don't exhaust your mental and physical energy. Overworking can lead to burnout, which diminishes productivity and reduces the quality of your work.

2. **Avoid Ignoring Feedback:**

Example:

Jake was deeply passionate about his project and believed in his vision so much that he ignored any feedback that contradicted his ideas. While his passion gave him the drive to continue, his refusal to listen to suggestions from mentors and clients led to a product that didn't resonate with the market. The project failed because he didn't incorporate essential feedback.

What to avoid:

Passion can sometimes make you overly protective of your ideas, leading you to ignore valuable feedback. This tunnel vision can limit your growth. It's crucial to remain open to constructive criticism, as it often helps refine and improve your work.

3. **Avoid Perfectionism:**

Example:

Amanda, a writer, was passionate about completing her first novel. However, her desire for perfection led her to constantly revise her work, never feeling it was "good enough" for publication. Years passed, and she never published the book because she was stuck in the cycle of perfecting it.

What to avoid:

Perfectionism, driven by passion, can prevent you from finishing tasks or launching projects. Sometimes, being "good enough" and taking action is better than waiting for perfection. Progress is often achieved by learning from mistakes and iterations, not from waiting until everything is flawless.

4. **Avoid Unrealistic Expectations:**

Example:

David was passionate about becoming a professional musician and believed that his talent alone would guarantee overnight success. He invested all his time and resources without creating a strategic plan, and when success didn't come immediately, he became frustrated and lost motivation.

What to avoid:

Passion can sometimes blind you to the time, effort, and patience needed to achieve long-term success. Setting realistic expectations and working steadily toward your goals is important. Passion should be combined with practicality and strategic planning.

5. **Avoid Comparing Yourself to Others:**

Example:

Lisa was passionate about her fitness journey and regularly posted about it on social media. However, she began comparing her progress to others, feeling discouraged when she saw influencers achieving faster results. Her passion turned into frustration, and she started losing confidence in her own progress.

What to avoid:

Comparison can be detrimental, especially when you are passionate about your own journey. Everyone's path to success is different, and comparing yourself to others can lead to self-doubt and loss of motivation. Focus on your progress, celebrate small victories, and avoid the trap of comparison.

Aspect	With Passion and Focus	Without Passion and Less Focus
Quality of Work	High-quality output; attention to detail	Variable quality; may overlook important details
Creativity	Increased creativity; innovative ideas	Limited creativity; may stick to conventional methods
Motivation	Strong intrinsic motivation; driven to excel	Lack of motivation; may feel indifferent
Efficiency	Highly efficient; effective time management	Less efficient; often procrastinate or get sidetracked
Problem-Solving	Proactive approach to challenges; finds solutions easily	Reactive approach; struggles to find effective solutions
Engagement	Fully engaged; enthusiastic about tasks	Disengaged; lacks enthusiasm for tasks
Collaboration	Open to collaboration; encourages teamwork	Less collaborative; may work in isolation
Resilience	More resilient; bounces back quickly from setbacks	Less resilient; may give up easily when faced with obstacles
Customer Satisfaction	Higher customer satisfaction due to attention and care	Lower customer satisfaction; may overlook customer needs
Long-Term Results	Sustainable success; builds a strong reputation	Inconsistent results; may harm reputation over time

This table illustrates how the presence of passion and focus significantly enhances the quality of delivery across various aspects, while their absence can lead to poorer outcomes.

Chapter 6
Consistency

Motivation will not be effective unless you take timely and effective action. Conversely, action alone will not lead to success unless you are motivated to go above and beyond what you are paid for. End-to-end responsibility, accountability, ownership, and the development of winning habits ensure consistent success. Success is not just about achieving a milestone once; it involves overcoming difficult situations with a positive mindset and skilful actions to win repeatedly. This approach, combined with skill, experience, and collaboration, ensures that you achieve sustainable success.

According to research, any business development or personal growth initiative typically fails due to a lack of consistent effort. Multiple failures, unfavourable conditions, and intense competition can demotivate individuals, leading them to quit in the middle of their journey. Those who possess tolerance, patience, and acceptance tend to succeed in the long run. They leverage their learning experiences to innovate and implement different strategies to achieve success.

Situation	Utilizing Opportunities with Consistency	Losing Opportunities without Consistency
Career Development	Regularly updating skills through training and networking leads to promotions and new job offers.	Failing to attend workshops or training can result in stagnation and missed promotions.

Situation	Utilizing Opportunities with Consistency	Losing Opportunities without Consistency
Health and Fitness	Consistently exercising and maintaining a healthy diet leads to improved physical health and well-being.	Inconsistent exercise and poor diet can lead to health issues and missed fitness goals.
Financial Planning	Regular saving and investing can grow wealth and provide security for the future.	Irregular saving habits can lead to financial instability and missed investment opportunities.
Personal Relationships	Consistently nurturing relationships through communication and quality time strengthens bonds.	Lack of consistent effort in maintaining relationships can result in misunderstandings and estrangement.
Business Growth	Regularly engaging with customers and improving services leads to repeat business and referrals.	Inconsistent customer service and engagement can result in lost clients and negative reviews.
Academic Success	Consistent study habits and participation in class lead to better grades and learning.	Inconsistent studying and lack of participation can lead to poor performance and missed opportunities for scholarships.
Skill Development	Regular practice and seeking feedback improve skills, leading to mastery and new opportunities.	Inconsistent practice can hinder skill development and result in missed job or project opportunities.
Networking	Attending industry events and maintaining connections leads to collaborations and new projects.	Inconsistent networking can result in missed opportunities for partnerships and job leads.
Creative Projects	Consistently dedicating time to creative work leads to completed projects and increased visibility.	Inconsistent effort can lead to unfinished projects and missed opportunities for recognition.

Situation	Utilizing Opportunities with Consistency	Losing Opportunities without Consistency
Community Involvement	Regularly volunteering and participating in community events builds connections and opens doors for collaboration.	Infrequent involvement can result in missed opportunities to contribute and gain support from the community.

This table highlights how consistency in various areas of life can lead to the successful utilization of opportunities, while a lack of consistency can result in missed chances and setbacks.

Story: The Bamboo and the Gardener – A Tale of Consistent Effort and Success

In a peaceful village nestled between the mountains, lived a wise old gardener named Rohan. He was known far and wide for his beautiful garden, where exotic plants and flowers bloomed year-round. However, there was one part of his garden that was seemingly barren. In this patch, he had planted bamboo seeds.

Every morning, Rohan would rise early, water the soil, tend to it with care, and ensure that the patch was getting the right amount of sunlight. Days turned into weeks, and weeks into months, but not a single bamboo shoot emerged from the ground. Curious villagers would pass by, and some began to question his efforts.

The Doubt and the Patience

"Why do you bother with that empty patch, old man?" they would say. "Nothing is growing there. You should plant something else!"

But Rohan was unfazed. He simply smiled and responded, "Bamboo takes time. You must be patient."

Months turned into years, and still, there was no sign of bamboo. Villagers started to laugh at his daily routine. "It's been years! You're wasting your time!" they said. Even Rohan's family began to worry, suggesting he abandon the bamboo patch and plant something else that would grow faster.

But Rohan continued to water the soil **every single day** without fail. He believed in the bamboo, even though there was no visible progress. His actions were consistent, even in the face of doubt and ridicule.

The Bamboo Miracle

Then, in the fifth year, something miraculous happened. One day, tiny green bamboo shoots began to peek through the soil. And within weeks, the bamboo grew—**not just a little, but up to 90 feet tall!**

The villagers were astounded. "How is this possible?" they asked. "It didn't grow at all for years, and now it's towering over everything!"

Rohan explained with a smile, "The bamboo wasn't doing nothing all those years. It was growing underground, developing a strong root system that would support its height. Without those years of nurturing and rooting, it wouldn't have been able to grow so tall, so quickly. Success, like the bamboo, takes time and consistent effort."

The Lesson of the Bamboo

This story of Rohan and his bamboo patch spread throughout the village, becoming a symbol of patience, perseverance, and the power of consistent effort. While everyone else saw the surface and gave up too soon, Rohan understood that success is often invisible in its early stages. Growth happens beneath the surface, out of sight, until one day, the results of all that hard work finally burst forth.

Lessons from the Story:

1. **Success takes time**: Like bamboo, many things in life take time to show results. Just because you can't see immediate progress doesn't mean nothing is happening.

2. **Consistent effort pays off**: Rohan's daily watering of the bamboo patch may have seemed pointless to others, but it was essential for the bamboo to eventually thrive.

3. **Foundation matters**: Just as the bamboo was building its root system underground, our consistent efforts help lay the foundation for future success, even if the results are not immediately visible.

4. **Patience is key**: Rohan's unwavering belief in the bamboo and his willingness to stick with his daily routine are what ultimately led to his success.

Real-World Application:

Whether it's learning a new skill, pursuing a career, or achieving a personal goal, **consistent effort** is the key to long-term success. While it may take months or years before you see the results, every small action contributes to your growth. Like the bamboo, your success is rooted in the foundation you build through dedication, even when progress seems invisible.

This story reminds us that with consistent effort, even the tallest of ambitions can be reached, just like the towering bamboo.

Chapter 7

The Success Blueprint Model

What is the definition of success? In summary, if your presence helps people make a visible difference, leading to an improvement in their quality of life or the resolution of their ongoing problems, and you enjoy growing together with an uplifted mindset, then you can be considered a successful person. Once you establish the habit of success, milestone achievements become a byproduct of your mature actions, which occur more easily as you gain clarity, visibility, and align your strategy with confident execution. Over time, you accumulate knowledge and experience, achieving excellence through uplifting and collaborative approaches.

Let's say you are at position X, which represents your current situation today. You aspire to become a highly successful person and the best version of yourself in five years, reaching position Y. To transition from position X to position Y, what do you essentially need? These are known as the Pillars of Success. They are labeled as the Pillars of Communicative Leadership, meaning that what you say to yourself will define the strength of each pillar and contribute to the robustness of your positive growth and learning journey. The stronger the pillars are, based on your communicative leadership styles and your positive vibes, the more effectively you can redefine your strategy according to your circumstances, ultimately enriching your sustainability.

Pillars of your communicative leadership excellence for consistent success:

- Pillar 1: You need **Good Health**. Healthy body with positive energy will enable you to contribute more and becoming creative to explore unlimited possibilities.

- Pillar 2: You need healthy mind with aspiring spirit and belief of confidence with Can do attitude (**Mindset**)

- Pillar 3: You need the **Skills** for behavioral efficiency to interact effectively with the external world.

- Pillar 4: **Observation and Modelling** – How others are doing what you are intended to do.

- Pillar 5: **Execution Excellence** – how you put your knowledge, skills into practice with attitude to serve.

- Pillar 6: **Financial Stability and Wealth**.

Each pillar are correlated with each other. When they are in harmony, results are outstanding. Since external environment are truly dynamic, changing in every moment, it is your responsibility and duty to adjust the pillars to keep the momentum upright so that your positive spirit will always win over all the negative emotions and road blockers, and you will be always with keep growing attitude in the success journey.

At the current moment, please put your score of each pillar out of 10 such that your current position will have self-assessment:

____

____

____

____

____

____

____

____

____

____

____

____

Specify top 3 pillars you want to improve by next year to upgrade your position into desired level:

____

____

____

____

____

____

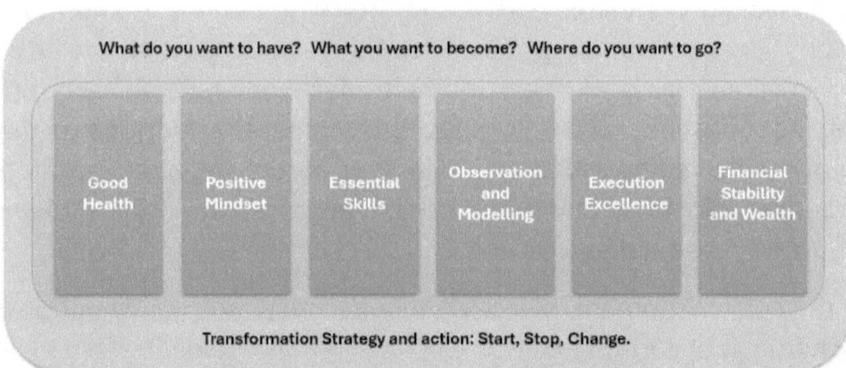

Chapter 8

Your Mind Power and Good Health

Your good health will provide you a better living experience such that you will be ready to focus on your important actions to achieve the milestones towards your dream life. Age is just a number, it is not necessarily mean that as you grow older, you will lose your good health, using Mind programming you can achieve better way of living to be different.

Almighty has blessed us with physical body which is the hardware. Mind is the software part which is to run the hardware efficiently. The physical body will grow over the period of time naturally with nutrition. But the Mindpower development and cognitive ability upliftment is our responsibility to enhance as we grow older.

By default, human mind is similar to monkey mind, it runs very fast travelling here and there without concentrating on one thing and thus our action is not in general always in positive aspect of life. Mind very frequently attracts the negativity and time, energy and other resources are misused and our main goals towards good health are missed.

While mind will procrastinate, tomorrow will start good having healthy food, quit negative habits, start morning walk, deep breath, exercise, meditation etc. and usually the next day never comes so easily. Even if it comes, with great enthusiasm practices are started for good health, lack of disciplined action usually fails to provide expected result.

For good health it is very important for you to understand from the core of the heart why do you need the good health. What will you do with the good health. Then only your strategy, your action, your focus, your aspiration will be aligned with your good health. In auto pilot mode, you will perform whatever important for you, you will escape habit even if it is pleasant but not for your good health. Discipline and control can make difference. Whatever you will do for your good health, you should keep on enjoying otherwise there will be immense inner conflict, and you will be controlled by your negative hormones even if you do all the hard work to live well. Be with the nature, be peaceful, happy, mindful to be ready to make right decision on time and act quickly such that external ups and downs will not impact your internal stability.

A survey was conducted, and few persons were selected who are more than 100 years old. They were questions what are the inspiration and secret of their happy peaceful healthy long life? There were 5 common answers were found:

- They are focused on what they love to do.

- They expanded their skill what they are good at.

- They tried to align their contribution on their work area where there was demanding social need.

- They tried to give more in problem solving space where people was happy to pay to get rid of burning situation – this they has financial sustainability.

- They are always connected to the nature and society with growing together mindset.

Now take a pen and paper. Sit down in a comfortable place. Take a glass of water and drink gently. List down 10 current issues of your health you are undergoing which is bothering you. What is the most important issue on your priority list that you want to get rid by next year?

____

____

What 3 actions you were planning since last 2 years and unable to do regularly which can help to get rid of the above issue?

What are the main obstacles that stopped you continuing the essential practice? Please don't specify that you have lack of time, you don't have lack of motivation as results are not coming fast, you have ignorance and lethargy, your indiscipline approach. You are the creator of your own destiny, please specify what will be your top 3 actions that you will start from today? Who will assist you to start and continue the actions?

The first step regarding your health is to select a knowledgeable doctor who can assist you in assessing your physical body and through required test, you will understand the current situation. Based on the given advice by doctor, physio, dietitian, maintain healthy lifestyle.

Next is your wellness from Mind perspective. Maintain regular deep breathing practice. Breath in slowly, belly will go expand first then chest. Hold the breath for few seconds and breath out slowly. Continue at least 10 times a set and 3 sets per day which will help your nerves to be relaxed for your stress relief and harmony of your hormonal balance. This practice will make your system in order removing the disorder conditions.

Practice regular visualization - meditation technique with muscle relaxation techniques. Sit comfortably. Take few deep breaths. Assume that you are in your favorite place. You are sitting in a safe and comfortable place in the nature. Weather is beautiful and you are enjoying the place. You assume light sunlight is coming to you to enlighten, it is giving your courage, it is giving you knowledge, wisdom of blessings are you are enjoying being there.

Now you take slow and deep breath. When you breath in, contract your foot muscles. Hold for few seconds. And you exhale slowly and relax your food muscle. Now again breath in slowly, make your foot muscle and cough muscle, make it contracted strong and when you breath out, relax the muscle slowly.

Each time you take slow deep breath in, gradually you tight the muscles one by one, knee, heap, belly, chest, neck, head and with your breath our relax the muscles. It is recommended to have guided start; in our workshop we help people to learn and then practice. This will make your body mind harmonized; muscles get more energy and pain and stress are getting relief by regular practice. Your energy level will boost up. Your gut mind axis will have a better rejuvenation, and you will be achieving enhanced wellness.

Story: The Mind's Power – How Ravi Transformed His Health

Ravi was a 35-year-old man working in a demanding corporate job in a bustling city. His days were filled with endless meetings, tight deadlines, and late nights at the office. Over time, he developed unhealthy habits – eating junk food, skipping exercise, and losing sleep. It wasn't long before these habits took a toll on his body. Ravi gained weight, became lethargic, and constantly felt fatigued. Worse, his doctor diagnosed him with high blood pressure and early signs of diabetes.

Ravi felt stuck. No matter how many diets he tried or gym memberships he signed up for, he would eventually fall back into his old habits. His health continued to decline, and he began to feel hopeless.

The Turning Point: Discovering Mind Programming

One day, while strolling through social media, Ravi came across an article about **mind programming** and the power of the mind to influence physical health. Intrigued, he read about how the subconscious mind controls habits, behaviours, and even the body's healing process. The article explained that by changing the way you think and perceive your health, you could reprogram your mind to adopt healthier behaviours and improve your well-being.

Determined to change his life, Ravi decided to learn more about **mind power** and how to use it to his advantage. He signed up for a workshop on **Neuro-Linguistic Programming (NLP)** and **positive visualization**, which taught techniques to rewire the mind.

Step 1: Visualization and Affirmations

One of the key techniques Ravi learned was **visualization.** He was taught that the brain responds to mental images and, when done consistently, the mind begins to align thoughts with reality. Every morning, Ravi would sit quietly for 10 minutes and visualize himself in his ideal state of health. He imagined himself with a fit body, full of energy, and free of disease. He pictured himself running on the beach, enjoying fresh, healthy meals, and feeling light and happy.

Along with visualization, Ravi began practicing **positive affirmations**. Instead of telling himself, "I'm unhealthy" or "I'll never lose weight," he replaced those negative thoughts with positive affirmations like "I am in control of my health," "My body is strong and vibrant," and "I choose healthy habits every day." These repeated affirmations started to reprogram his subconscious mind, changing his relationship with his body.

Step 2: Subconscious Reprogramming

Ravi learned that most unhealthy habits were deeply rooted in his subconscious mind – patterns that had formed over years. His cravings for junk food, his tendency to avoid exercise, and his procrastination around health were all linked to subconscious beliefs about what he thought he could or couldn't achieve.

Using **NLP techniques**, Ravi started to reframe his thoughts. He associated unhealthy foods with negative feelings – sluggishness, fatigue, and regret – and healthy foods with positive emotions like energy and vitality. He used **anchor techniques**, where he would snap his fingers and immediately visualize himself rejecting unhealthy habits, reminding his brain to make better choices.

Step 3: Building Consistency and Habits

By consistently visualizing his ideal health and using positive affirmations, Ravi began to notice changes. He started craving healthier foods and no longer felt drawn to fast food. Instead of forcing himself to go to the gym, he genuinely looked forward to his daily workout because he associated it with positive energy and self-care. His mind had been reprogrammed to see exercise as something enjoyable rather than a chore.

Ravi also practiced **meditation** and **mindfulness**, which helped reduce his stress levels. With lower stress, his blood pressure naturally improved. He became more aware of his body and its needs, such as when to rest and when to push harder. His quality of sleep improved as he practiced deep breathing exercises before bed, calming his mind and preparing his body for rest.

The Transformation

Over the next few months, Ravi experienced a dramatic transformation. Not only had he lost weight and improved his physical appearance, but his energy levels soared. His blood pressure returned to normal, and his doctor was amazed at how well his body had responded. Even his early signs of diabetes had been reversed through a healthier lifestyle.

But the real change was in Ravi's **mindset**. By using the power of mind programming, Ravi had trained his brain to view health as a priority. What had once seemed impossible—getting in shape, managing stress, and eating well—was now a natural part of his life. He realized that his mind had always held the key to unlocking his potential for good health.

The Lesson: Mind Programming and Health

Ravi's story demonstrates how **mind power** can play a critical role in achieving good health. By changing the way you think, reprogramming your subconscious, and aligning your actions with positive mental images, you can overcome unhealthy habits and create lasting change in your life.

Mind programming techniques like visualization, affirmations, and mindfulness are powerful tools that can:

1. **Shift your mindset**: Replace limiting beliefs with empowering ones.

2. **Rewire your habits**: Make healthier choices a natural part of life rather than a struggle.

3. **Reduce stress**: Achieve a calm, focused mind that supports your physical well-being.

In the end, Ravi realized that health wasn't just about what he ate or how much he exercised—it was about aligning his **mind** with his **actions** and using his mental power to shape the life he truly wanted.

Key Takeaways from Ravi's Story:

1. **Mind programming can break old patterns**: By reprogramming his subconscious mind, Ravi overcame unhealthy habits that had persisted for years.

2. **Visualization helps manifest success**: Ravi's consistent mental imagery of good health motivated him to make the right choices.

3. **Affirmations create positive beliefs**: By replacing negative thoughts with affirmations, Ravi changed his internal narrative and empowered himself.

4. **Consistency is key**: Daily focus on visualizations, affirmations, and mindfulness led to lasting change.

The mind has immense power over the body. When used correctly, it can be the greatest tool for achieving optimal health.

To stay healthy and fit, your mind must control several key aspects such as cravings, discipline, stress, motivation, and mindset. Each of these plays a crucial role in maintaining a balanced and healthy lifestyle. Below are detailed explanations with examples of how controlling these factors is essential for overall health and fitness:

1. **Control Over Cravings and Impulse Eating**

   Example:

   Anna is trying to maintain a healthy diet but often finds herself craving junk food, especially during the late afternoon. Her mind tends to justify unhealthy snacks with thoughts like, "I've worked hard today, I deserve a treat." Over time, these unhealthy eating habits contribute to weight gain and lower energy levels.

What the mind must control:

To stay fit, the mind must control cravings and impulse eating. This can be done by identifying triggers (like stress, boredom, or fatigue) and practicing mindful eating. Anna began to control her cravings by drinking water when she felt hungry between meals, taking a moment to assess whether she was truly hungry, and replacing unhealthy snacks with fruit or nuts. By managing her cravings, she could stick to her nutritional goals and see positive changes in her fitness.

2. **Discipline and Consistency with Exercise**

Example:

David is committed to his fitness goals, but some days after work, he feels exhausted and his mind convinces him to skip the gym, thinking, "I'll make up for it tomorrow." However, this lack of consistency leads to missed workouts, and eventually, he struggles to maintain progress.

What the mind must control:

Discipline is key for staying fit. The mind must control the desire to skip workouts or be lazy. David realized that discipline meant doing his workout even on the days when he didn't feel like it. He created a mental routine to remind himself of how good he felt after exercising, and he set small, achievable goals like 30-minute workouts. Over time, by controlling his urge to skip workouts, David saw significant improvements in his fitness level and overall health.

3. **Managing Stress and Emotional Eating**

Example:

Lisa has a stressful job, and when she's overwhelmed, she turns to comfort food, such as sweets and fast food. Her mind tells her that eating these foods will make her feel better, but this habit leads to weight gain and low energy levels, affecting her overall well-being.

What the mind must control:

Stress can lead to emotional eating, where the mind associates food with comfort. To stay healthy, Lisa needed to control her stress-induced cravings. She began practicing meditation and deep breathing exercises to manage her stress instead of turning to food. Additionally, she started keeping a journal to track her feelings and learned to channel stress through exercise. By controlling emotional eating and stress, Lisa was able to maintain a balanced diet and improve her fitness.

4. **Overcoming Procrastination and Laziness**

Example:

Mark often plans to go for a run every morning, but when the alarm goes off, his mind convinces him to hit the snooze button, thinking, "I'll just do it later." This constant procrastination leads to skipped workouts, and he struggles to meet his fitness goals.

What the mind must control:

Procrastination is a common barrier to fitness. To succeed, the mind must control the urge to delay or avoid exercise. Mark realized that he needed to set clear intentions the night before, laying out his workout clothes and setting multiple alarms. By visualizing the benefits of staying active and focusing on how much better he felt after a run, he trained his mind to resist procrastination. As a result, Mark started running regularly and saw improvements in his stamina and health.

5. **Maintaining a Positive and Growth-Oriented Mindset**

Example:

Sarah is trying to lose weight, but after several weeks of effort, she doesn't see the results she expected. Her mind starts to tell her, "This isn't working, I should just give up." Frustrated, she considers quitting her fitness routine.

What the mind must control:

To stay fit, it's essential to control negative thoughts and maintain a positive, growth-oriented mindset. Sarah decided to shift her focus from the numbers on the scale to how she felt—stronger, more energetic, and healthier. By celebrating small victories and embracing progress rather than perfection, Sarah stayed motivated and continued her journey. Over time, her positive mindset helped her achieve her long-term fitness goals.

6. **Controlling Sleep and Rest Patterns**

Example:

John is passionate about working out and staying fit, but he often sacrifices sleep to fit more activities into his day. Over time, his lack of sleep affects his recovery and reduces the effectiveness of his workouts, leading to fatigue and low performance.

What the mind must control:

Sleep and recovery are vital for maintaining health and fitness. The mind must resist the temptation to cut back on rest. John realized that overworking his body without proper sleep led to diminishing returns in his fitness progress. He adjusted his schedule to prioritize 7-8 hours of sleep each night, ensuring his body had time to recover. By controlling his sleep patterns, John was able to enhance his workout performance and improve his overall health.

Chapter 9

Positive Mindset – the key to success

Success is not just like a T20 cricket match; it is a continuous series of matches throughout one's lifespan. Ups and downs are inevitable. Failure is natural, and learning from failure, along with corrective measures, reduces the probability of experiencing severe setbacks again. Change is the only constant. A cloudy sky can turn day into night, but nothing is permanent; clouds will pass, rain will stop, the sun will rise again, and a blue sky will reappear. This is the rule of nature.

Accepting reality, letting go of uncontrollable failures, and starting afresh with a new strategy—while dynamically adjusting your actions based on circumstances—requires courage and accountability, ultimately leading to favourable results. It is often said that familiar things provide survival, while challenging experiences expand your creative abilities, encouraging you to explore new horizons of possibility. Every significant innovation starts from zero; ideas are first sketched on paper, and through engineering techniques, they are transformed into reality, creating those "wow" moments.

Aspect	People with a Positive Mindset	People with a Negative Mindset
Attitude	Proactive and optimistic, believing in their ability to succeed.	Reactive and pessimistic, doubting their chances of success.

Aspect	People with a Positive Mindset	People with a Negative Mindset
Goal Setting	Sets clear, achievable goals and creates actionable plans.	Often sets vague or unrealistic goals without a clear plan.
Approach to Challenges	Sees challenges as opportunities for growth and learning.	Views challenges as obstacles and feels overwhelmed by them.
Effort and Consistency	Demonstrates consistent effort and resilience in pursuing goals.	Lacks consistency and may give up easily when faced with setbacks.
Learning from Failure	Embraces failure as a valuable learning experience.	Fears failure and often sees it as a confirmation of their inadequacy.
Action Orientation	Takes decisive actions to move towards their goals.	Tends to procrastinate or wait for the "right moment" to act.
Mindset Towards Opportunities	Actively seeks out and creates opportunities for success.	Waits for opportunities to come without taking initiative.
Self-Reflection	Regularly reflects on progress and adjusts strategies as needed.	Rarely reflects on their actions or learns from past experiences.
Support Systems	Builds and nurtures positive relationships and networks for support.	May isolate themselves or surround themselves with negativity.
Celebration of Achievements	Celebrates small wins and uses them as motivation for future success.	Downplays or ignores achievements, focusing only on what went wrong.

This table highlights how a positive mindset fosters proactive habits that lead to success, while a negative mindset results in passivity and missed opportunities.

Story: Meera's Leap into the Unknown – How a Positive Mindset Created Wow Results

Meera was a marketing professional in her early thirties, living in Mumbai. For the past decade, she had been working in corporate marketing, handling advertising campaigns for big brands. She was good at her job, but deep inside, she felt restless. Meera had always loved **baking**, and in her spare time, she would whip up cakes, cookies, and pastries for her family and friends. Over the years, her hobby had grown into a passion, but it was just that—**a hobby**.

One day, after a particularly stressful week at work, Meera started to think seriously about following her heart. What if she could turn her passion for baking into a business? The idea excited her, but it also terrified her. She had no experience running a business, no formal training in baking, and no idea where to begin.

Despite these doubts, something inside Meera told her that she needed to take the leap. She decided to approach her new venture with a **positive mindset**, focusing on possibilities rather than fears. She didn't know the outcome, but she was determined to put her best foot forward.

The Shift to Positivity

Meera realized that in order to succeed, she needed to believe in herself and her vision. So, instead of being overwhelmed by the challenges, she made a **commitment to stay positive** through every step of the journey. Here's how she transformed her mindset:

1. **Focus on Growth, Not Fear:**

2. Meera knew she lacked business experience, but instead of seeing that as a limitation, she saw it as an opportunity to learn. She started reading books on entrepreneurship, joined a local business network, and took online courses on baking techniques and business management.

3. **Visualizing Success**:

4. Every morning, Meera practiced **visualization**. She would close her eyes and imagine the bakery she dreamed of—a cozy space filled with the smell of fresh bread and pastries, happy customers coming in for treats, and her name being known for unique, delicious baked goods. This positive visualization fueled her daily efforts and gave her confidence, even when obstacles arose.

5. **Affirmations for Self-Belief**:

6. Meera adopted daily **affirmations** to help maintain her positive mindset. She would tell herself things like:

7. *"I am capable of running a successful bakery."*

8. *"I have the talent, creativity, and determination to make this dream come true."*

9. *"Every challenge is an opportunity for growth."*

10. These affirmations helped her replace self-doubt with self-belief.

The Challenges

Starting the bakery wasn't easy. Meera had to figure out **finances**, **find suppliers**, and set up a website to market her new business. Initially, she faced some failures: her first batch of cookies for a big event was overbaked, her online orders were few and far between, and many days were quiet at her pop-up shop.

But Meera didn't give up. Her **positive mindset** kept her going. Every time something went wrong, she reframed it as a learning experience. For example, instead of being discouraged by the cookie disaster, she spent a week perfecting the recipe and received rave reviews when she offered the revised version at her next event.

The Wow Moment

About six months into her journey, Meera got an unexpected call. A **popular food blogger** had tried her pastries at a local farmers' market and was incredibly impressed. The blogger wanted to feature Meera's bakery on her website, which had thousands of followers.

The feature was a game-changer. Within days, Meera's online orders skyrocketed. People started flocking to her pop-up events, and soon, she had a loyal customer base that spread the word about her business. What was once a side hobby had now turned into a full-fledged success.

But the real "wow" moment came a few months later when a well-known restaurant group approached her to supply desserts for their chain of restaurants. Meera had gone from being a corporate employee with no business experience to running a thriving bakery that was getting attention from major industry players—all because she maintained a **positive mindset** and believed in her ability to succeed.

The Power of Positivity

Meera's story highlights the power of a **positive mindset** in navigating new and uncertain territory. It wasn't her background or business experience that made her bakery a success—it was her belief in herself, her ability to see challenges as opportunities, and her unwavering focus on her goals.

Key Lessons from Meera's Story:

1. **Positive Mindset Fuels Growth**:

2. Meera didn't let her lack of business experience hold her back. Instead, she embraced the learning process, which opened doors to new skills and opportunities.

3. **Reframing Challenges as Opportunities**:

4. Each time Meera faced an obstacle, she viewed it as a lesson rather than a failure. This helped her grow and improve with every step.

5. **Visualizing Success Leads to Action**:

6. Meera's consistent practice of visualizing her success gave her the motivation and confidence to take action, even when the path was unclear.

7. **Affirmations Build Confidence**:

8. Daily affirmations reinforced Meera's belief in herself, helping her stay positive and resilient, even when things got tough.

9. **Consistency in Positivity Yields Results**:

10. By maintaining her positive mindset consistently, Meera's hard work and belief eventually manifested in "wow" results—being featured by a popular blogger, gaining customers, and securing a major business deal.

Conclusion:

Meera's leap into the unfamiliar world of entrepreneurship is a testament to the power of the **mind**. A **positive mindset** doesn't just make you feel better—it **drives action, builds resilience**, and opens up possibilities that would otherwise seem out of reach. By focusing on growth, visualizing success, and believing in her abilities, Meera transformed her passion into a thriving business, achieving **wow results** in a completely new area of her life.

Keeping your mind away from negative emotions and focusing on positive, aspiring vibes requires intentional practice and strategies. It involves cultivating emotional resilience, mindfulness, and adopting habits that steer your thoughts toward positivity. Here's how you can achieve this, with practical steps:

1. **Practice Mindfulness and Meditation**

   How it works:

   Mindfulness involves paying attention to the present moment without judgment. It helps in recognizing when negative emotions arise and allows you to address them calmly, without letting them take control. Meditation strengthens your ability to stay present and focused on positive thoughts.

Practical Step:

Start your day with 5-10 minutes of meditation. Focus on your breathing or repeat a positive affirmation. For example, "I am capable, calm, and moving towards my goals." This daily practice helps clear your mind and create space for positive energy.

Example:

Susan, a busy executive, used to start her day stressed and overwhelmed with negative thoughts about her workload. She began practicing mindfulness, taking a few moments in the morning to focus on deep breathing and gratitude. Over time, this practice helped her start the day with clarity and positive energy, leading to more productive and optimistic days.

2. **Identify and Reframe Negative Thoughts**

How it works:

Often, we're not aware of our negative thought patterns. By becoming conscious of these thoughts, you can actively reframe them into more positive or constructive ones.

Practical Step:

When you catch yourself thinking something negative, ask: "Is this thought helpful?" For example, if you think, "I can never do this," reframe it to, "This is challenging, but I'm capable of learning and improving."

Example:

John often thought, "I'm not good enough," especially in his professional life. He started practicing reframing, changing his thought to, "I'm still learning, and every challenge is an opportunity to grow." This shift in mindset helped him reduce anxiety and approach his work with more confidence and enthusiasm.

3. **Surround Yourself with Positive Influences**

How it works:

The people and environment you surround yourself with have a significant impact on your emotional state. Positive energy from uplifting individuals, inspiring content, or a harmonious environment can keep you focused on positivity.

Practical Step:

Surround yourself with supportive people who encourage your growth. Also, consume positive content—books, podcasts, or videos that inspire you and align with your goals. Limit time spent with negative influences, whether it's people or media.

Example:

Emily felt drained and negative after spending time with certain friends who were always critical or complaining. She made a conscious effort to spend more time with colleagues and friends who were optimistic and encouraging. This change uplifted her mood and gave her the motivation to pursue her personal goals with more enthusiasm.

4. **Practice Gratitude**

How it works:

Focusing on what you're grateful for shifts your mind from dwelling on what's lacking or going wrong to what's already good in your life. Gratitude rewires your brain for positivity.

Practical Step:

Keep a gratitude journal and write down 3 things you're grateful for each day. This practice will help you focus on the positives, even during tough times.

Example:

Sarah started writing down daily moments of gratitude—simple things like a good conversation with a friend, or a task she accomplished at work. Gradually, she found herself looking for more things to be thankful for, which reduced her focus on minor frustrations and increased her sense of happiness.

5. **Engage in Physical Activity**

How it works:

Exercise not only improves your physical health but also releases endorphins—natural mood lifters that help reduce stress, anxiety, and depression.

Practical Step:

Incorporate regular physical activity into your routine, even if it's just a 20-minute walk or a quick home workout. It helps in channelling negative emotions into something productive and positive.

Example:

Mike found himself feeling anxious and irritable after a long day at work. He started going for a 30-minute run every evening, which helped him release tension and shift his mindset from negative thoughts to feeling refreshed and positive.

6. **Set Realistic Goals and Celebrate Small Wins**

How it works:

Setting achievable goals keeps your mind focused on progress and positivity. Celebrating small successes boosts your confidence and motivates you to stay on track.

Practical Step:

Break your larger goals into smaller, actionable steps, and celebrate each accomplishment. This could be as simple as finishing a task you've been procrastinating on or completing a workout. Reward yourself with something meaningful, like taking time for self-care or enjoying a hobby.

Example:

Rachel was working on a long-term project, and the lack of visible progress made her feel discouraged. She started setting smaller weekly goals and celebrating each win—like completing a report or hitting a fitness milestone. These small victories helped her stay motivated and focused on the positive aspects of her journey.

7. **Limit Exposure to Negative News and Social Media**

How it works:

Constant exposure to negative news, social media comparison, or toxic conversations can trigger negative emotions like fear, jealousy, or anger. Reducing this exposure helps maintain a balanced, positive mindset.

Practical Step:

Set limits on your social media usage, and take breaks from consuming negative news. Instead, curate your feed with inspirational content, educational material, or uplifting stories that align with your values.

Example:

Adam noticed that after scrolling through social media, he often felt anxious or envious, comparing himself to others' seemingly perfect lives. He decided to take social media breaks and limited his exposure to news that was overly negative. Instead, he subscribed to newsletters focused on personal growth and positivity. This shift helped him stay focused on his own progress and feel more content.

8. **Practice Positive Affirmations**

How it works:

Positive affirmations are statements that help reprogram your mind toward self-belief, positivity, and optimism. Repeating them reinforces positive thinking and helps eliminate self-doubt and negativity.

Practical Step:

Choose affirmations that resonate with you, such as "I am capable of handling whatever comes my way," or "I am worthy of happiness and success." Repeat them each morning or whenever you feel negative thoughts creeping in.

Example:

Whenever Megan faced a challenging day, she would stand in front of the mirror and repeat affirmations like "I am strong, and I can overcome any challenge." Over time, this practice boosted her self-esteem and helped her approach difficulties with a more positive mindset.

9. **Help Others and Be of Service**

How it works:

Acts of kindness and helping others can elevate your mood and shift focus away from your problems. Being of service cultivates a sense of fulfilment and positivity.

Practical Step:

Find small ways to help others—whether it's offering support to a friend, volunteering, or simply doing something kind for a stranger. These acts of kindness promote a sense of connection and positivity.

Example:

Jake, feeling overwhelmed by personal challenges, started volunteering at a local shelter once a week. The act of giving back shifted his perspective, and the gratitude and joy he experienced from helping others brightened his outlook on life and reduced his stress.

Chapter 10

Essential Skill Development

Once your mind is energized and ignited, you are ready to effectively interact with the external world. This is purely an inside-out practice for achieving behavioural excellence. Essential skills are key elements that empower you to behave with maturity and create favourable situations. These essential skills include leadership behaviour, communication skills, interpersonal skills, decision-making skills, conflict resolution skills, time management skills, collaboration skills, and more. Together, these skills ensure that the desired tasks are delivered on time.

Aspect	Skilful People	Unskilled People
Mindset	Adopt a growth mindset, believing they can improve with effort.	Often have a fixed mindset, believing their abilities are static.
Approach to Challenges	View challenges as opportunities to learn and grow.	See challenges as threats, leading to avoidance or discouragement.
Problem-Solving	Use analytical thinking to assess situations and develop solutions.	May struggle to find effective solutions and rely on trial and error.
Decision-Making	Make informed decisions based on data and experience.	Tend to make impulsive decisions without sufficient information.

Aspect	Skilful People	Unskilled People
Learning from Failure	Embrace failure as a learning opportunity to improve.	Fear failure and may become discouraged, leading to inaction.
Collaboration	Actively seek collaboration and value diverse perspectives.	Prefer to work independently and may resist input from others.
Time Management	Prioritize tasks effectively and manage time efficiently.	Struggle with prioritization and often miss deadlines.
Adaptability	Quickly adapt to new situations and adjust strategies as needed.	Resist change and may stick to ineffective methods.
Self-Reflection	Regularly reflect on their performance to identify areas for growth.	Rarely reflect on their actions or learn from past experiences.
Goal Setting	Set clear, achievable goals and create actionable plans.	Often set vague goals without a clear plan for achievement.
Communication	Communicate effectively and actively listen to others.	May struggle with clear communication and lack listening skills.
Confidence	Exhibit confidence in their abilities and decisions.	Often display self-doubt and lack confidence in their skills.

This table highlights the contrasting thought processes and actions of skilful versus unskilled individuals, showcasing how these differences can influence their effectiveness and success.

Below are top 50 essential skills that you should emphasize to uplift your personal life and professional career.

1. **Self-discipline**

   Story: John had a dream to run a marathon, but he had never run more than 2 miles in his life. By waking up at 5 AM every day and sticking to a strict training plan, he gradually increased his stamina. After 6 months of consistent effort, he completed his first marathon.

2. **Time management**

   Story: Sarah was balancing college with a part-time job. She used planners and to-do lists to block time for study, work, and personal activities. Her planning allowed her to maintain a high GPA while excelling at her job.

3. **Goal setting**

   Story: Amit set a goal to save ₹50,000 in 12 months. By creating a detailed budget and sticking to his plan, he avoided unnecessary expenses and reached his savings goal by the end of the year.

4. **Adaptability**

   Story: Maya worked as a graphic designer in print media, but when her company moved to digital formats, she quickly learned new software. Her willingness to adapt led her to a promotion in the digital design department.

5. **Resilience**

   Story: After losing his job, Arjun faced financial hardship. Instead of giving up, he focused on learning new skills and building connections. Within a year, he started his own successful consulting firm.

6. **Emotional intelligence**

   Story: In a heated meeting, Priya noticed a colleague was becoming frustrated. Instead of arguing, she listened empathetically, diffused the tension, and helped the team reach a compromise.

7. **Stress management**

   Story: During exams, Deepika felt overwhelmed. She began practicing yoga and meditation, which helped her stay calm and focused, ultimately allowing her to perform well in her tests.

8. **Mindfulness**

   Story: Raj used to work on autopilot, missing details in his work. After learning mindfulness techniques, he began staying present during tasks, which improved his productivity and creativity at work.

9. **Growth mindset**

   Story: Despite failing his first programming exam, Sameer believed he could improve. He took extra courses, practiced daily, and eventually became the top student in his class.

10. **Self-motivation**

    Story: Tina started an online business selling handmade jewellery. Even when sales were slow, she kept creating and promoting her work. Her persistence paid off when her brand got featured in a major fashion magazine.

11. **Critical thinking**

    Story: Faced with declining sales, Ria analysed market trends and customer behaviour, identifying a gap in her company's product line. Her critical thinking helped the business pivot, leading to a successful product launch.

12. **Problem-solving**

    Story: When his company's system crashed, Sandeep quickly diagnosed the problem, implemented a temporary solution, and worked with the IT team to prevent future issues, minimizing downtime.

13. **Decision-making**

    Story: As a manager, Aliya had to decide whether to invest in new software. After researching, she confidently chose the one that improved efficiency and reduced costs.

14. **Leadership**

    Story: As team lead, Varun encouraged open communication and built a collaborative environment. His team exceeded their targets and received the "Best Team of the Year" award.

15. **Innovation and creativity**

    Story: Neha, an event planner, turned a tight budget wedding into a fairy-tale experience by using recycled materials and creative lighting, impressing everyone with her innovation.

16. **Strategic planning**

    Story: Vijay wanted to expand his local coffee shop into a chain. By carefully planning his location strategy, marketing, and operations, he opened five successful branches in two years.

17. **Financial literacy**

    Story: Ravi took control of his personal finances by learning about budgeting, investments, and debt management. This allowed him to pay off loans and start investing in the stock market.

18. **Negotiation**

    Story: When negotiating a contract with a vendor, Priyanka skilfully balanced her company's needs with the vendor's interests, resulting in a deal that benefited both parties.

19. **Project management**

    Story: Anika was tasked with launching a new product. Using her project management skills, she coordinated teams, set timelines, and managed the budget, delivering the project ahead of schedule.

20. **Technical proficiency**

    Story: Ashok became the go-to person at his workplace for troubleshooting software issues because of his deep knowledge of the tools they used, which led to a promotion in IT.

21. Communication

Story: Raj's ability to clearly explain complex ideas in simple terms made him a valuable resource at work. His presentations were always engaging and easy to understand, which helped close major deals.

22. Collaboration

Story: Aisha was known for bringing people together in her company. By encouraging collaboration across departments, she helped improve processes and innovation.

23. Networking

Story: At a business conference, Vishal made meaningful connections with industry leaders. A few months later, one of those connections helped him land a dream job at a prestigious firm.

24. Empathy

Story: As a customer service representative, Anjali's ability to empathize with frustrated customers helped her resolve complaints quickly, leading to higher customer satisfaction ratings.

25. Conflict resolution

Story: In her role as a mediator, Saira helped two employees with ongoing tensions resolve their differences through active listening and compromise, restoring harmony to the team.

26. Perseverance

Story: Kunal applied to multiple engineering programs but faced rejection from his top choices. Instead of giving up, he improved his skills and re-applied the next year, eventually gaining admission.

27. Public speaking

Story: Rohan was terrified of public speaking, but after practicing consistently, he gave a TEDx talk that received a standing ovation and led to more speaking engagements.

28. Active listening

Story: During team meetings, Rashmi was known for her ability to listen intently to everyone's opinions before offering thoughtful insights, which made her a respected leader.

29. Creativity

Story: As an advertising copywriter, Lakshmi brainstormed a creative campaign that resonated deeply with consumers, leading to a significant increase in product sales.

30. Initiative

Story: When the office supply system was inefficient, Nitin took the initiative to develop a better system. His efforts were recognized, and he was promoted to operations manager.

31. Confidence

Story: Meena believed in her ability to launch her own clothing line. Her confidence in her designs and marketing helped her create a successful business in a competitive industry.

32. Attention to detail

Story: Manish's precision as an architect ensured every building he designed met safety standards, earning him the trust of high-profile clients.

33. Flexibility

Story: During the pandemic, Priya, a dance teacher, shifted to offering virtual classes. Her flexibility helped her maintain her business and reach a global audience.

34. Resourcefulness

Story: With limited funding, Sohail used free online tools and a volunteer network to build a website for his nonprofit, successfully raising awareness and donations for his cause.

35. Learning agility

Story: Neeraj learned new coding languages quickly when his company transitioned to a new technology stack, ensuring he stayed relevant in his role.

36. Curiosity

Story: Sneha's natural curiosity about technology led her to explore AI and machine learning, which opened doors to an exciting career in tech innovation.

37. Self-awareness

Story: Through reflection and feedback, Arvind became aware of his leadership weaknesses and actively worked on them, transforming himself into a more effective leader.

38. Decision-making under pressure

Story: During a crisis at the hospital, Dr. Ayesha made quick, life-saving decisions under immense pressure, showcasing her ability to remain calm and focused.

39. Work ethic

Story: Vikram's reputation for being reliable and putting in extra effort helped him rise through the ranks in his company, earning him a leadership position.

40. Delegation

Story: As a manager, Reema learned to trust her team by delegating tasks effectively, which not only improved productivity but also empowered her team to grow.

41. Negotiation

Story: During salary negotiations, Sunita researched industry standards and presented her value confidently, securing a raise that reflected her contributions.

42. Risk-taking

Story: Kiran took the calculated risk of leaving a secure job to start her own business. The risk paid off as her startup grew into a profitable enterprise within a few years.

43. Accountability

Story: When a project at work went wrong, Dev owned up to his mistakes and worked on solutions, which earned him the respect of his peers and boss.

44. Coaching and mentoring

Story: As an experienced software engineer, Varsha regularly mentored junior developers, helping them advance in their careers and improving team dynamics.

45. Cultural competence

Story: Having worked with diverse teams globally, Sanjay understood the importance of cultural sensitivity, which made his international collaborations smooth and successful.

46. Listening to feedback

Story: Riya actively sought feedback from her colleagues and clients to improve her services, leading to continuous growth in her freelancing business.

47. Persuasion

Story: Arnav's persuasive communication helped convince a major investor to back his startup, ensuring the business had the financial support it needed.

48. **Adaptability**

   Story: When unexpected changes in regulations affected his business, Suresh quickly pivoted his business model, ensuring continued growth.

49. **Patience**

   Story: Karthik's patience in building his blog paid off after three years when it became one of the top resources in his niche, attracting thousands of visitors daily.

50. **Humility**

   Story: After achieving great success, Shalini stayed humble and continued learning from others, earning her the respect and admiration of her peers.

Among all skills, time management is one of the critical aspects where you need to focus on what is important but non-urgent so that you can concentrate on long-term goals. Your goals should be SMARTIES: Specific, Measurable, Achievable, Realistic, Timeline-oriented, Enthusiastic, Emotionally connected, and Success-oriented. Non-urgent, non-important tasks should be avoided, urgent but important tasks should be prioritized, and urgent but non-important tasks should be delegated.

Conflict resolution techniques can lead to a wealth of ideas that open up creative solution options. Be open to listening to the perspectives of others, and present your point of view for improving the situation. Your communication should follow a structured approach, such as problem-solution-benefit or past-present-future. Deliver your message in a way that others can easily understand, ensuring they can complete the task on time. The effectiveness of your communication is reflected in the results you achieve. Often, we struggle to convey our messages effectively, leading to frustration when we do not get the expected outcomes. Therefore, setting the right expectations is essential: clarify what you need, when you need it, in what format, why you need it, and the potential consequences if the desired task is not completed. Clearly articulate the value the person will add by delivering the task on time to inspire them.

Every individual is unique in terms of learning style, personality, and social interaction. Some people learn quickly through audio-visual materials, while others learn through feeling and experience. Some individuals are bold and lead from the front, while others are shy and introverted. Some have analytical minds, some judge others, and some rely on intuition. Your communication must align with the other person's style to create maximum impact. By observing eye-accessing cues, you can assess whether someone is recalling or constructing a situation, helping you gauge their truthfulness.

Communication relies heavily on body language. When you successfully build rapport with another person through mirroring, matching, and pacing, the bridge of communication will be well established, making it easier to convey your message. The tonality of your voice is also important; you should adjust the modulation based on your audience. Choose your words wisely, using a positive tone to enhance the quality of your communication.

Leadership skills encompass all of the above competencies, along with the right mindset, ensuring you set an example as a role model for problem-solving abilities. To solve problems effectively, you must first understand and define the problem, assess its impact by questioning the risk elements, and seek potential solutions. Understand the root cause and source of the problem. Investigate whether it is a recurring issue or the first occurrence. Critically evaluate why certain solution options may not work, and select the best option, whether it involves a workaround or complete mitigation of the root cause. The main objective of problem-solving skills is to take precautions to avoid similar issues in the future, along with maintaining proper documentation and transitioning knowledge within the team to ensure that anyone can address similar issues effectively.

Essential skills can lead to extraordinary results, combining perseverance, creativity, leadership, and more to transform challenges into successes.

1. **The Power of Perseverance and Self-discipline: Rohan's Coding Journey**

The Challenge:

Rohan was an average student when he first started learning coding in college. While his peers picked up programming languages easily, Rohan struggled. His grades were average, and during his first internship, he failed to meet the expectations of his mentor. He felt discouraged and doubted his ability to succeed in the tech industry.

The Skill: Perseverance and Self-discipline

Rohan decided not to give up. He realized that while he may not have been the most naturally gifted, he could achieve his goals if he put in consistent, focused effort. Every day, he set a strict schedule to study coding for at least three hours outside of his regular classes. He practiced solving coding problems online, participated in coding challenges, and dedicated weekends to learning new programming languages.

The Breakthrough:

Months later, his hard work paid off. Rohan entered an international coding competition and placed in the top 5% out of 10,000 participants. His extraordinary result didn't come from natural talent but from his **perseverance** and **self-discipline**. After the competition, he was invited to interview at a leading tech company, where his deep understanding of programming earned him a job offer.

The Lesson:

Consistent effort and discipline, even in the face of difficulty, can lead to extraordinary results. While talent may open doors, perseverance and dedication unlock real success.

2. The Role of Creativity and Adaptability: Maya's Art Business

The Challenge:

Maya was a talented artist, but after graduating, she found it difficult to earn a living selling her artwork. Her initial approach of showcasing her work in galleries wasn't yielding enough sales. The market was competitive, and she struggled to stand out. She was on the verge of quitting her dream and getting a regular job.

The Skill: Creativity and Adaptability

Instead of giving up, Maya decided to approach her problem differently. She tapped into her **creativity** and **adaptability**, brainstorming new ways to market her art. She began sharing her work on social media platforms like Instagram and TikTok, creating time-lapse videos of her paintings. She also started offering **customized artwork** based on her followers' preferences, something unique that no other artist was doing at the time.

The Breakthrough:

Within a few months, Maya's online presence grew rapidly. Her time-lapse videos went viral, and she gained thousands of new followers. People from all over the world started commissioning her for custom artwork. Her once-fledgling art business turned into a thriving online enterprise, and she earned far more than she had imagined through gallery sales alone.

The Lesson:

By **adapting to changing circumstances** and using **creativity** to differentiate yourself, you can achieve extraordinary results even in challenging and competitive environments.

3. **Leadership and Emotional Intelligence: Rahul's Team Transformation**

The Challenge:

Rahul was promoted to team leader in a fast-growing tech startup. He inherited a team that was demotivated, constantly missing deadlines, and had poor collaboration. Rahul quickly realized that unless he turned things around, the team's underperformance could damage the company's reputation and hinder his career growth.

The Skill: Leadership and Emotional Intelligence

Instead of focusing only on deadlines and productivity, Rahul used his **emotional intelligence** to connect with each team member. He set up one-on-one meetings to understand their individual challenges, frustrations, and motivations. He noticed that one team member felt underappreciated, while another was overwhelmed with their workload.

Rahul restructured tasks based on people's strengths and interests. He also introduced flexible work hours, created an open space for sharing feedback, and made a point of celebrating small wins to boost morale. By **leading with empathy** and supporting the team emotionally, he cultivated a positive and collaborative work environment.

The Breakthrough:

Within three months, the team's performance improved significantly. They not only met deadlines but exceeded expectations by delivering high-quality work ahead of schedule. The team's turnaround was so remarkable that the company won a major client contract, and Rahul's leadership was credited as a key factor in the success.

The Lesson:

Leadership grounded in **emotional intelligence** can inspire and motivate teams to achieve extraordinary results. When leaders focus on understanding and empowering their team members, it leads to higher productivity and a sense of shared success.

As a mindful aspiring iconic leader, few critical aspects you should avoid which will help you get consistent success regularly. Below is the list that you should follow in your daily practice:

1. **Avoid Ego and Arrogance**

   Why it matters:

   Ego can be the downfall of many leaders. Arrogance can alienate team members, cause friction, and close you off from learning and growth. A mindful leader values humility and openness to feedback.

   What to do instead:

   Practice humility, no matter your level of success. Be open to the idea that you can always learn from others, whether they are colleagues, mentors, or even competitors. A leader who is grounded in humility is more approachable and capable of leading a team toward collective success.

   Example:

   An iconic leader who avoids ego listens to their team's input before making decisions. For example, if a company is facing a challenge, this leader would consult key team members for their insights and ideas, fostering collaboration and collective problem-solving, rather than dictating a solution from a place of ego.

2. **Avoid Micromanagement**

   Why it matters:

   Micromanagement stifles creativity and innovation, and it can frustrate team members. It signals a lack of trust in others, which can lead to disengagement and decreased productivity.

What to do instead:

Delegate tasks and trust your team to deliver. Provide guidance and resources but allow them the autonomy to approach tasks in their own way. This creates an environment where team members feel empowered and motivated.

Example:

A mindful leader empowers their team to take ownership of projects. Instead of micromanaging, they set clear goals and deadlines but give the team the freedom to execute the work. This fosters creativity and strengthens team morale, leading to better performance and results.

3. **Avoid Overcommitment**

Why it matters:

Taking on too many responsibilities or overcommitting can lead to burnout, poor decision-making, and subpar execution of projects. Aspiring leaders often want to prove themselves, but spreading yourself too thin can diminish your effectiveness.

What to do instead:

Prioritize and focus on key areas where you can have the most impact. Practice saying no when necessary to maintain balance and focus on high-priority tasks that align with your long-term goals.

Example:

An aspiring leader might be tempted to take on every project to showcase their capabilities, but a mindful leader recognizes the importance of focus. They avoid overcommitting by choosing only the most strategic projects where their leadership can add the most value, ensuring they deliver high-quality results.

4. **Avoid Reactivity and Impulsiveness**

Why it matters:

Quick, emotional decisions made without careful consideration can lead to mistakes and damage relationships. Being reactive often results in short-sighted solutions that don't address the root cause of problems.

What to do instead:

Take a step back, breathe, and assess situations mindfully before acting. Practice emotional regulation, especially in stressful or high-pressure situations. This allows for clearer, more rational decision-making.

Example:

A leader who avoids reactivity listens calmly when faced with unexpected challenges or conflicts. Instead of immediately reacting, they gather all necessary information, consult their team, and then make a well-informed decision. This thoughtful approach leads to better outcomes and fosters trust within the team.

5. **Avoid Blame and Finger-Pointing**

Why it matters:

Blaming others for failures or challenges creates a toxic work environment and undermines trust. It shifts the focus away from solutions and learning, which is critical for growth and success.

What to do instead:

Take responsibility for both successes and failures. When things go wrong, focus on solutions and what can be learned from the situation, rather than assigning blame. This builds a culture of accountability and continuous improvement.

Example:

A mindful leader takes responsibility when a project doesn't go as planned. Instead of blaming team members, they ask, "What can we learn from this, and how can we improve for the future?" This approach encourages problem-solving and ensures the team feels supported even when mistakes are made.

6. **Avoid a Fixed Mindset**

Why it matters:

Leaders who believe their abilities or intelligence are fixed tend to avoid challenges, fear failure, and resist new ideas. This limits growth and the ability to adapt in a rapidly changing environment.

What to do instead:

Embrace a **growth mindset**—the belief that abilities and intelligence can be developed through dedication and hard work. Be open to new ideas, feedback, and continuous learning.

Example:

A leader with a growth mindset sees failure as an opportunity to learn. If a product launch doesn't succeed, instead of seeing it as a setback, they review what went wrong and how the team can improve. This creates a culture of resilience and continuous improvement, driving long-term success.

7. **Avoid Negative Thinking and Self-Doubt**

Why it matters:

Negative thinking can sap motivation and prevent you from taking the necessary risks to succeed. Self-doubt can lead to inaction, missed opportunities, and a lack of confidence that others will sense in your leadership.

What to do instead:

Cultivate a positive mindset by focusing on possibilities, solutions, and lessons learned from challenges. Practice self-compassion and recognize your accomplishments, big or small.

Example:

When faced with a difficult decision, an aspiring leader might doubt their ability to make the right call. Instead of succumbing to self-doubt, a mindful leader focuses on their past successes, consults with their trusted team, and moves forward with confidence. This inspires others to trust in their leadership.

8. **Avoid Complacency**

Why it matters:

Success can sometimes lead to complacency, where leaders stop pushing themselves or their teams to innovate and grow. This can result in stagnation and losing a competitive edge.

What to do instead:

Continuously seek out new challenges, invest in learning, and encourage innovation. Foster a culture of continuous improvement and adaptability.

Example:

After achieving great success with a product, an iconic leader doesn't rest on their laurels. Instead, they challenge their team to explore new opportunities for innovation, pushing for the next breakthrough. By avoiding complacency, they maintain their company's competitive edge and drive future growth.

9. **Avoid Lack of Empathy**

Why it matters:

Leaders who lack empathy may struggle to connect with their team, making it difficult to inspire and motivate others. This can lead to disengagement, low morale, and high turnover.

What to do instead:

Practice **empathic leadership**—take time to understand your team's perspectives, emotions, and challenges. Show genuine care and support, both personally and professionally.

Example:

During a challenging period, a mindful leader takes the time to check in on their employees, understanding the personal and professional stress they may be experiencing. By offering flexibility and support, they build loyalty and a strong, motivated team, ensuring long-term success.

10. **Avoid Stagnant Leadership Styles**

Why it matters:

Leadership isn't static, and sticking to outdated or rigid leadership styles can prevent growth and adaptation, especially in a fast-paced, evolving environment.

What to do instead:

Be adaptable and open to change in your leadership approach. Stay up-to-date with new trends, technologies, and leadership philosophies. Flexibility and innovation in your leadership style can foster success.

Example:

A leader in the tech industry regularly updates their leadership approach based on new methodologies and trends like agile leadership or remote team management. This openness to evolving their style ensures they remain effective in a constantly changing environment.

Chapter 11

Observation and modelling Skill

Let's say your dream is to visit the Himalayan range, and this December, your school friends are organizing a trip. It will be very cold during the winter, making the journey challenging. However, you aspire to climb to the summit and host the national flag. It would be a moment of glory for you to stand at such an altitude with your school friends, feeling proud of your nation while holding the flag.

The weather conditions may be harsh, and the journey could involve trekking through snow. You may face difficulties with oxygen levels, and since this is your first visit, you feel utterly nervous and scared, unsure of how to achieve your dream, even though it is incredibly special to you.

You have already paid the advance amount, which is a significant investment for you, but your confidence is low. In this moment, one skill will be particularly helpful: observation and modelling methodology.

What you can do is start extensive research on those who have already completed similar journeys. In your friend circle or among your friends' acquaintances, find anyone who has visited that area. Investigate what they did during difficult times and how they achieved their goals. What proactive measures did they take to prepare for unforeseen situations? What are the typical weather trends during that month in those specific areas? What risk factors should you be aware of, and what mitigation strategies do they recommend?

Look into those who failed to complete the journey and returned. What were the root causes of their failures? Did they lack physical fitness or the necessary equipment? By observing and modelling the successes of others, as well as learning from their failures, you can enhance your chances of success on your dream journey.

Aspect	Learning from Observing Excellent Communication	Missed Opportunities When Ignoring
Effective Techniques	Learn techniques for clear and concise messaging	Miss out on strategies for effective communication
Active Listening Skills	Understand the importance of active listening and engagement	Fail to appreciate the value of listening in conversations
Non-Verbal Cues	Observe body language and tone that enhance communication	Overlook the impact of non-verbal communication on interactions
Persuasion and Influence	Discover how to persuade and influence others effectively	Struggle with gaining buy-in and support for your ideas
Empathy and Understanding	Learn to convey empathy and build rapport with others	Miss opportunities to connect emotionally with others
Clarity and Structure	Understand how to organize thoughts for clarity	Communicate in a confusing manner, leading to misunderstandings
Feedback Skills	Observe how to give and receive constructive feedback	Avoid learning how to improve based on feedback

Aspect	Learning from Observing Excellent Communication	Missed Opportunities When Ignoring
Conflict Resolution	Learn techniques for managing and resolving conflicts	Struggle to navigate disagreements effectively
Cultural Sensitivity	Gain insights into culturally appropriate communication styles	Miss the chance to connect with diverse audiences
Adaptability	See how skilled communicators adjust their style to different audiences	Remain fixed in your communication style, missing engagement opportunities

This table outlines the valuable lessons you can gain from observing effective communication in others, contrasted with the lost opportunities that come from ignoring those observations. If you need any further changes or specific details added, just let me know!

Similarly in your personal and professional life, lets assume you want to achieve one mission. But somehow you are stuck. Look around and check who are the people extremely successful on that field. Enquire what approach they have followed in their strategy definition and action. What was their plan B approach as fall back option. When a failure situation happened, how they did respond, what action they took to bounce forward. Note down. From the modelling exercise, what are the top 3 approach you can adapt which will help you to come out from the stuck in stage to move forward to get the desired outcome.

____

____

____

____

____

The Power of Modelling and Observation: A Story of Successful Transformation

The Challenge:

Ananya was a marketing manager at a mid-sized company. While she was good at her job, she felt like something was holding her back from reaching the next level. Despite her hard work, she noticed that her colleague, Rohan, consistently outperformed her. He effortlessly closed bigger deals, inspired his team, and consistently exceeded targets. Ananya was frustrated and began doubting her abilities.

She realized that her current strategies weren't yielding the results she wanted. Instead of continuing to struggle, she decided to adopt a different approach: **modelling and observation**.

The Skill: Modelling and Observation

In NLP, **modelling** is the process of studying the behaviours, thought patterns, language, and strategies of successful individuals to replicate their success. Rather than reinventing the wheel, Ananya chose to model Rohan's behaviour and habits.

Step 1: Observation

Ananya began by carefully observing Rohan's actions and communication style at work. She noticed the following patterns:

- **Body Language**: Rohan always maintained confident, open body language. Whether he was talking to a client or leading a team meeting, he made strong eye contact, smiled often, and used gestures to emphasize points.

- **Communication Style**: Rohan spoke in clear, concise sentences, and often used metaphors or analogies to explain complex ideas. He asked powerful, open-ended questions that engaged his audience, making them feel heard and valued.

- **Emotional State**: Rohan seemed calm and collected, even under pressure. Ananya realized that his ability to stay composed in stressful situations allowed him to think clearly and make better decisions.

Step 2: Modelling

Once Ananya had thoroughly observed Rohan's behaviours and mental strategies, she began to **model** them in her own work. She took the following steps:

1. **Body Language**: Ananya consciously adopted a more confident posture in meetings. She began making eye contact and smiling more, which gave her a natural sense of authority and positivity. This change immediately helped her connect better with her team and clients.

2. **Communication Patterns**: She started using some of the communication techniques she had observed. She practiced asking more open-ended questions, which encouraged deeper conversations with clients and colleagues. This not only improved her rapport but also helped her uncover important insights that were critical to her marketing strategies.

3. **Emotional State**: Ananya learned how to maintain a calm emotional state, especially when dealing with difficult clients or tight deadlines. She incorporated simple NLP techniques like **anchoring**, where she associated a confident feeling with a specific gesture (pressing her fingers together) so she could access that feeling in high-pressure situations.

Step 3: Replication and Adaptation

Rather than imitating Rohan blindly, Ananya **adapted** what worked for her. She combined Rohan's strategies with her own unique strengths. For instance, while Rohan excelled in persuasive communication, Ananya added her analytical strength to back her claims with data, making her pitches even more impactful.

The Breakthrough:

Over time, Ananya's efforts paid off. She noticed that her interactions with clients were smoother and more engaging, and her ability to maintain composure helped her close more deals. Her team became more motivated, and she successfully launched multiple marketing campaigns that exceeded expectations. Within a year, Ananya was promoted to head of marketing, achieving the extraordinary success she had longed for.

The most significant change was not in the tactics she used but in **how she modelled the mental and behavioural patterns** of success. Through careful **observation** and strategic **modelling,** she was able to replicate and internalize winning strategies that transformed her professional performance.

The Lesson:

modelling and observation can provide powerful tools for achieving success. By observing successful individuals and adopting their thought patterns, communication styles, and behaviours, you can bypass years of trial and error. The key to success through modelling is not only imitation but also adapting those strategies to fit your unique context and strengths.

This approach teaches us that success leaves clues, and by studying those who have already achieved what you aspire to, you can **model their excellence** to achieve extraordinary results in your own life.

Chapter 12

Execution Excellence

Whatever your goal may be, how powerful your strategic planning may be, until you execute or implement effectively, your desired outcome will not be fulfilled in reality in satisfactory manner. Thus it is very important to put focus how do you do what you do. That makes key difference in way of delivering things and makes the delivery amazing such that your customer will say "Just WoW"!

When you implement any project, what are the top 5 key best practice you follow such that your implementation will be successful?

____

____

____

____

____

____

In order to achieve excellence in your implementation, your first job is to understand the goal, what exactly you need to deliver, why you need to deliver, who all will be involved and what are the bigger pictures in the ecosystem for your delivery. What is the expected timeline and what will be the impact if the timeline or quality or budget is missed.

Once the goal is clear, your next step is to align your belief system with focus to accomplish the tasks. Make a strong believer that you have the ability to deliver with quality by learning and collaborating. Peet into deep your earlier achievements to go with your positive anchors.

Pre execution phase is very important. That starts with strategy and planning. Write down, what to do what not to do by chunking down your goals to smaller achievable milestones. Make yearly or half yearly planner. Write down. Make that broken into monthly, weekly and daily planner. Then it should be broken into hourly planner in each week so that your timeslot will be fully occupied result oriented and always you will be associated with handful task for your 8 – 12 hours of productive work. In parallel focus on your health, good sleep family time so that you can empower the quality of your work life balance.

Your planning will include setting up right expectation, don't overcommit, take some buffer to deliver within the timeline and to avoid unnecessary escalation. Maintain transparency to inform abut the situations, dependencies so that you client will be on the same page and help you to get help. Remember your contribution is the key business enabler of your customer to run their business, if you deliver on time, they will win with growing together model.

Below are few best practices that you must follow as proven method to enhance your quality of service delivery:

1. Forward looking approach: Think today for netter tomorrow.

Forward-Looking Thinking: A Story of Success

The Challenge:

Akshay, a young entrepreneur, had started a small tech startup specializing in app development. In the first two years, his business did fairly well by securing small projects from local companies. However, Akshay quickly realized that the industry was evolving faster than his business. Competitors were introducing cutting-edge technologies like AI integration and blockchain, while Akshay's company was still focusing on standard mobile app development.

Akshay knew that if he continued with his current strategy, his company might fall behind, losing clients to more innovative firms. He had to think beyond immediate success and develop a **forward-looking approach** if he wanted his business to thrive long-term.

The Skill: Forward-Looking Thinking and Approach

Forward-looking thinking involves anticipating future trends, challenges, and opportunities. It requires planning for not just the present but also considering how today's actions will shape tomorrow's outcomes. Akshay decided to adopt this mindset to take his company to the next level.

Step 1: Anticipating Industry Trends

Akshay began researching the future of technology in app development. He noticed that clients were becoming more interested in:

- **Artificial Intelligence (AI)** to personalize user experiences.

- **Blockchain** for secure data transactions.

- **Augmented Reality (AR)** for immersive customer engagement.

Instead of reacting to these trends later when they were mainstream, Akshay decided to invest in learning about these technologies immediately. He enrolled in courses on AI and blockchain, attended industry conferences, and collaborated with experts who were already using these technologies.

Step 2: Strategic Planning for the Future

Armed with knowledge of future trends, Akshay created a **forward-thinking business strategy**. He shifted his focus from simply building apps to creating smart, future-ready solutions. He began offering AI-driven features in apps, such as chatbots and predictive analytics, to give his clients a competitive edge. He also explored blockchain technology for building secure payment systems and started working on AR for retail apps.

Instead of aiming for short-term projects that paid the bills, Akshay targeted companies that were interested in **long-term innovations** and were willing to invest in the future. This helped him secure contracts with larger, more forward-thinking companies.

Step 3: Building a Team for the Future

Akshay understood that the success of his vision depended on the skills of his team. He hired developers with expertise in AI, blockchain, and AR, ensuring his company would be able to lead the market in these areas. He also encouraged continuous learning and upskilling within his company so that his team would stay on top of technological advancements.

The Breakthrough:

Within two years, Akshay's company was no longer a small local player but an emerging leader in the tech space. By being **proactive** and **forward-looking**, Akshay secured a major contract with a global retail chain to develop an AI-driven AR app that allowed customers to virtually try on clothes using their smartphones.

His forward-thinking approach set his company apart from competitors, who were still focused on basic app development. Akshay's ability to look ahead, anticipate future needs, and position his company for future trends resulted in a **30% growth in revenue** and multiple contracts with industry giants.

The Lesson:

Forward-looking thinking enables you to anticipate and prepare for future challenges and opportunities, putting you ahead of competitors who are focused solely on immediate results. It requires:

1. **Anticipation of trends**: Understanding where your industry is headed and staying ahead of the curve.
2. **Strategic long-term planning**: Making decisions today that will bear fruit in the future.

3. **Investing in future skills and technology**: Continuously upgrading yourself and your team to handle tomorrow's challenges.

Example of a Forward-Looking Approach: Elon Musk's SpaceX

A real-world example of forward-thinking is **Elon Musk's SpaceX**. When Musk founded SpaceX in 2002, the idea of privately funded space travel was considered unrealistic. However, Musk wasn't focused on the current limitations; he was looking far into the future. His vision of **colonizing Mars** and creating reusable rockets was revolutionary.

By anticipating future space exploration needs, investing in new technologies, and setting a bold long-term goal, Musk turned SpaceX into one of the leading aerospace companies. The forward-thinking approach allowed SpaceX to:

- Develop reusable rockets, drastically reducing the cost of space travel.

- Secure contracts with NASA and other major players in the space industry.

- Lead the conversation on humanity's future in space.

This kind of **forward-looking thinking**, focused on long-term vision rather than immediate challenges, demonstrates how thinking ahead can create **extraordinary success**.

Key Takeaways:

1. **Anticipate the future**: Always think about where your industry is headed and what skills or innovations will be valuable in the future.

2. **Plan for the long-term**: Don't focus solely on short-term gains. Make decisions that align with your long-term vision.

3. **Invest in future capabilities**: Continuously upgrade yourself and your resources to stay relevant in the ever-changing world.

In both Akshay's startup and Elon Musk's SpaceX, a forward-looking approach led to success that far surpassed immediate expectations, opening doors to opportunities that wouldn't have been possible otherwise.

2. Proactiveness: Avoiding the risk of failure

The Software Startup's Breakthrough

A young software startup, **TechWave**, had developed a promising new app that allowed users to collaborate on projects in real-time, much like an advanced virtual whiteboard. The team had invested a year into designing the app, and they were confident it would be a hit. They planned to launch the product at a major tech conference where hundreds of potential investors and customers would see it for the first time.

The founder, **David**, was thrilled about the launch and believed the app's functionality would speak for itself. He was eager to make a big impression. However, **Sophie**, the head of product development, was more cautious. She had seen enough launches in her career to know that even the best apps could face unexpected problems. She wasn't satisfied with launching without ensuring that everything was prepared.

David's Approach:

David, driven by enthusiasm, was focused on impressing investors and maximizing the marketing campaign. He believed that **"launch fast, fix later"** was the way to go. His plan was simple: launch at the conference, get as much exposure as possible, and then worry about bugs or issues after the initial feedback.

Sophie's Proactive Plan:

Sophie, however, advocated for a proactive strategy, one that would reduce the risks of failure during such an important launch. Here's what she proposed:

1. **Early Beta Testing**: Sophie suggested opening the app to a small group of early users two months before the big launch.

These beta testers would help identify any bugs, usability issues, or technical problems. While David was concerned this would delay the excitement of a big public release, Sophie believed that catching and fixing issues early would ensure a smoother launch.

2. **Stress Testing**: Sophie also recommended testing the app under high-demand conditions. She knew that during the conference, there would be hundreds of people accessing the app at once, so her team simulated heavy user traffic on their servers. They discovered that the current server setup wouldn't handle the expected load, leading them to upgrade their infrastructure in advance.

3. **Preparing a Backup Plan**: Sophie insisted on creating a backup plan for the conference in case anything went wrong during the live demo. She arranged to have a pre-recorded demonstration of the app, just in case there were connectivity issues or technical difficulties. This way, they wouldn't be completely reliant on a flawless live performance.

4. **User Support Readiness**: Understanding that first impressions matter, Sophie set up a small team to monitor user feedback during the launch and provide real-time support. She believed that being proactive in responding to any immediate issues would demonstrate to potential customers that TechWave was reliable and customer-focused.

The Outcome:

The conference day arrived, and hundreds of tech enthusiasts, investors, and media representatives gathered to see TechWave's app in action. During the live demo, the servers briefly experienced an unexpected load spike, causing a momentary delay. Thanks to Sophie's proactive stress testing and server upgrades, the issue was resolved within seconds. Even better, when it occurred, Sophie's team was able to switch to the pre-recorded demo seamlessly, so the audience barely noticed any interruption.

The early beta testing had also paid off. Many of the usability issues had been addressed ahead of time, so users found the app intuitive and responsive. Feedback from the conference was overwhelmingly positive, and TechWave secured several deals with investors who were impressed not only with the app but with how smoothly the launch had been handled.

Meanwhile, other startups at the conference that hadn't planned as thoroughly faced challenges—apps crashed, bugs appeared in front of investors, and the chaos cost them valuable opportunities.

The Lesson:

Sophie's proactive approach saved the day for TechWave. By testing the app thoroughly, preparing for potential challenges, and having a backup plan, she avoided the risk of failure during their high-stakes launch. David's enthusiasm was important, but Sophie's foresight ensured that the product's debut was not marred by technical difficulties or unforeseen problems.

This story shows that **being proactive is about identifying potential risks early, preparing for the worst-case scenarios, and ensuring everything is ready for smooth implementation**. By thinking ahead and addressing possible issues before they arise, Sophie helped TechWave succeed when it mattered most.

3. Flexibility: Working dynamically, available on time based on demand with supportive attitude.

The Adaptable Architect and the Skyscraper Challenge

In a bustling city eager to modernize its skyline, a prestigious architectural firm was hired to design and construct the tallest skyscraper the city had ever seen. The project was not only ambitious but also symbolic of the city's growth and future potential. The client wanted the building to reflect innovation, strength, and modernity, and they hired **Julian**, one of the best architects in the field, to lead the project.

Julian initially designed an awe-inspiring, sleek structure with glass panels, state-of-the-art facilities, and eco-friendly technology. His original plans were praised for their creativity and beauty, and construction began on schedule. However, a few months into the project, **unexpected problems** started to arise.

Challenges Along the Way:

1. **Unforeseen Environmental Conditions**: Halfway through the construction, it was discovered that the land was more prone to soil erosion than previously thought. If Julian stuck rigidly to the original design, the foundation might not hold up well in the long term. The project risked collapse, which would be disastrous.

2. **Change in Regulations**: While construction was underway, the city updated its building regulations, requiring stricter sustainability standards, including a new energy-efficient design for all new structures. Julian's original design didn't fully meet these new requirements, so he needed to make significant changes to comply.

3. **Client's Evolving Vision**: As construction progressed, the client's vision shifted. They wanted a more unique and artistic element to distinguish the skyscraper from other modern buildings in the city. The original design, while impressive, no longer fit their desire for a more creative, signature element.

Julian's Flexibility:

Julian could have insisted on sticking to his original design, but he knew that success in such a complex project required adaptability. Instead of viewing the changes as setbacks, he saw them as opportunities to innovate and demonstrate his flexibility.

1. **Redesigning the Foundation**: Julian consulted with geotechnical experts and reworked the building's foundation to account for the new environmental findings. Instead of

the typical deep-set foundation, he integrated an advanced support system that dispersed weight more evenly, preventing erosion damage and increasing long-term stability. This added months to the construction timeline, but it ensured the building would be structurally sound.

2. **Incorporating Sustainable Elements**: In response to the new sustainability regulations, Julian revisited the plans and made the building even more eco-friendly. He incorporated **solar panels, wind turbines**, and a **rainwater harvesting system**. These not only met the city's regulations but also helped lower the building's operational costs, making it more appealing to future tenants and giving the building a futuristic edge.

3. **Adding Artistic Flair**: For the client's evolving vision, Julian collaborated with a famous local artist to incorporate a **giant, spiraling sculpture** into the building's design. The sculpture wrapped around the exterior of the tower like a ribbon, making the building iconic and visually striking. This creative addition wasn't in the original plan, but Julian was open to exploring new possibilities that made the project even more impressive.

The Outcome:

Because of Julian's flexibility, the skyscraper became an instant landmark upon completion. It wasn't just a towering structure— it was a sustainable, resilient, and artistically unique building that represented the city's forward-thinking aspirations. The client was thrilled, the city hailed the project as a symbol of modern engineering, and the skyscraper became a global attraction.

Other architects in Julian's position might have resisted making so many adjustments to the original plan. Some might have stuck to the initial design, fearing the extra work and changes would reflect poorly on their leadership. But **Julian's willingness to adapt, embrace change, and see challenges as opportunities made the project a huge success.**

The Lesson:

Flexibility in execution can be the difference between mediocrity and greatness. Julian's adaptability allowed him to:

- **Overcome unforeseen challenges** (environmental and regulatory changes),

- **Enhance the project** with even better solutions (sustainability features),

- **Exceed client expectations** by evolving the design into something even more unique.

This story demonstrates that **success is often a result of how well you can pivot, respond to changing circumstances, and transform obstacles into new pathways to innovation**. Flexibility adds immense value by allowing one to stay aligned with evolving conditions without losing sight of the ultimate goal.

4. Standardization and quality of service delivery – what is the minimum standard you will maintain and what you must not do even if no one is watching. Thus, your reputation and character will be improved, and you will be recognized and appreciated in the industry.

The Auto Manufacturer's Breakthrough

In a rapidly growing auto industry, **Velocity Motors**, a mid-sized car manufacturer, was struggling to keep up with the demands of the market. They had a reputation for producing innovative cars, but their manufacturing process was plagued with issues. **Inconsistent quality**, frequent delays, and high production costs were preventing them from competing with the larger brands.

The company had recently launched a new electric car model called the **Velocity V1**, which had great potential. Customers loved the car's design, features, and eco-friendliness, but there were problems on the production line. Faulty components, variations in assembly quality, and missed deadlines led to negative reviews and frustrated customers. Velocity Motors needed to find a way to standardize their processes and enhance the quality of their product if they wanted to stay in the game.

Enter Maria: The Quality Expert

The company hired **Maria**, a seasoned expert in **quality management and process standardization**, to lead the turnaround. Maria had worked with some of the top automakers and was known for her ability to transform inefficient production lines into well-oiled machines.

Maria's first step was to conduct a thorough audit of the production process for the Velocity V1. She discovered several key issues:

1. **Lack of Standardization**: Each team on the assembly line had developed its own way of doing things. One team used slightly different techniques for assembling the battery packs, while another team varied in how they handled the wiring. This inconsistency led to quality control issues—some cars ran smoothly, while others had electrical problems.

2. **Supplier Variations**: The parts being sourced from different suppliers varied slightly in quality. While some components were top-notch, others were subpar, leading to a high rate of returns and repairs.

3. **Quality Control Weaknesses**: The quality checks at the end of the production line were insufficient. They caught major defects but missed smaller, yet critical, issues that affected the car's performance and customer satisfaction.

Maria's Plan for Standardization and Quality Enhancement

Maria knew that to improve the company's project delivery, she had to introduce **standardization** and raise the **quality of both the process and the final product**. Here's how she did it:

1. **Standardized Workflows**: Maria worked with each department to **create clear, standardized workflows** for every stage of

production. From battery assembly to painting and wiring, every step was documented and optimized. She introduced **Standard Operating Procedures (SOPs)** that outlined the best practices for each task. This ensured that every team followed the same process, reducing variability and errors.

2. **Supplier Quality Standards**: Maria developed a set of **rigorous quality standards** for all suppliers. She worked closely with the parts suppliers, ensuring they met these new standards consistently. If a supplier couldn't meet the new criteria, Velocity Motors would no longer work with them. This improved the reliability of the parts coming into the factory, reducing the number of faulty components.

3. **Enhanced Quality Control**: Maria overhauled the quality control process. Instead of only checking cars at the end of the line, she introduced **quality checkpoints** throughout the production process. Each section of the assembly line now had its own quality inspectors, who checked every step of the build. If a defect was found early, it could be fixed immediately, reducing the number of cars that needed major repairs later.

4. **Continuous Improvement**: Maria also implemented a **Continuous Improvement Program**, where every employee was encouraged to contribute ideas for improving processes. The company held regular meetings to discuss these ideas and make adjustments to the workflows as needed. This created a culture of constant refinement and focus on quality.

The Results

Within six months, the impact of Maria's standardization and quality enhancement efforts was remarkable:

1. **Increased Consistency**: The Velocity V1 was now being produced with a much higher level of consistency. Every car leaving the factory met the same quality standards, leading to fewer defects and higher customer satisfaction.

2. **Reduced Costs**: By standardizing the production process, Velocity Motors reduced waste and inefficiencies. Fewer faulty components meant less rework, and the company saved money on repairs and recalls. The production line became faster and more efficient, which also reduced overall costs.

3. **Improved Reputation**: Customer reviews of the Velocity V1 began to improve as the quality issues were resolved. The car's reliability became a selling point, and word spread that Velocity Motors had turned things around. Sales began to rise, and the company's reputation improved significantly.

4. **Faster Delivery Times**: With the production process running smoothly, Velocity Motors was able to **meet delivery deadlines** more consistently. This made dealers and customers happy, further boosting the brand's image.

The Lesson

By focusing on **standardization and quality enhancement**, Maria helped Velocity Motors turn a failing project into a success story. Standardizing the production process reduced variability and errors, while enhancing quality control ensured that only the best cars left the factory. These changes not only improved the quality of the product but also reduced costs, improved customer satisfaction, and ultimately led to successful project delivery.

This story shows that **standardization creates a foundation of consistency**, and **quality enhancement ensures excellence**. Together, they can transform a struggling project into one that delivers outstanding results.

5. Resiliency, Disaster Recovery and business continuity: Finding alternate route in your planning to overcome bottlenecks of execution.

The Global Data Company's Crisis

DataVerse, a leading global company specializing in cloud data storage and management, had built a reputation for providing fast, reliable data services to businesses worldwide. Their clients ranged from small startups to multinational corporations, all relying on DataVerse to store their critical data securely. With millions of gigabytes of data flowing through their systems daily, any disruption could have severe consequences—not just for DataVerse, but for all its clients.

For years, DataVerse had operated smoothly, but then came **The Incident**—an unexpected, catastrophic event that could have crippled the company.

The Catastrophic Event:

One afternoon, a powerful **cyberattack** hit DataVerse's primary data centre. Hackers exploited a vulnerability in the system, causing major parts of the infrastructure to go offline. To make matters worse, a **freak storm** hit the region, causing massive flooding, knocking out the local power grid, and damaging the physical hardware at the data centre.

Within minutes, DataVerse's clients began experiencing service outages, and critical systems were down. Businesses that relied on their cloud storage for financial transactions, customer data, and business operations were suddenly unable to access their data.

The potential losses were staggering—clients were at risk of losing irreplaceable data, and DataVerse's reputation was on the line. A crisis of this scale could drive clients away, lead to lawsuits, and ultimately, bring the company to its knees.

Enter the Resiliency, Disaster Recovery, and Business Continuity Plan

Fortunately, DataVerse had **invested heavily** in preparing for exactly this kind of crisis. Years earlier, under the guidance of their COO, **Rachel**, they had developed a comprehensive approach focused on **resiliency, disaster recovery**, and **business continuity**. These three pillars now played a crucial role in how the company would respond and recover from the crisis.

1. **Resiliency: Building Strength in Advance**

   Rachel believed that **resiliency** wasn't just about bouncing back after a disaster but being prepared to handle it without significant disruption. With that mindset, she led initiatives to strengthen DataVerse's infrastructure long before any crisis hit.

   - **Multi-Region Redundancy**: DataVerse had multiple **data centers spread across different geographic regions**. This meant that if one center was compromised, others could take over without the company losing access to critical data. When the attack and storm took out the primary data center, the backup centers automatically started handling the data traffic.

   - **Regular Stress Testing**: Resiliency requires regular testing, so DataVerse conducted **simulated disaster scenarios** at least once a quarter. These stress tests ensured the systems and staff were prepared to handle unexpected situations, from cyberattacks to natural disasters. When the crisis happened, the team had already practiced how to react quickly and calmly.

   Because of these resilient designs, **95% of DataVerse's services remained operational** even as the primary data center failed.

2. **Disaster Recovery: Bouncing Back from Chaos**

   Though resiliency helped mitigate the immediate damage, the disaster still caused significant disruption. The flooded data center was crucial to DataVerse's overall capacity, and without it, their remaining data centers would soon become overwhelmed by the massive surge in traffic. This is where the **Disaster Recovery (DR) plan** kicked in.

   - **Rapid Data Recovery**: Rachel's team had implemented a **cloud-based disaster recovery system**. This system took hourly snapshots of all data in the primary data center and stored it in **offsite servers** that were untouched by the storm or cyberattack. As soon as the attack was detected, the recovery system restored the most recent version of the data to the active data centers, minimizing data loss.

- **Failover Mechanism**: DataVerse had also invested in an **automatic failover mechanism**, which rerouted traffic to unaffected data centers instantly when the primary center went down. While some clients experienced brief delays, the failover prevented a total service outage.

Within **24 hours**, the critical functions of the damaged data centre were restored to full operation thanks to the disaster recovery plan, allowing DataVerse to prevent long-term disruption to their clients' businesses.

3. **Business Continuity: Ensuring Stability Through Crisis**

While resiliency and disaster recovery addressed the technical side, **business continuity** ensured that DataVerse could continue to operate and support clients during the disaster.

- **Predefined Response Teams**: Rachel had established a **business continuity team** composed of employees from all departments—IT, communications, legal, and customer service. Each person had a specific role during a crisis. When the attack and storm hit, this team immediately mobilized. The IT team focused on restoring services, while the communications team kept clients informed about the status of the recovery process.

- **Clear Communication with Clients**: One of the key components of the business continuity plan was **transparent communication**. Clients needed to know what was happening, what was being done, and when they could expect full services to return. The continuity team used multiple channels (emails, social media, phone support) to send out frequent updates, which helped calm clients' fears and maintain trust.

- **Alternative Work Arrangements**: Even as the crisis was unfolding, DataVerse's employees continued working without interruption. Rachel had implemented a **remote work policy** that allowed employees to work from anywhere if the main office or data centre was inaccessible. This ensured that the team could still collaborate and manage the crisis, even when the physical office was affected by the storm.

By having a well-prepared business continuity plan in place, DataVerse **never stopped operating** during the disaster, keeping clients reassured and maintaining its reputation as a reliable service provider.

The Outcome

Thanks to their **resiliency**, **disaster recovery**, and **business continuity** approach, DataVerse emerged from the crisis stronger than before. The company's ability to bounce back and continue providing services to clients during a major disaster not only prevented significant losses but also **strengthened their client relationships**.

In fact, after the crisis, DataVerse saw an **increase in new clients**. Word spread that they had managed to handle a catastrophic situation with minimal disruption, which attracted businesses looking for a stable, trustworthy data partner.

The Lesson:

Resiliency, disaster recovery, and business continuity are not just "insurance policies" for businesses—they are active components of success. By building resilient systems, having a solid disaster recovery plan, and ensuring business continuity, companies can **survive and even thrive during a crisis**. These strategies allow businesses to protect their operations, maintain customer trust, and bounce back quickly, ensuring that disruptions don't turn into long-term failures.

6. Risk assessment and preparedness with mitigating action plan

The Solar Power Plant Project

A renewable energy company, **EcoPower Solutions**, was awarded a contract to build a large-scale **solar power plant** in an arid region. The project was of national importance as it would provide clean energy to over 100,000 homes and serve as a model for future solar projects. The timeline was tight, and the government was keen to see it completed on schedule.

The project appeared straightforward on the surface—after all, the location was ideal for solar energy. However, **Jasmine**, the project manager, was experienced enough to know that major infrastructure projects rarely go exactly as planned. She insisted that before breaking ground, the team should perform a thorough **risk assessment** and develop a **preparedness and mitigation action plan** to ensure smooth execution.

Step 1: Risk Assessment

Jasmine and her team conducted a detailed **risk assessment**, identifying potential risks that could impact the project's timeline, budget, and quality. Here's what they found:

1. **Supply Chain Disruptions**: The solar panels and critical equipment were being sourced from overseas suppliers. Delays in shipping or manufacturing could cause significant project setbacks.

2. **Extreme Weather**: While the region was generally dry and sunny, **seasonal sandstorms** could cause temporary halts in construction or damage sensitive equipment.

3. **Regulatory Delays**: Navigating local regulations and securing permits from multiple government agencies could take longer than expected.

4. **Labor Shortages**: The project was located in a remote area, and finding skilled workers for certain technical roles might be a challenge.

5. **Security Concerns**: The remote location made the site vulnerable to theft or vandalism, especially given the high value of solar panels and equipment.

Step 2: Preparedness and Mitigating Action Plan

Once the risks were identified, Jasmine developed a **mitigating action plan** for each risk. This plan was aimed at either reducing the likelihood of the risks occurring or minimizing their impact if they did occur.

1. **Supply Chain Contingencies**:

   - Jasmine secured **secondary suppliers** for critical equipment and materials. If the primary suppliers faced delays, they could quickly switch to alternate providers.

   - She arranged for **early orders** of long-lead items like solar panels, so they would arrive well before installation was set to begin.

   - Jasmine also set up **real-time tracking systems** for shipments, so they could quickly identify and address any delays.

2. **Weather Contingency Plans**:

   - The team created a **weather monitoring system** to provide early warnings of potential sandstorms. If a storm was predicted, they could halt work temporarily and take protective measures to safeguard equipment.

   - Jasmine also arranged for **temporary protective covers** for the solar panels and equipment to minimize potential damage from wind and sand.

3. **Regulatory Risk Mitigation**:

   - Jasmine's team assigned a dedicated **legal and compliance specialist** to work closely with the local government agencies and navigate the permit process more efficiently.

- The team built **extra time** into the project schedule for potential regulatory delays, ensuring that if approval took longer than expected, the timeline wouldn't be severely impacted.

4. **Addressing Labor Shortages**:

   - To address the shortage of skilled workers, Jasmine partnered with local vocational training centres to **train workers** in specific skills needed for the project.

   - She also brought in **technical experts** from other parts of the country to lead specialized tasks and reduce dependence on hard-to-find local talent.

5. **Security Measures**:

   - Jasmine arranged for **24/7 security patrols** at the construction site and installed **security cameras** and motion detectors to deter theft and vandalism.

   - She also negotiated with the insurance company for comprehensive **theft and damage insurance** to minimize financial loss if any incidents occurred.

Step 3: Execution and Monitoring

As the project unfolded, Jasmine's risk assessment and mitigation plan proved invaluable.

- **Supply Chain Success**: When an unexpected strike at the port delayed shipments from their primary supplier, Jasmine immediately activated the secondary supplier, ensuring that construction materials arrived on time. The pre-ordered equipment was delivered early, allowing the installation to begin smoothly.

- **Weather Management**: A severe sandstorm hit the region in the middle of the construction phase, but thanks to the **weather monitoring system**, the team had been given advance warning. They halted construction in time, covered the solar panels with protective covers, and resumed work as soon as the storm passed. No equipment was damaged, and no significant time was lost.

- **Regulatory Hurdles Cleared**: There was a delay in securing environmental clearance, but because Jasmine had factored this into the schedule and her compliance team was proactively engaging with local authorities, the project timeline was not seriously affected.

- **Labor Force Solutions**: Initially, it was difficult to find enough skilled workers, but the partnership with local training centres began to pay off. Within weeks, a steady stream of qualified workers was available, and Jasmine had flown in the technical experts for the more complex parts of the project. This reduced any potential delays from labour shortages.

- **Security in Action**: There was an attempted break-in at the site late one night, but thanks to the security patrols and cameras, the intruders were caught, and no equipment was stolen. The insurance in place also meant the company faced no significant financial loss.

Step 4: Successful Completion

Because of the **thorough risk assessment** and **mitigation plans**, Ecopower Solutions completed the solar power plant **ahead of schedule** and **under budget**. The project was a success, with minimal delays and no major incidents. The government praised the company for its efficiency, and new opportunities opened up for similar projects across the country.

Jasmine's leadership and foresight were the key to the project's success. By preparing for potential risks and putting mitigation plans in place, she ensured that even when challenges arose, they were managed effectively without jeopardizing the overall outcome.

7. Reporting: Measuring and showing the progress over the period and taking corrective measures to improve. Data analytics plays

a pivotal role on which you should put focus to quantify your progress, areas of avoidance to save resources.

The Smart City Initiative

MetroNext, a large metropolitan city, embarked on a multi-year project to transform itself into a **smart city** by upgrading its infrastructure with modern technologies. The goal was to create a more efficient, sustainable, and livable environment for its citizens by integrating smart traffic management systems, energy-efficient street lighting, and data-driven public services.

The project was highly ambitious, with several stakeholders involved, including the city's government, private contractors, and technology vendors. The success of this project would greatly impact the city's future reputation, its ability to attract businesses, and its overall liability.

The Role of Analytics and Management Reporting

Maya, the project director, understood that delivering on the technical aspects of the project was only half the battle. The other half was ensuring that the stakeholders—particularly the city officials and the public—could see and **understand the project's value** at each phase of its implementation.

To achieve this, Maya decided to leverage **analytics and management reporting** as a strategic tool to brand the project as a success, even before its final completion. Here's how she did it:

Step 1: Data Collection and Analytics

Maya knew that for a project of this scale, data was essential for measuring progress, performance, and impact. She worked with her team to establish a system for **real-time data collection** across all project components:

1. **Smart Traffic Management**:
   - Sensors were installed across the city to monitor traffic flow, congestion, and vehicle speeds.

- Analytics tracked how traffic patterns improved after new systems were implemented. They measured metrics like average commute time, reduction in traffic jams, and changes in accident rates.

2. **Energy-Efficient Street Lighting**:

- The new streetlights were equipped with sensors to measure energy usage, and the data was fed into a central system that tracked energy consumption before and after the upgrades.

- Analytics provided insights into how much energy was saved, the cost reductions, and the impact on carbon emissions.

3. **Public Service Efficiency**:

- Data was gathered from various public services, like waste collection and water management, to analyze how responsive and efficient the services were after integrating smart technologies.

The team set up **dashboards** that collected data in real time, turning complex raw data into **digestible insights** through graphs, charts, and reports.

Step 2: Management Reporting to Stakeholders

Once the data was collected and analyzed, Maya knew it was crucial to keep all stakeholders informed through **transparent, regular reporting**. She didn't want stakeholders to only find out about the project's success after it was completed—she wanted them to see the progress and feel confident at every stage.

1. **Regular Progress Reports**:

- Maya's team generated **monthly management reports** that showed detailed updates on project milestones, budget utilization, and timelines. These reports broke down each component of the smart city project and highlighted key performance indicators (KPIs) like traffic flow improvements and energy savings.

- The reports included **data visualizations**, such as graphs showing the reduction in commute times and heatmaps displaying changes in traffic density. This helped city officials understand the practical benefits of the project in a visual, easy-to-read format.

2. **Executive Dashboards for City Officials**:

- Maya set up **executive dashboards** for city leaders that provided a real-time overview of the project's status. These dashboards presented the most critical metrics at a glance, such as energy savings in kilowatt-hours and percentage reductions in traffic accidents.

- City officials could log in at any time and see real-time data, which gave them confidence that the project was on track and delivering results. The dashboard also allowed them to **adjust resources** and **make decisions** based on actual data.

3. **Public Transparency**:

- Maya understood that the project's success also depended on the **perception of the public**. To keep the citizens engaged and informed, her team developed **public-facing reports** that were posted on the city's website.

- These reports highlighted key achievements, such as how the smart traffic system had reduced commute times by 15% during peak hours, or how the energy-efficient streetlights were saving the city millions in energy costs annually.

- The reports were made user-friendly, with infographics and interactive maps that showed changes in real time. This level of transparency helped foster **public trust** and built excitement about the improvements in their daily lives.

Step 3: Continuous Improvement and Branding the Success

By using analytics and management reporting, Maya was able to **brand the project as a success** long before it was finished. Here's how this approach helped ensure the project's success:

1. **Identifying Early Wins:**

   - Analytics revealed that the **smart traffic management system** had significantly reduced congestion in key areas within just a few months. Maya highlighted these early wins in her reports, making sure stakeholders knew the project was already delivering tangible benefits.

   - These early successes created **positive momentum** and helped Maya secure additional funding and support for the remaining phases of the project.

2. **Mitigating Risks Through Data:**

   - By constantly monitoring key metrics, Maya's team could **identify potential risks** early. For example, they noticed that energy savings in one district were lower than expected due to faulty installations. The data helped them quickly address the issue before it became a larger problem.

   - Regular reporting allowed Maya to communicate these adjustments to stakeholders, showing that the team was proactive in resolving issues. This further strengthened stakeholder confidence.

3. **Public and Political Support:**

   - Through clear, data-backed reporting, Maya ensured that both the public and city officials understood the project's impact. The public saw real, measurable improvements in their day-to-day lives, such as faster commute times and better street lighting, which generated **positive media coverage.**

   - City leaders, seeing the **data-driven success**, began to view the project as a model for future urban development.

The positive results helped them **garner political support** for additional smart city initiatives.

4. **Positioning the City as a Leader**:

- As the project continued to meet its targets, the city began to attract attention from **other cities and tech companies**. Maya and the city's leadership used the **analytics and reports** to demonstrate their success at conferences and in the media, branding MetroNext as a **pioneer in smart city development**.

The Outcome:

Thanks to the use of **analytics and management reporting**, Maya was able to **brand the smart city initiative as a resounding success**. The combination of data-driven insights, clear reporting, and public transparency turned a complex infrastructure project into a model of efficiency and innovation.

By the time the project reached its final phases, it was already seen as a success, with tangible benefits delivered early on. The use of analytics helped stakeholders see the value being created at every step, and the continuous reporting ensured that the project stayed on track, mitigated risks, and fostered trust and enthusiasm.

8. Ontime Escalation: to avoid delays

Story: The Construction Project Turnaround

Setting the Scene:

A mid-sized construction company, **BuildWell**, had recently won a contract to construct a new office building for a tech firm in a bustling urban area. The project was ambitious, with a tight deadline of six months to complete the work. **Mike**, the project manager, was experienced and confident in his team's abilities. However, he understood the importance of monitoring the project's progress closely to avoid any potential setbacks.

The Challenge:

About halfway through the project, Mike noticed that the excavation phase was falling behind schedule due to unexpected underground rock formations. As a result, the timeline for the subsequent phases was at risk, and the construction crew was facing increasing pressure to catch up. Initially, Mike thought it was a manageable delay and believed that they could make up for lost time in later phases.

The Warning Signs:

As the weeks passed, the team struggled to keep up with the excavation schedule. The equipment needed to remove the rock was taking longer than anticipated to arrive, and the crew's morale was beginning to wane due to the mounting pressure. Mike sensed that the delay was becoming a more significant issue but hesitated to escalate the problem, fearing it might reflect poorly on his leadership.

However, during a routine progress meeting, several team members expressed their concerns about the delays, and some suggested that the project might need additional resources or support to stay on track. Mike realized that the situation could quickly escalate beyond repair if not addressed immediately.

The Escalation:

Recognizing the potential consequences of inaction, Mike decided to take proactive steps. He escalated the issue to **Rachel**, the company's regional director, outlining the specific challenges the team faced, the potential risks to the project timeline, and the solutions he believed could help. Mike proposed:

- **Increasing the excavation crew** to expedite the process.

- **Renting additional heavy machinery** to speed up the rock removal.

- **Revising the project schedule** to reflect the new timeline, while also outlining contingency plans.

Rachel appreciated Mike's transparency and swift action. Together, they convened a meeting with the executive team to discuss the escalation. They approved the additional resources and strategized on how to support the construction team effectively.

The Result:

With the new resources in place, the excavation crew worked around the clock to tackle the unexpected challenges. Within a few weeks, they had cleared the rock formations, and the project was back on track. The additional machinery and workforce helped the team not only catch up but also finish the excavation phase ahead of schedule.

Because Mike had escalated the issue promptly, the company managed to avoid a significant delay that could have jeopardized the entire project. The rest of the construction phases progressed smoothly, and the building was completed on time, impressing the tech firm with both the quality of work and the adherence to the timeline.

Conclusion:

This experience reinforced the importance of timely escalation in project management. By addressing issues early and involving higher management, when necessary, Mike not only prevented potential failure but also demonstrated strong leadership skills. His willingness to escalate challenges fostered a culture of transparency and collaboration within Build Well, ultimately leading to successful project delivery.

9. Get the job done by establishing shared vision and delegating the tasks with accountability and ownership.

Story: The Marketing Campaign Success

Setting the Scene:

Trendsetters, a mid-sized marketing agency, was tasked with launching a new product for a popular eco-friendly skincare brand.

The project had a tight deadline of just six weeks, and the stakes were high—failure could mean losing the client and damaging the agency's reputation. **Emma**, the project lead, was known for her positive attitude and collaborative approach to leadership.

The Challenge:

As the team kicked off the project, they faced several challenges:

- The client had a vague vision for the campaign, leading to confusion about the direction.

- The graphic designer was overloaded with work from other projects, causing delays in producing necessary visuals.

- Some team members felt overwhelmed by the tight timeline and were beginning to lose motivation.

Instead of succumbing to stress, Emma saw this as an opportunity to strengthen her team's collaboration and maintain a positive outlook.

The Approach:

1. **Fostering Open Communication:**

   - Emma organized a brainstorming session, encouraging every team member to voice their ideas and concerns. She made it clear that every opinion was valued, creating an open atmosphere for discussion.

   - By acknowledging the team's frustration with the timeline, Emma fostered trust, allowing team members to express their feelings without fear of judgment.

2. **Setting Clear Goals:**

   - Together, they broke the project down into smaller, manageable tasks, assigning clear responsibilities to each team member. This structure helped clarify the project's direction and alleviate feelings of being overwhelmed.

   - Emma emphasized the importance of celebrating small victories along the way, which helped boost morale.

3. **Encouraging Collaboration:**

   - To address the graphic designer's workload, Emma proposed a buddy system where team members could assist one another. The copywriters, for example, worked with the designer to create visual content that aligned with the messaging.

   - Emma also organized daily check-ins to track progress and address any roadblocks. These short meetings kept everyone aligned and motivated.

4. **Maintaining a Positive Attitude:**

   - Throughout the process, Emma consistently highlighted the team's strengths and progress. She recognized individual contributions during team meetings, fostering a sense of accomplishment.

   - Her enthusiasm was infectious, encouraging team members to maintain a positive mindset despite the pressures they faced.

The Result:

Thanks to Emma's leadership and the team's collaborative spirit, they managed to not only complete the project on time but also exceed the client's expectations. The campaign was a hit, receiving praise for its creativity and impact.

The client was thrilled with the results, leading to an extension of their contract and a long-term partnership with the agency. Emma's ability to cultivate a positive attitude and encourage teamwork proved to be a critical factor in their success.

Conclusion:

This story highlights how a positive attitude and a collaborative approach can transform challenges into opportunities. By fostering open communication, setting clear goals, encouraging teamwork, and maintaining a supportive environment, Emma empowered her team to succeed. Their collective effort, driven by a shared commitment to get the job done, resulted in a successful marketing campaign and strengthened their relationship with the client.

4o mini

10. Associated and de associated:

Story: The Product Launch Dilemma

Setting the Scene:

Innovatech Solutions, a tech startup, was preparing to launch a groundbreaking new app designed to streamline project management for small businesses. **David**, the project manager, was excited about the launch but quickly realized that the team was becoming overwhelmed with multiple tasks that were not essential to the product's success.

The Challenge:

As the launch date approached, the team faced numerous distractions and "energy drags":

- The marketing team was caught up in extensive social media campaigns that were not effectively targeting their audience.

- The development team was spending time on minor bugs that did not significantly impact the app's functionality.

- There were frequent, unproductive meetings that drained team energy without yielding tangible results.

David recognized that these distractions were hindering progress and could jeopardize the app's successful launch.

The Approach:

1. **Prioritizing Key Tasks:**
   - David called for a team meeting to reassess priorities. He facilitated a discussion on which tasks would have the

most significant impact on the app's launch and which ones could be postponed or eliminated.

- Together, they created a **Priority Matrix**, categorizing tasks into four quadrants: "Urgent and Important," "Important but Not Urgent," "Urgent but Not Important," and "Neither Urgent nor Important." This visual helped the team see where to focus their energy.

2. **Assigning Roles and Responsibilities:**

- Based on the matrix, David assigned specific roles to team members for the critical tasks. He encouraged team members to focus on what they did best, ensuring everyone was aligned with the key objectives.

- For example, the marketing team shifted their focus to creating targeted campaigns that reached their ideal audience rather than spreading themselves thin across multiple platforms.

3. **Eliminating Energy Drags:**

- David identified unproductive meetings and proposed a new approach. Instead of lengthy discussions, he implemented **stand-up meetings**—brief, focused sessions where team members shared updates and addressed immediate concerns.

- He also encouraged the team to adopt a "no-meeting day" once a week, allowing everyone to dedicate uninterrupted time to critical tasks.

4. **Regular Progress Check-Ins:**

- To keep the momentum going, David established weekly progress check-ins to evaluate the effectiveness of the prioritized tasks and make necessary adjustments. This provided a platform for celebrating successes and addressing challenges in real-time.

The Result:

By focusing on key tasks and de-prioritizing energy-draining activities, the team made significant progress in the weeks leading up to the launch. The marketing campaign was refined, effectively generating buzz and engagement with their target audience. The development team streamlined their efforts to address critical bugs, resulting in a more polished app.

On launch day, Innovatech Solutions introduced the app to the market with confidence. The event was a success, drawing in substantial media attention and exceeding initial download projections.

Conclusion:

This story illustrates the importance of associating with key tasks and de-associating from energy drags for project success. By prioritizing effectively, assigning roles, eliminating unnecessary distractions, and maintaining focus on the objectives, David and his team were able to deliver a successful product launch. Their experience highlighted that strategic focus and clarity in responsibilities are vital to achieving goals and driving project success.

11. Effective decision making: Pain vs Gain analysis with ecological check and taking decision to change the situation.

Story: The Championship Basketball Game

Setting the Scene:

The **Riverside Eagles**, a high school basketball team, were in the finals of the state championship. Under the guidance of their coach, **Coach Thompson**, they had a stellar season. The team was facing their biggest rival, the **Valley Sharks**, in a closely contested game. As the game progressed, the tension in the gym was palpable, with the score tied and only a few minutes remaining on the clock.

The Challenge:

With two minutes left in the game, the Eagles were struggling with their offense. Their star player, **Mike**, was being heavily guarded by the Sharks, and his usual plays weren't working. The team's morale began to dip as they missed several critical shots, and it seemed like the momentum was shifting toward the Sharks.

Coach Thompson faced a critical decision:

1. **Stick to their original game plan**, relying on Mike to break through the defense, hoping he could turn the game around.

2. **Change the strategy**, moving Mike to a different position and involving other players in the offense to spread the defense.

The Decision-Making Process:

Recognizing the urgency of the situation, Coach Thompson took a moment to assess the game dynamics. He considered the following factors:

- **Current Performance:** Mike was being double-teamed and was visibly frustrated, which affected his confidence and performance.

- **Team Dynamics:** Other players, like **Jordan** and **Emily**, had been scoring well earlier in the game and were ready to step up.

- **Game Flow:** The Sharks were gaining confidence, and the Eagles needed to regain their momentum quickly.

Understanding the stakes, Coach Thompson decided to **change the strategy**. He called a timeout to gather the team and shared his new plan. He explained that Mike would play a different role, allowing Jordan and Emily to take more shots and drive to the basket, while Mike would act as a facilitator.

The Execution:

After the timeout, the Eagles implemented Coach Thompson's new strategy. With Mike drawing defenders away from the basket, Jordan and Emily found open opportunities to shoot. The team moved the ball more fluidly, and the Sharks struggled to adapt to the sudden change.

In the last minute, Jordan hit a crucial three-pointer that put the Eagles ahead by three points. The Sharks tried to respond but were unable to make significant plays as the Eagles' defense tightened. Finally, in the last seconds of the game, Emily secured a steal and scored a fast-break layup, sealing the victory for the Riverside Eagles.

The Outcome:

The Eagles won the championship, thanks to Coach Thompson's critical decision-making. By recognizing when to adapt their strategy and empowering other players to step up, he effectively shifted the game's momentum. The team celebrated their victory, not just as a group of players but as a cohesive unit that learned the importance of adaptability and teamwork under pressure.

Conclusion:

This story illustrates how critical decision-making can influence success in a game. Coach Thompson's ability to assess the situation, make timely adjustments, and empower his players to take charge of the moment was pivotal in securing the victory. In high-stakes situations—whether in sports, business, or life—the ability to make effective decisions can mean the difference between winning and losing.

12. Optimization of resources to save money, time, energy.

Story: The Solar Energy Project

Setting the Scene:

Green Solutions, a renewable energy firm, was awarded a contract to install solar panels on a large commercial building. The project had a budget of $500,000 and a timeline of four months. **Lisa**, the project manager, understood that optimizing resources—time, money, and energy—was crucial for ensuring the project's success and establishing a reliable reputation for future projects.

The Challenge:

As the project commenced, Lisa encountered a few challenges:

- The site preparation was taking longer than anticipated due to unforeseen weather conditions.

- Labor costs were rising because the installation team was working overtime to meet deadlines.

- Material costs fluctuated, and suppliers were inconsistent in their delivery times.

Lisa realized that if she didn't optimize these resources effectively, the project could exceed the budget and timeline, potentially harming future opportunities for the company.

The Approach:

1. **Time Optimization:**

   - **Scheduling:** Lisa reviewed the project schedule and identified opportunities to overlap tasks. For instance, she scheduled site preparation and equipment procurement simultaneously. By doing this, she ensured that when the site was ready, the materials would already be on hand, minimizing idle time.

   - **Delegation:** Lisa empowered her team leads to take ownership of specific tasks, allowing her to focus on critical decision-making and strategic adjustments. This approach helped streamline processes and improved team morale.

2. **Money Optimization:**

   - **Budget Review:** Lisa conducted a thorough review of the project budget and identified non-essential expenses that could be trimmed. For example, she opted for more cost-effective materials that met the required standards without compromising quality.

- **Supplier Negotiation:** Recognizing the fluctuating material costs, Lisa negotiated bulk purchasing agreements with suppliers. By committing to a larger order upfront, she secured a discount that saved the project $25,000.

3. **Energy Optimization:**

- **Efficient Practices:** Lisa implemented energy-efficient practices on-site. She arranged for the installation team to use solar-powered tools whenever possible, reducing electricity costs and promoting a culture of sustainability.

- **Break Management:** To ensure the team remained energized and productive, Lisa introduced structured breaks and wellness activities, such as brief stretching sessions and hydration reminders. This helped maintain high energy levels throughout the workday.

The Result:

Through these optimization strategies, the project was completed on time and under budget. The total cost came in at $450,000, leaving a surplus that the company could reinvest in future projects. The efficient management of resources also led to high-quality installation, which impressed the client.

The successful completion of the solar energy project not only solidified Green Solutions' reputation but also resulted in referrals and new contracts. The company secured two additional projects in the following months, thanks to positive testimonials from the satisfied client.

13. Emotional intelligence, working with empathy and cognitive creativity

Story: The Community Centre Renovation

Setting the Scene:

Community Builders, a nonprofit organization, was working on a project to renovate an old community centre in a neighbourhood that needed a space for events, classes, and youth programs. The project team consisted of diverse members, including architects, volunteers, and local community leaders. **Tina**, the project manager, recognized the potential for conflict due to differing opinions and backgrounds, and she believed that emotional intelligence (EI) and empathetic behaviour were essential for fostering excellent teamwork.

The Challenge:

As the renovation process began, tensions arose among team members:

- The architects wanted to prioritize modern design elements, while some community leaders were more focused on preserving the building's historical character.

- Volunteers felt underappreciated and voiced concerns that their contributions were being overlooked.

- Disagreements escalated into heated discussions during meetings, causing a divide between the professional team and the community members.

Tina knew that if these conflicts continued, the project would suffer, and the team's morale would plummet.

The Approach:

1. **Cultivating Emotional Intelligence:**

   - **Active Listening:** Tina scheduled a team-building workshop focused on emotional intelligence. She taught the team the importance of active listening, encouraging everyone to genuinely hear and understand each other's perspectives.

   - **Self-Awareness Exercises:** During the workshop, Tina facilitated activities that helped team members identify their own emotions and triggers. This created a safe space for everyone to express themselves without judgment.

2. **Fostering Empathy:**

   - **Sharing Stories:** Tina encouraged team members to share personal stories about why the community centre was meaningful to them. This exercise helped build emotional connections and fostered empathy among team members, as they began to see the project through each other's eyes.

   - **Recognizing Contributions:** Tina made it a point to acknowledge and celebrate the contributions of each member, especially the volunteers. She organized "shout-out" moments during meetings where team members could recognize each other's hard work, reinforcing a culture of appreciation.

3. **Mediating Conflicts:**

   - **Open Dialogue:** When conflicts arose during meetings, Tina intervened with a calm and empathetic approach. She facilitated discussions by asking team members to express their concerns and desires openly. She ensured that each voice was heard, prompting others to consider different perspectives.

   - **Collaborative Problem-Solving:** Tina encouraged brainstorming sessions focused on finding common ground. For instance, when debating design choices, she suggested a hybrid approach that incorporated both modern elements and historical features, allowing both sides to feel valued and respected.

The Result:

Over time, the team began to work more cohesively. Emotional intelligence and empathetic behaviour broke down barriers, allowing team members to communicate openly and resolve conflicts amicably. As they embraced collaboration, they developed innovative solutions that reflected the needs and values of the entire community.

14. New technology adaptation for fast and quick delivery with accuracy

Story: The Greenfield Housing Development Project

Setting the Scene:

EcoBuild Inc., a construction company, had been awarded a contract to develop a sustainable housing project in a rapidly growing suburban area. The project involved building 200 eco-friendly homes within 18 months, with a budget of $15 million. The project manager, **Alice**, was determined to leverage new technologies to ensure fast execution, high accuracy, and reduced overall costs.

The Challenge:

As the project began, EcoBuild faced several challenges:

- **Tight Timeline:** The local government had set a firm deadline for the completion of the homes due to increasing housing demand.

- **Budget Constraints:** Rising material costs and labor shortages threatened to exceed the allocated budget.

- **Complexity of Coordination:** The project involved multiple contractors, suppliers, and subcontractors, making communication and coordination critical.

The Approach:

To address these challenges, Alice implemented several new technologies that added significant value to the project:

1. **Building Information Modelling (BIM):**

   - Alice introduced BIM software, which allowed the entire project team to create a detailed digital representation of the housing development.

   - The 3D modelling enabled all stakeholders, including architects, engineers, and contractors, to visualize the project before construction began, identifying potential design conflicts early on. This proactive approach minimized costly changes during construction, enhancing accuracy.

2. **Drones for Surveying and Monitoring:**

- EcoBuild utilized drones for aerial site surveys. The drones provided real-time data and high-resolution images of the construction site, enabling Alice to monitor progress accurately and make quick adjustments as needed.

- This technology eliminated the need for extensive manual surveying, saving time and labour costs. Drones also facilitated better communication among teams by providing a clear view of the site's status.

3. **Project Management Software:**

- The team adopted cloud-based project management software to streamline communication and collaboration among all stakeholders. This platform allowed real-time updates on project progress, task assignments, and timelines.

- With everyone on the same platform, the chances of miscommunication were greatly reduced, leading to more efficient workflows and timely decision-making.

4. **Prefabrication Techniques:**

- EcoBuild implemented prefabrication methods for building components, such as wall panels and roof trusses, which were manufactured off-site in a controlled environment.

- This approach accelerated the construction timeline as the prefabricated elements could be quickly assembled on-site, reducing labor costs and minimizing waste.

The Result:

By leveraging these new technologies, EcoBuild successfully completed the Greenfield housing development ahead of schedule and under budget. The project was finished in just 15 months, allowing the homes to be occupied three months earlier than planned.

The total project cost came in at $13 million, well below the $15 million budget, thanks to the efficiency gained through technology. The use of BIM and drones improved accuracy, reducing costly errors and rework during construction. Additionally, the eco-friendly features of the homes received praise from the community, positioning EcoBuild as a leader in sustainable construction.

Conclusion:

This story illustrates how new technologies can significantly enhance project success through fast execution, accuracy, and reduced cost ownership. By embracing innovative solutions, Alice and her team at EcoBuild were able to navigate the complexities of the Greenfield housing development project effectively, delivering a high-quality product that met the needs of the community while setting the stage for future projects.

15. Creating value in every step and give more than you are paid for

Story: The Community Health Initiative

Setting the Scene:

HealthFirst, a nonprofit organization, was tasked with delivering a community health initiative aimed at improving access to healthcare services in an underserved neighborhood. **Emma**, the project manager, understood that to achieve extraordinary success, her team would need to adopt an attitude of giving more than what was expected.

The Challenge:

The initiative faced several challenges:

- **Limited Resources:** HealthFirst had a constrained budget and a small team.

- **Community Trust:** Many residents were skeptical about the initiative due to past experiences with healthcare providers.

- **Time Constraints:** The project had to be completed within six months, with specific milestones to meet.

The Approach:

1. **Going Above and Beyond:**

   - Emma encouraged her team to adopt a mindset of giving more than what was required. Instead of simply organizing basic health services, they decided to include additional services like mental health counselling, nutritional workshops, and fitness classes.

   - The team also volunteered their own time outside of regular working hours to set up community events and informational sessions, creating a stronger connection with the residents.

2. **Engaging the Community:**

   - To build trust, Emma and her team organized community meetings to listen to residents' concerns and needs. Instead of dictating what the initiative would provide, they involved the community in the planning process.

   - They collaborated with local leaders and organizations to identify key health issues, ensuring that the services offered were relevant and valuable to the residents.

3. **Empowering Volunteers:**

   - Emma recognized the potential of local volunteers. She trained residents to assist in organizing events and providing health education, creating a sense of ownership among community members.

   - This empowerment not only increased participation in the initiative but also fostered a spirit of collaboration and support within the community.

4. **Exceptional Service Delivery:**

   - During the initiative's execution, the team went the extra mile to ensure that every resident felt valued. They provided personalized health assessments and follow-ups, making sure that no one was left behind.

   - The team members actively sought feedback and adjusted their approach based on community responses, demonstrating a commitment to continuous improvement.

The Result:

The attitude of giving more led to extraordinary success for the community health initiative:

- **High Participation Rates:** The initiative exceeded its target of reaching 500 residents; over 800 people participated in the health services offered.

- **Improved Community Trust:** Residents began to trust HealthFirst and the services they provided, leading to long-term relationships that continued beyond the initiative's completion.

- **Sustainable Impact:** Due to the community's engagement, many residents took the initiative's lessons to heart, forming support groups and continuing health education within the neighbourhood.

Emma's commitment to giving more not only enhanced the project's impact but also fostered a culture of collaboration and trust within the community. The initiative became a model for similar projects in other neighbourhoods, establishing HealthFirst as a leader in community health advocacy.

Conclusion:

This story illustrates how an attitude of giving more can lead to extraordinary project success. By prioritizing the needs of the community, engaging residents, and empowering volunteers, Emma and her team at HealthFirst created a lasting impact that went beyond the initial goals of the initiative. Their dedication to going above and beyond not only ensured the project's success but also strengthened community ties and improved the overall well-being of the neighbourhood.

16. Operate in high demand area and be agile.

Story: The Mobile App Development Company

Setting the Scene:

Tech Innovations, a mobile app development company, specialized in creating apps for small businesses. As demand for mobile solutions surged, especially in the e-commerce sector, the company faced intense competition from both established firms and startups. To stay ahead, the management decided to adopt an **Agile approach** to enhance flexibility, speed, and responsiveness to customer needs.

The Challenge:

The team at Tech Innovations was working on a new e-commerce app aimed at helping local businesses improve their online sales. However, the project faced several challenges:

- **Changing Market Dynamics:** The e-commerce landscape was evolving rapidly, with customer preferences shifting frequently.

- **Tight Deadlines:** Potential clients were eager to see prototypes and quick turnarounds to make purchasing decisions.

- **Limited Feedback Loops:** The traditional development cycle led to long gaps between feedback and implementation, making it difficult to adjust to new requirements.

The Agile Approach:

To overcome these challenges, Tech Innovations implemented the Agile methodology, focusing on iterative development, collaboration, and customer feedback.

1. **Iterative Development:**

   - Instead of attempting to deliver a fully finished product after several months, the team divided the project into smaller, manageable **sprints** of two weeks. Each sprint focused on developing specific features of the app.

   - After each sprint, they showcased the completed features to stakeholders, allowing them to provide immediate feedback and suggest adjustments.

2. **Frequent Collaboration:**

   - Tech Innovations established daily **stand-up meetings** to discuss progress, address challenges, and align on priorities. This ensured that the team remained focused and agile in their approach.

   - The development team worked closely with a **design team** to ensure that user experience (UX) and user interface (UI) considerations were integrated from the start, resulting in a more cohesive product.

3. **Customer Involvement:**

   - The company invited small business owners to participate in feedback sessions after each sprint. This allowed real users to test features and provide insights on usability, ensuring that the app truly met their needs.

   - This ongoing engagement fostered a sense of ownership among customers and built loyalty, as they felt their input directly influenced the app's development.

The Result:

By adopting the Agile approach, Tech Innovations gained a competitive advantage in several ways:

1. **Faster Time to Market:**

   - The iterative development process enabled the company to deliver the initial version of the app within just three months, compared to the six months typical in their previous approach. This quick turnaround allowed them to launch ahead of competitors.

2. **Enhanced Flexibility:**

   - With regular feedback and the ability to pivot quickly based on customer input, Tech Innovations could adapt features to better meet user needs. For instance, after a few sprints, they learned that local businesses wanted integrated payment solutions, which they prioritized in subsequent iterations.

3. **Improved Customer Satisfaction:**

   - The collaborative process and frequent updates kept customers engaged and satisfied. When the app was officially launched, it received rave reviews from users who appreciated its usability and features tailored to their needs.

4. **Increased Market Share:**

   - As a result of their success, Tech Innovations attracted more clients, expanding their market share in the competitive mobile app development space. They became known for delivering high-quality, user-focused apps quickly, which set them apart from competitors.

Conclusion:

This story demonstrates how an Agile approach in a high-demand area can provide a significant competitive advantage. By embracing iterative development, fostering collaboration, and involving customers in the process, Tech Innovations not only met market demands but also built a reputation for responsiveness and quality. The Agile methodology allowed them to navigate the fast-paced e-commerce landscape successfully, positioning them as a leader in mobile app development for small businesses.

17. Creating awareness to be alerted

Story: The Rise of QuickFix Tech Support

Setting the Scene:

QuickFix, a tech support company, specialized in providing troubleshooting services for software and hardware issues. As the demand for their services grew, the team realized that customer satisfaction was declining due to long wait times and inconsistent service quality. To turn things around, the management decided to focus on **learning and sharing knowledge** within the team to enhance the customer experience.

The Challenge:

QuickFix faced several challenges:

- **High Volume of Support Requests:** With an increasing number of customers, the support team was overwhelmed, leading to longer response times and frustrated clients.

- **Knowledge Gaps:** New hires often struggled with complex issues because they lacked the experience and knowledge of senior technicians.

- **Inconsistent Solutions:** Different technicians provided varied solutions to the same problems, resulting in confusion and dissatisfaction among customers.

The Approach:

To address these challenges, QuickFix implemented a comprehensive learning and knowledge-sharing strategy:

1. **Creating a Knowledge Base:**

   - The team developed an internal knowledge base that documented common issues, troubleshooting steps, and solutions. This resource was regularly updated and included input from all technicians.

   - Technicians were encouraged to contribute their experiences and solutions to the knowledge base, fostering a culture of collaboration and continuous improvement.

2. **Regular Training Sessions:**

   - QuickFix instituted bi-weekly training sessions where technicians could learn about new technologies, software updates, and best practices. Senior team members led these sessions, sharing their expertise and real-world experiences.

   - These training sessions not only improved the skill sets of newer employees but also reinforced the importance of teamwork and shared learning.

3. **Mentorship Program:**

   - The company established a mentorship program pairing experienced technicians with new hires. Mentors guided mentees through complex issues and provided hands-on training, creating a supportive learning environment.

   - This program helped new employees feel more confident and capable in their roles, reducing the time it took for them to become fully productive.

4. **Feedback Loop:**

   - QuickFix implemented a feedback system where customers could provide input on their support experience. This feedback was shared with the team during meetings, allowing everyone to learn from both successes and areas needing improvement.

- Technicians were encouraged to discuss customer feedback openly and brainstorm solutions to recurring issues.

The Result:

By focusing on learning and sharing, QuickFix significantly increased customer satisfaction:

1. **Faster Response Times:**

   - With a centralized knowledge base, technicians could quickly access solutions to common problems, reducing the time spent searching for answers. Average response times decreased by 40%.

2. **Consistent and Effective Solutions:**

   - The shared knowledge and training ensured that all technicians provided consistent solutions to customer issues, which improved the overall service quality. Customers began to notice that their problems were being resolved faster and more effectively.

3. **Higher Customer Satisfaction Ratings:**

   - Customer satisfaction ratings soared. QuickFix received numerous positive reviews highlighting the knowledgeable and friendly support staff. The company's Net Promoter Score (NPS) rose from 30 to 75 in just six months.

4. **Increased Employee Engagement:**

   - Technicians felt more empowered and engaged in their roles, knowing they had access to valuable resources and support. This sense of community and shared purpose led to lower turnover rates and a more positive work environment.

Conclusion:

This story illustrates how learning and sharing can significantly enhance customer satisfaction. By prioritizing knowledge sharing, training, and collaboration, QuickFix transformed its operations and created a more efficient and effective support team. As a result, they not only improved their service quality but also fostered stronger relationships with their customers, leading to long-term loyalty and success in the competitive tech support industry.

18. Exploring the new possibilities in inter disciplinary areas

Three Interdisciplinary Areas for Business Growth

In today's rapidly evolving business landscape, leveraging interdisciplinary approaches can significantly enhance solutions and drive growth. Companies that integrate insights from different fields can address complex challenges more effectively and innovate better. Here, we'll explore three key interdisciplinary areas: **Technology, Marketing, and Operations**, with a real-world example of how a company successfully combined them to achieve business growth.

Example: The Transformation of GreenBites

Background: GreenBites, a startup specializing in healthy snacks, was facing stagnant sales and increasing competition in the health food market. To differentiate themselves and drive growth, the company decided to integrate three key disciplines: **Technology, Marketing**, and **Operations**.

1. **Technology: Data Analytics and Product Development**

     - **Implementation:** GreenBites adopted advanced data analytics tools to analyze consumer preferences, buying patterns, and feedback from social media and online reviews. They invested in machine learning algorithms to identify trends and predict which types of snacks would be in demand.

     - **Outcome:** By leveraging technology, GreenBites developed new product lines that catered specifically to emerging trends, such as gluten-free and plant-based snacks. This allowed them to launch products that were not only innovative but also tailored to customer desires.

2. **Marketing: Social Media and Influencer Partnerships**

   - **Implementation:** The marketing team collaborated with food bloggers and health influencers to create a targeted social media campaign. They utilized the data insights from the technology team to determine the best platforms and messaging that resonated with their target audience.

   - **Outcome:** The influencer partnerships helped boost brand visibility, and the social media campaign led to a significant increase in engagement. GreenBites experienced a 150% increase in followers on Instagram, translating into higher website traffic and, ultimately, sales.

3. **Operations: Streamlined Supply Chain Management**

   - **Implementation:** The operations team worked on optimizing the supply chain by integrating technology that tracked inventory levels in real-time and managed supplier relationships more effectively. They implemented a just-in-time inventory system to reduce waste and improve cash flow.

   - **Outcome:** With a streamlined supply chain, GreenBites could respond quickly to market demands without overproducing, reducing costs and improving margins. This operational efficiency meant they could offer competitive pricing while maintaining quality.

The Results of Interdisciplinary Collaboration:

By working at the intersection of Technology, Marketing, and Operations, GreenBites achieved significant business growth:

- **Increased Sales:** Within a year, GreenBites saw a **200% increase in sales**, driven by the successful launch of new products and effective marketing strategies.

- **Enhanced Brand Loyalty:** The targeted marketing efforts and engagement with influencers created a loyal customer base, with repeat purchases rising by 60%.

- **Operational Efficiency:** The improved supply chain management not only reduced costs but also increased the speed of delivery, enhancing customer satisfaction.

19. Be the master of one – area of specialization

Story: Dr. Maya Chen and the Quest for Renewable Energy

Setting the Scene:

Dr. Maya Chen was a passionate and dedicated scientist specializing in renewable energy. After earning her PhD in environmental science, she became obsessed with the idea of creating affordable solar energy solutions for underserved communities. Her deep passion for renewable energy and commitment to mastering this field drove her to innovate tirelessly.

The Challenge:

Despite her expertise, Maya faced significant challenges:

- **Limited Access:** Many low-income communities had little access to affordable energy sources, relying on expensive fossil fuels.

- **Skepticism:** There was skepticism about solar energy's viability in regions with less sunlight.

- **Funding Issues:** Securing funding for her research and development projects was difficult due to the focus on more traditional energy sources.

The Approach:

Maya decided to take a pioneering approach, focusing intensely on mastering solar technology to create innovative solutions that could change the landscape of renewable energy:

1. **Innovative Research:**

   - Maya immersed herself in research, studying various solar panel technologies and energy storage solutions. She spent countless hours in the lab, experimenting with materials and designs that would maximize energy efficiency while reducing costs.

   - Her groundbreaking research led to the development of a new type of solar panel made from locally sourced materials, which was cheaper and more effective than traditional options.

2. **Community Engagement:**

   - Understanding the importance of community buy-in, Maya organized workshops in underserved neighborhoods to educate residents about the benefits of solar energy. She listened to their concerns and tailored her approach to address specific community needs.

   - By involving the community in the design process, she created solar solutions that resonated with their values and lifestyles.

3. **Collaboration with Local Governments:**

   - Maya collaborated with local governments to secure funding and support for her projects. Her deep knowledge and passion for renewable energy convinced officials of the potential benefits for their communities.

   - She established partnerships with nonprofits to help distribute solar panels and provide training for local residents on installation and maintenance.

The Result:

Through her passionate mastery of renewable energy, Maya achieved extraordinary success:

1. **Affordable Solar Solutions:**

   - Maya's solar panels became a game changer for low-income communities, providing reliable and affordable energy. Over 1,000 homes adopted her solar technology within the first year of launch.

2. **Pioneering Recognition:**

   - Her innovative work caught the attention of national media and energy organizations. Maya became a recognized pioneer in the field of renewable energy, receiving awards for her contributions and dedication to sustainability.

3. **Inspiration for Future Generations:**

   - Maya's success inspired many young scientists and engineers to pursue careers in renewable energy. She established a scholarship fund to support students from underserved communities interested in STEM fields, furthering her mission of promoting clean energy solutions.

20. Appreciation and Feedback

Story: The Transformation of Creative Solutions Inc.

Setting the Scene:

Creative Solutions Inc. was a mid-sized marketing agency known for its innovative campaigns. However, despite its creative potential, the work environment had become stagnant and demotivating. Employees felt overwhelmed by tight deadlines and often received little recognition for their efforts. The leadership team realized that fostering a more positive culture through feedback and appreciation was crucial for improving morale and productivity.

The Challenge:

The agency faced several issues:

- **Low Employee Morale:** Many employees felt their hard work went unnoticed, leading to decreased motivation and engagement.

- **Lack of Collaboration:** Team members were reluctant to share ideas or provide constructive feedback, fearing criticism or negative repercussions.

- **High Turnover Rates:** The lack of a supportive culture contributed to high turnover, with talented employees leaving for more positive environments.

The Approach:

To address these challenges, Creative Solutions Inc. implemented a comprehensive strategy focused on **feedback** and **appreciation**:

1. **Feedback Training:**

   - The leadership introduced training sessions on giving and receiving constructive feedback. Employees learned how to communicate their thoughts in a positive and supportive manner, emphasizing growth rather than criticism.

   - The focus was on the **"sandwich method"**, where constructive feedback was framed between two positive comments. This helped create a more balanced and encouraging feedback culture.

2. **Regular Recognition Programs:**

   - The company established a monthly recognition program called **"Shining Stars,"** where employees could nominate colleagues for their outstanding contributions. Winners received public acknowledgment during team meetings, along with small rewards like gift cards or extra time off.

- This initiative encouraged employees to appreciate each other's efforts and fostered a sense of community within the workplace.

3. **Open Communication Channels:**

- Management implemented weekly check-in meetings, allowing team members to discuss ongoing projects, share challenges, and celebrate successes. This open forum encouraged collaboration and strengthened team bonds.

- Employees were also encouraged to provide feedback to management, creating a two-way communication street that made everyone feel valued.

The Result:

The focus on feedback and appreciation transformed the work culture at Creative Solutions Inc.:

1. **Increased Employee Morale:**

- Employees reported feeling more motivated and engaged in their work. The monthly recognition program boosted morale significantly, with many stating they felt valued for their contributions.

2. **Enhanced Collaboration:**

- Team members became more open to sharing ideas and providing constructive feedback. The fear of negative criticism diminished, leading to increased collaboration and creativity in projects.

- Projects improved as a result, with team members feeling empowered to voice their opinions and contribute innovative ideas.

3. **Lower Turnover Rates:**

- The positive changes in the work environment led to a noticeable decrease in turnover rates. Talented employees chose to stay, contributing to a more experienced and cohesive team.

- New hires expressed excitement about joining a company that prioritized recognition and collaboration, further enhancing the agency's reputation.

4. **Improved Overall Performance:**

- The positive culture translated into better project outcomes. The agency saw a 30% increase in client satisfaction ratings and a 25% increase in project completion rates within deadlines.

Conclusion:

This story illustrates how appreciation and positive feedback can create a healthy work culture. By fostering an environment where feedback is constructive and recognition is valued, Creative Solutions Inc. transformed its workplace from one of stagnation to one of innovation and collaboration. The shift not only motivated employees but also led to improved performance and retention, showcasing the powerful impact of appreciation in creating a thriving organizational culture.

21. Lead by iconic example

Story: The Rise of Emma Johnson: A Communicative Leader

Setting the Scene:

Emma Johnson, the newly appointed CEO of **TechWave**, a software development company, faced a critical challenge. After years of steady growth, the company was experiencing stagnation, and morale among employees was low. Team members felt disconnected from the company's vision and were uncertain about their roles in driving innovation. Emma recognized that effective leadership required not only vision but also strong communication skills to inspire and engage her team.

The Challenge:

TechWave was grappling with several issues:

- **Lack of Direction:** Employees felt that they were working in silos without a clear understanding of the company's goals or their contributions to those goals.

- **Decreased Innovation:** With no collaborative environment, the flow of new ideas had diminished, leading to a lack of innovative products and solutions.

- **Low Employee Engagement:** Many employees felt undervalued and disengaged, resulting in high turnover rates and decreased productivity.

The Approach:

Emma decided to embrace **communicative leadership** to tackle these challenges head-on:

1. **Vision Sharing:**

   - Emma organized a company-wide town hall meeting to communicate her vision for TechWave. She articulated her goals for innovation and collaboration, sharing specific strategies for how the company could achieve them.

   - During this meeting, she encouraged employees to voice their thoughts and concerns, ensuring that everyone felt heard. She emphasized that every team member played a crucial role in the company's success.

2. **Open-Door Policy:**

   - Emma established an open-door policy, inviting employees to discuss their ideas, challenges, or feedback directly with her. She made it clear that she valued transparency and wanted to build trust within the organization.

   - To facilitate this, she held regular **"Coffee with Emma"** sessions, where employees could drop in for informal discussions. This initiative fostered open communication and helped break down hierarchical barriers.

3. **Interactive Team Meetings:**

- Rather than traditional status update meetings, Emma transformed team meetings into interactive brainstorming sessions. Each meeting began with a review of current projects, followed by a segment where team members could share innovative ideas or solutions.

- Emma encouraged participation by highlighting and building on team members' suggestions, demonstrating that she genuinely valued their input.

4. **Recognition and Feedback:**

- Emma implemented a peer recognition program called **"TechWave Kudos,"** where employees could publicly acknowledge their colleagues' contributions during team meetings. This created a culture of appreciation and motivated employees to engage and support each other.

- She also sought feedback on her leadership style and communication methods, showing her commitment to continuous improvement.

The Result:

Through her communicative leadership approach, Emma transformed TechWave into an iconic organization known for its innovative culture:

1. **Increased Employee Engagement:**

- Employees reported feeling more connected to the company's vision and goals. Surveys indicated a 40% increase in employee engagement scores within six months, with team members expressing enthusiasm for their work and pride in their contributions.

2. **Enhanced Collaboration:**

   - The interactive meetings and open-door policy fostered a collaborative atmosphere. Team members began to work together more effectively, sharing ideas and solving problems collectively. This led to the development of innovative software solutions that attracted new clients.

3. **Lower Turnover Rates:**

   - As a result of the positive work environment, turnover rates dropped significantly. Talented employees who had considered leaving decided to stay, contributing to a more experienced workforce.

4. **Recognition in the Industry:**

   - TechWave gained recognition as a leader in innovation within the tech industry. Their new products, developed through collaborative efforts, won several prestigious awards, further enhancing the company's reputation.

5. **Emma's Legacy:**

   - Emma's communicative leadership style earned her respect and admiration not only within TechWave but also in the broader business community. She became an iconic figure, known for her ability to inspire and empower others, demonstrating the profound impact of effective communication in leadership.

Conclusion:

Emma Johnson's story exemplifies how communicative leadership can create a thriving organizational culture and drive success. By prioritizing open communication, collaboration, and recognition, she transformed TechWave from a stagnating company into an innovative powerhouse. Emma's ability to connect with her team and inspire them to embrace the company's vision made her an iconic leader, proving that action-oriented communication is at the heart of effective leadership.

22. Focus what you can control

Welcome to this guided meditation for self-control and inner peace. Find a quiet and comfortable space where you can relax without distractions. You may sit or lie down in a position that feels best for you. When you're ready, gently close your eyes and take a deep breath in... and out.

[Body]

1. **Cantering the Breath**

    (Pause for a few moments)

    Narrator:

    Begin to focus on your breath. Inhale deeply through your nose, feeling your abdomen rise. Hold it for a moment... and then exhale slowly through your mouth, feeling your abdomen fall. Let's do this together. Inhale... hold... and exhale.

    (Pause)

    Continue to breathe in this manner, allowing each breath to bring you deeper into a state of relaxation.

2. **Visualization of Calm**

    (Pause)

    Narrator:

    Now, imagine a warm, golden light surrounding you. This light represents your inner peace and self-control. As you breathe in, visualize this golden light entering your body, filling you with warmth and tranquility. With each exhale, imagine releasing any tension, stress, or distractions.

3. **Affirmations for Self-Control**

(Pause)

Narrator:

As you continue to breathe, I will say a series of affirmations. Repeat them silently in your mind or aloud, allowing their meaning to resonate within you.

- I am in control of my thoughts and actions.

- I embrace calmness and clarity in my mind.

- I am strong, focused, and resilient.

- Each challenge I face strengthens my self-control.

- I choose peace over chaos.

(Pause for a few moments after each affirmation)

4. **Letting Go of Distractions**

(Pause)

Narrator:

Now, let's take a moment to acknowledge any distractions or negative thoughts that may be lingering in your mind. Imagine these thoughts as leaves floating on a stream.

As you inhale, visualize gently placing each thought on a leaf. As you exhale, watch the leaves drift away, carrying your distractions downstream.

(Pause for a few moments)

With each breath, feel a sense of liberation as you release what no longer serves you.

5. **Cultivating Inner Peace**

(Pause)

Narrator:

Focus on the sensation of inner peace growing within you. Picture yourself in a serene environment—a tranquil beach, a peaceful forest, or a quiet garden. Feel the calmness of this space surrounding you.

Let this peace fill every part of your being. Embrace the stillness and serenity, allowing it to empower your self-control and clarity.

(Pause for a few moments)

6. **Closing the Meditation**

(Pause)

Narrator:

As we begin to close this meditation, take a moment to reflect on the feelings of self-control and inner peace you have cultivated. Know that you can return to this state whenever you need.

Now, gently bring your awareness back to your breath. Take a deep inhale, feeling the energy and peace within you, and exhale slowly.

Begin to wiggle your fingers and toes, bringing gentle movement back into your body. When you're ready, open your eyes, and take a moment to notice how you feel.

(Pause)

[Conclusion]

Narrator:

Thank you for joining this meditation for self-control and inner peace. Carry this sense of calm with you throughout your day, knowing that you are empowered to make choices that reflect your true self. Remember, you are strong, and you can embrace your inner peace at any time.

23. Use case reference as stepping stone of next project success:

Example: Digital Transformation Project in Retail

Project Background: Retail Innovations Inc. is a mid-sized retail chain that has successfully implemented a digital transformation project in one of its flagship stores, leading to increased sales and improved customer satisfaction. With plans to expand this initiative to all locations, the company aimed to leverage its past experiences to ensure the success of the next phase of digital transformation.

Learning from Previous Project Experience

Previous Project: Digital Transformation of the Flagship Store

1. **Project Overview:**

   - The flagship store underwent a digital transformation that included the integration of mobile payment options, digital signage, an online inventory system, and a customer loyalty app.

   - The goal was to enhance the customer shopping experience and streamline operations.

2. **Successes:**

   - After implementing the digital solutions, the store saw a **25% increase** in foot traffic and a **15% rise** in overall sales within the first quarter.

   - The customer loyalty app resulted in a **40% increase** in repeat purchases, demonstrating enhanced customer engagement.

3. **Challenges:**

   - Initial resistance from staff who were not familiar with the new technology led to operational inefficiencies during the rollout.

   - Some technical issues arose with integrating the new systems, causing temporary disruptions in service and inventory management.

Applying Lessons to the Company-Wide Digital Transformation

Next Project: Digital Transformation Rollout Across All Locations

1. **Preparation Phase:**

   - **Utilizing Feedback:** The project team conducted a series of debrief meetings to gather feedback from employees and customers regarding the flagship store's digital changes. This input highlighted the need for comprehensive staff training and more seamless integration of technology.

   - **Identifying Key Metrics:** The team analyzed performance metrics from the flagship store, focusing on what drove the increases in sales and customer satisfaction. This data helped define success criteria for the rollout across other locations.

2. **Training and Support:**

   - To address the resistance from staff encountered in the flagship store, the company developed a robust training program that included hands-on workshops, video tutorials, and ongoing support.

   - Store managers were trained to become "digital champions," enabling them to support their teams better and answer questions during the transition.

3. **Pilot Testing:**

   - Before rolling out the digital transformation to all locations, the company decided to implement a pilot program in two additional stores. This allowed them to test the systems, gather data, and make necessary adjustments based on real-world experiences.

   - The pilot revealed additional areas for improvement, such as optimizing the layout for digital signage and refining the mobile app interface based on customer feedback.

4. **Ongoing Evaluation:**

   - The project team established a process for continuous feedback and improvement, including regular check-ins with staff and customers to evaluate the effectiveness of the new systems. Metrics from the flagship store informed ongoing adjustments and enhancements.

Outcome of the Next Project

By leveraging the experiences from the previous digital transformation project, Retail Innovations Inc. achieved several positive outcomes:

1. **Successful Rollout:**

   - The digital transformation was successfully implemented across all stores within six months, resulting in an overall sales increase of **20%** and a **30% increase** in customer satisfaction scores across the board.

2. **Enhanced Employee Engagement:**

   - The comprehensive training and support led to higher employee confidence and satisfaction, with staff feeling empowered to use the new technology effectively.

3. **Improved Customer Experience:**

   - Customers enjoyed a more cohesive shopping experience, with streamlined payments, real-time inventory updates, and engaging digital displays that enhanced their shopping journey.

4. **Stronger Data-Driven Decisions:**

   - The insights gained from the initial flagship store project helped Retail Innovations Inc. make data-driven decisions that improved marketing strategies and inventory management, ultimately leading to sustained growth.

Conclusion

This example illustrates how the experiences from a previous project can provide a fundamental understanding that informs and enhances the success of subsequent projects. By analysing successes and challenges, gathering feedback, and applying lessons learned, Retail Innovations Inc. was able to execute a seamless and effective digital transformation across all its locations, leading to significant improvements in sales, customer satisfaction, and employee engagement.

24. Continuous learning attitude

Maria's Journey in the Competitive World of Graphic Design

Background: Maria is a graphic designer working for a medium-sized advertising agency. In a field where creativity and innovation are paramount, she noticed that many of her peers were stagnating in their skills. To stand out in a competitive market, Maria adopted a continuous learning attitude that not only enhanced her skill set but also made her a valuable asset to her team and clients.

Continuous Learning in Action

1. **Investing in New Skills:**

   - **Online Courses:** Maria enrolled in online courses to learn the latest design software and tools, such as Adobe Illustrator and Sketch. While her colleagues primarily used traditional methods, she took the initiative to explore advanced techniques in digital design.

   - **Workshops and Webinars:** She attended design workshops and webinars hosted by industry experts, covering topics like user experience (UX) design, animation, and branding strategies. This commitment to learning kept her updated on trends and best practices.

2. **Networking and Feedback:**

   - **Design Communities:** Maria joined online design communities and forums where she shared her work, received feedback, and learned from others. Engaging with other designers allowed her to broaden her perspective and adopt new approaches to her projects.

   - **Mentorship:** She sought mentorship from senior designers in her agency and outside. Through this mentorship, she gained insights into effective design strategies, project management, and client relationships.

3. **Experimentation and Application:**

   - **Side Projects:** Maria took on side projects that allowed her to experiment with different styles and techniques. She worked on personal branding for small businesses, allowing her to apply what she learned in real-world scenarios. This not only boosted her portfolio but also helped her refine her skills.

   - **Incorporating Feedback:** With every project, Maria sought feedback from clients and peers. She viewed constructive criticism as an opportunity for growth, adapting her designs based on the input she received.

Achievements and Competitive Edge

1. **Innovative Portfolio:**

   - As Maria expanded her skills and knowledge, her portfolio became a showcase of diverse styles and cutting-edge designs. Clients began to notice her unique approach, and her work stood out in a saturated market.

2. **Recognition and Opportunities:**

   - Maria's dedication to continuous learning earned her recognition within her agency. She was entrusted with high-profile projects that required innovative solutions, and her designs received accolades from clients and peers alike.

- As she became known for her creative and effective design strategies, Maria was invited to speak at industry conferences, sharing her insights on the importance of continuous learning and adaptability.

3. **Increased Client Satisfaction:**

- Maria's ability to stay ahead of trends and incorporate the latest techniques into her work led to increased client satisfaction. Clients appreciated her innovative ideas and ability to deliver designs that aligned with their brand visions.

- This satisfaction translated into repeat business and referrals, helping her build a robust client base.

Conclusion

Maria's continuous learning attitude set her apart in the competitive graphic design industry. By investing in her skills, actively seeking feedback, and embracing new challenges, she not only enhanced her creativity but also positioned herself as a thought leader in her field. Her journey illustrates how a commitment to lifelong learning can lead to exceptional personal and professional growth, allowing individuals to stand out in a competitive landscape.

25. Be a mentor to empower your team members

James's Journey as a Mentor in Software Development

Background: James is a mid-level software developer at a tech company specializing in mobile applications. After a few years of honing his skills in programming and project management, he was given the opportunity to mentor new interns joining the team. Initially hesitant, James soon realized that mentoring others would not only help them grow but also contribute significantly to his self-development.

Learning Through Mentoring

1. **Deepening Knowledge:**

   - **Teaching Concepts:** As James prepared to mentor his interns, he needed to revisit fundamental concepts and programming languages. Explaining complex topics, such as algorithms and data structures, required him to break them down into simpler terms, deepening his understanding of the material. This process solidified his knowledge and revealed gaps he hadn't realized existed.

   - **Staying Updated:** To provide the best guidance, James committed to staying current with industry trends and emerging technologies. He began reading books and taking online courses on new programming frameworks, ensuring that he could offer relevant insights to his mentees.

2. **Improving Communication Skills:**

   - **Tailoring Explanations:** Mentoring taught James the importance of adapting his communication style to suit his interns' varying levels of experience. He learned how to ask questions that encouraged critical thinking and problem-solving, enhancing his ability to convey complex ideas clearly.

   - **Active Listening:** James developed his active listening skills by paying attention to his mentees' concerns and challenges. This not only improved his communication but also helped him foster a supportive environment where interns felt comfortable asking questions and seeking help.

3. **Enhancing Leadership Qualities:**

   - **Responsibility and Accountability:** As a mentor, James felt a newfound sense of responsibility for his interns' success. He established regular check-ins, created a structured mentorship plan, and set goals with his mentees, which helped him develop strong organizational and leadership skills.

- **Conflict Resolution:** When conflicts arose between interns—such as differing opinions on project approaches—James learned how to mediate discussions and facilitate constructive dialogue. This experience equipped him with valuable conflict resolution skills that benefited his interactions with colleagues.

4. **Gaining Perspective:**

- **Fresh Ideas:** Working closely with interns exposed James to new ideas and perspectives. Their fresh approach to problem-solving and willingness to experiment with innovative solutions inspired him to think outside the box and consider alternative methods in his projects.

- **Understanding Different Learning Styles:** He learned that each intern had a unique learning style, which prompted him to adapt his mentoring approach. This awareness of diverse perspectives enriched his own understanding of teamwork and collaboration.

Outcomes of Mentoring

1. **Personal Growth:**

- Through mentoring, James gained confidence in his abilities, improved his leadership skills, and developed a deeper understanding of software development concepts. He became a more well-rounded professional, ready to take on greater responsibilities within his company.

2. **Building a Supportive Culture:**

- James's commitment to mentoring created a supportive culture within the team. His interns felt valued and motivated, leading to increased productivity and better team dynamics. This positive environment encouraged collaboration and knowledge sharing among team members.

3. **Career Advancement:**

- His success as a mentor did not go unnoticed. James's leadership skills and ability to nurture talent positioned him for promotions and greater opportunities within the organization. He was later offered a role as a team lead, where he could further implement his mentoring approach on a larger scale.

26. Environment friendliness and contribution to save earth: Whatever your areas of work, it is our duty to contribute save the mother earth and support go green project.

GreenTech Solutions – A Sustainable Development Initiative

Background: GreenTech Solutions is a fictional company focused on providing innovative technological solutions to promote sustainability and environmental protection. The company realized that its actions not only impacted its immediate business outcomes but also contributed to long-term sustainable development goals. They decided to implement a series of initiatives aimed at protecting the environment while driving growth.

Actions Taken for Long-Term Sustainable Development

1. **Adopting Renewable Energy Sources:**

- **Solar Power Installation:** GreenTech Solutions made a significant investment in solar energy by installing solar panels on the rooftops of their office buildings and production facilities. This move not only reduced the company's reliance on fossil fuels but also cut energy costs by 30%. The switch to renewable energy sources allowed the company to operate more sustainably and set a positive example for its community.

- **Energy Efficiency Initiatives:** In addition to solar power, they implemented energy-efficient lighting and HVAC systems in their facilities, further reducing energy consumption and lowering their carbon footprint.

2. **Sustainable Product Development:**

- **Eco-Friendly Products:** The company committed to developing a line of eco-friendly products, such as biodegradable packaging and energy-efficient devices. For instance, they created a smart thermostat that reduces energy consumption by learning users' habits and optimizing heating and cooling accordingly.

- **Lifecycle Analysis:** Each product underwent a lifecycle analysis to assess its environmental impact from production to disposal. This approach helped the company identify areas for improvement, ensuring that their products contributed positively to sustainable development.

3. **Waste Reduction and Recycling Programs:**

- **Zero Waste Goals:** GreenTech Solutions set a goal to achieve zero waste in their operations by implementing recycling and composting programs. They established a robust waste management system that sorted materials for recycling, composted organic waste, and minimized landfill contributions.

- **Employee Engagement:** The company encouraged employees to participate in waste reduction initiatives by providing training on recycling best practices and holding regular "green challenges" to promote sustainability awareness.

4. **Community Engagement and Education:**

- **Environmental Workshops:** GreenTech Solutions organized workshops and seminars for local schools and community groups to educate people about sustainability, renewable energy, and environmental protection. These initiatives helped raise awareness and fostered a culture of sustainability within the community.

- **Partnerships with Local Organizations:** The company partnered with local environmental organizations to participate in tree-planting events and cleanup drives, contributing to the beautification and preservation of natural spaces.

Outcomes of Sustainable Actions

1. **Positive Environmental Impact:**

   - As a result of their initiatives, GreenTech Solutions significantly reduced their carbon emissions and energy consumption. The solar panels alone generated enough energy to power their facilities, offsetting thousands of tons of CO_2 emissions over the years.

   - Their commitment to waste reduction and recycling resulted in diverting 90% of their waste from landfills, contributing to the circular economy.

2. **Enhanced Brand Reputation:**

   - GreenTech Solutions gained recognition as a leader in sustainability within their industry. Their efforts attracted environmentally conscious customers, leading to increased sales and loyalty.

   - The company's brand reputation improved, attracting top talent who wanted to work for an organization committed to social responsibility and environmental protection.

3. **Long-Term Business Sustainability:**

   - By integrating sustainable practices into their operations, GreenTech Solutions ensured long-term viability and profitability. Their innovative products and efficient processes positioned them well for future growth in an increasingly eco-conscious market.

4. **Community Benefits:**

   - The educational programs and community engagement initiatives led to a more environmentally aware community, fostering local support for sustainability initiatives and encouraging individuals to adopt eco-friendly practices in their daily lives.

Conclusion

GreenTech Solutions demonstrates how a company's actions and commitment to environmental protection can contribute to long-term sustainable development. By adopting renewable energy, developing eco-friendly products, reducing waste, and engaging with the community, they created a positive impact that benefited both the environment and the business. This holistic approach not only promotes sustainability but also sets a precedent for other companies to follow, reinforcing the importance of integrating environmental responsibility into corporate strategy for a better future.

27. If you are very serious, you are prone to mistake. Be Mindful not stressful.

Sarah's Experience in a High-Stakes Project

Background: Sarah is a project manager at a technology firm responsible for overseeing the development of a new software product. The project is high-stakes, with tight deadlines and significant investment from the company. Initially, Sarah approached the project with a very serious mindset, believing that focusing solely on the task at hand would lead to success. However, this approach quickly revealed its downsides.

The Serious Mindset

1. **Increased Stress:**

   - Sarah was deeply focused on meeting deadlines and delivering results. She often worked late, skipped breaks, and was constantly anxious about every detail of the project. This serious approach led to elevated stress levels, affecting her mental and physical well-being.

   - Her team noticed her tension and began to mirror her seriousness, creating a stressful work environment where everyone felt pressured to perform perfectly.

2. **Prone to Mistakes:**

   - As Sarah became more serious, she began to overlook minor details. For instance, during a crucial meeting with the client, she mistakenly presented outdated project timelines. This error not only embarrassed her in front of the client but also raised concerns about the team's professionalism.

   - Additionally, her serious demeanor stifled creativity within the team. Team members felt hesitant to share innovative ideas or solutions for fear of making mistakes, leading to missed opportunities for improvement.

Shifting Towards a Mindful Approach

Realizing that her seriousness was counterproductive, Sarah decided to adopt a more mindful approach to her work.

1. **Practicing Mindfulness:**

   - Sarah began incorporating mindfulness practices into her daily routine, such as meditation and deep-breathing exercises. These practices helped her manage stress and maintain a clearer perspective on her work.

   - She encouraged her team to take short breaks, engage in open discussions, and share their thoughts without fear of judgment. This shift fostered a more relaxed and creative atmosphere in the workplace.

2. **Emphasizing a Growth Mindset:**

- Instead of focusing solely on perfection, Sarah embraced the idea that mistakes are opportunities for learning. She started to celebrate small wins and encouraged her team to view challenges as chances to grow.

- When mistakes occurred, she facilitated discussions on what went wrong and how to improve in the future, reinforcing the idea that it's okay to make mistakes as long as they lead to learning and growth.

Outcomes of the Mindful Approach

1. **Improved Team Dynamics:**

- With a more mindful environment, the team became more cohesive and collaborative. Team members felt comfortable sharing ideas and taking calculated risks, leading to innovative solutions for the project.

- The overall morale improved, and team members reported feeling less stressed and more engaged in their work.

2. **Enhanced Productivity:**

- By reducing stress and fostering a culture of mindfulness, Sarah and her team became more productive. They met deadlines more effectively and produced high-quality work, ultimately leading to a successful project launch.

- The team learned to prioritize tasks, manage time effectively, and approach challenges with a positive mindset.

3. **Better Client Relationships:**

- With improved communication and collaboration, Sarah's team was better equipped to meet client expectations.

When presenting project updates, they provided accurate information and showcased their creativity, leading to increased client satisfaction.

- Clients appreciated the team's openness and willingness to learn from mistakes, reinforcing their trust in the company.

28. 360 Degree viewpoint: Is essentially required to see any situation from bird eye view such that selection of optimized option will be easy. Unbiased nutria decision accelerates growth of execution. Stay away from problem and find unbiased solution.

The Launch of EcoSmart, a Sustainable Product Line

Background: EcoSmart, a fictional consumer goods company, is preparing to launch a new line of sustainable household products. To ensure the success of the launch, the company decided to employ both a bird's eye view and a 360-degree view approach to gain unbiased clarity on its strategy, operations, and market positioning.

Bird's Eye View

1. **Strategic Overview:**

   - The leadership team at EcoSmart conducted a bird's eye view analysis, which provided a high-level perspective of the company's objectives and market landscape. This overview included an analysis of market trends, competitive positioning, and customer needs.

   - By examining industry reports, competitor strategies, and consumer behavior data, they identified the growing demand for eco-friendly products and recognized opportunities for differentiation in the marketplace. This clarity allowed them to define their unique value proposition clearly: high-quality, sustainable products at competitive prices.

2. **Setting Clear Objectives:**

   - The bird's eye view helped EcoSmart's leadership set clear, overarching goals for the product line launch, including targeted sales figures, marketing strategies, and sustainability benchmarks.

   - They aimed to not only launch the products successfully but also to position EcoSmart as a thought leader in sustainability, creating awareness and advocacy around their brand.

360-Degree View

1. **Comprehensive Analysis:**

   - EcoSmart employed a 360-degree view approach by gathering feedback from various stakeholders, including employees, customers, suppliers, and industry experts. This involved conducting surveys, focus groups, and interviews to understand different perspectives on the product line.

   - Employees provided insights into the production process, highlighting potential challenges in sourcing sustainable materials. Customers shared their expectations for eco-friendly packaging and transparency in product sourcing. Suppliers offered feedback on logistical considerations and cost implications.

2. **Unbiased Clarity:**

   - The 360-degree view enabled EcoSmart to identify potential pitfalls and opportunities that a single viewpoint might have overlooked. For instance, customer feedback revealed that while many consumers were excited about the product line, there were concerns about the price point and availability in stores.

   - By synthesizing this diverse feedback, EcoSmart was able to refine its product pricing strategy and develop a targeted marketing campaign that emphasized both sustainability and affordability.

Outcomes of Combining Both Views

1. **Informed Decision-Making:**

   - The combination of the bird's eye view and 360-degree view provided EcoSmart with a comprehensive understanding of the market landscape and internal dynamics. This informed decision-making process led to a well-rounded strategy for the product launch.

   - Leadership was able to align the goals set during the bird's eye analysis with the insights gained from the 360-degree feedback, ensuring that all stakeholders' perspectives were considered.

2. **Successful Product Launch:**

   - When EcoSmart launched the sustainable product line, it was met with positive feedback and strong initial sales. The thoughtful integration of stakeholder insights allowed them to address potential issues proactively, resulting in a smooth launch process.

   - The company's marketing campaign effectively highlighted their commitment to sustainability while assuring customers of the value and affordability of their products.

3. **Long-Term Benefits:**

   - By utilizing both perspectives, EcoSmart established a reputation as a responsible and innovative brand in the sustainable market. This reputation helped them build customer loyalty and differentiate themselves from competitors.

   - The company also created a feedback loop for future product developments, continuously integrating stakeholder perspectives into their strategy to maintain relevance and adaptability in a changing market.

29. Metaphor: Presentation is the key for communication regarding any project delivery. Use positive way of explaining the deviations, exceptions to get escalation to be transformed to acceptance.

Maria's Transformational Presentation at a Tech Conference

Background: Maria, a product manager at a leading software development company, was invited to present at an annual tech conference attended by industry experts, potential clients, and investors. Her goal was to introduce her company's latest software solution, aimed at enhancing team collaboration. Understanding the competitive nature of the conference, Maria knew she needed to create a presentation that would not only inform but also inspire and engage her audience.

The Approach

1. **Setting the Tone:**

   - Maria began her preparation by focusing on the energy and positivity she wanted to bring to her presentation. She envisioned a vibrant atmosphere where her audience would feel excited about her product. She decided to incorporate storytelling, humour, and relatable examples to create an emotional connection with her listeners.

   - To further enhance the positive vibe, Maria chose bright colors and dynamic graphics for her slides. She also included an upbeat soundtrack to play softly during her introduction, setting a lively tone right from the start.

2. **Engaging Content:**

   - Maria structured her presentation around a compelling narrative. She started by sharing a personal story about a time when her team struggled with collaboration and how it affected their project outcomes. This story resonated with the audience, as many could relate to similar challenges in their own workplaces.

- She then introduced her software solution, framing it as a game-changer that could transform team dynamics and productivity. Instead of diving straight into technical features, she focused on the benefits and real-world applications of the product, using anecdotes and testimonials from early users to illustrate its impact.

3. **Interactive Elements:**

   - To maintain audience engagement, Maria incorporated interactive elements throughout her presentation. She encouraged audience participation by asking questions and prompting them to share their experiences. For instance, she posed a question about their biggest challenges in team collaboration and invited a few attendees to share their thoughts.

   - Maria also included live polls where audience members could vote on various features they found most appealing in collaboration tools. This not only kept the energy high but also made the audience feel involved in the discussion.

The Impact

1. **Creating a Positive Atmosphere:**

   - The combination of her storytelling, interactive elements, and enthusiastic delivery created a positive and welcoming atmosphere. Attendees were smiling, nodding, and actively participating, which amplified the overall energy in the room.

   - The positive vibes created a sense of community among the audience, making them feel connected not only to Maria but also to each other.

2. **Captivating the Audience:**

   - By the end of her presentation, Maria had successfully captivated her audience. They were not only informed about the software solution but also inspired to think about how they could implement similar tools to improve their own team collaboration.

- Many attendees approached Maria afterward, eager to learn more about the product and discuss potential partnerships. The positive energy she radiated made her memorable, increasing the likelihood of follow-up conversations and collaborations.

3. **Miraculous Results:**

- Maria's presentation was deemed one of the highlights of the conference. Feedback from the attendees highlighted how her positive energy and engaging storytelling transformed a potentially dry topic into an inspiring session.

- As a result, her company saw a significant increase in interest for the software solution, leading to several new partnerships and sales inquiries. The presentation not only achieved its objective but also positioned Maria as a thought leader in the industry.

30. Think rationally and stop overthinking, adapt critical thinking for better collaboration with your customers:

The Launch of a New Marketing Campaign by TrendyWear

Background: TrendyWear, a fashion retail company, was preparing to launch a new marketing campaign for its upcoming fall collection. The marketing team was excited about the project but found themselves caught in a cycle of overthinking various elements, which began to hinder their progress. Recognizing the risk of delaying the campaign, they decided to refocus on rational thinking and clear decision-making to ensure timely delivery.

The Overthinking Scenario

1. **Complicated Decision-Making:**

- Initially, the team spent countless hours deliberating over minor details, such as the perfect color scheme for the promotional materials and the ideal time to post on social media. Each team member had different opinions, leading to endless discussions that went in circles.

- The project timeline started to slip, causing anxiety among team members as they felt pressure to finalize decisions. This overthinking created an atmosphere of uncertainty, and the team began to lose sight of the project's main objectives.

2. **Analysis Paralysis:**

- The marketing team fell into analysis paralysis, where they were so focused on analyzing data and gathering feedback that they failed to make concrete decisions. They conducted surveys to determine customer preferences, but the abundance of data only fueled further debate rather than clarity.

- The fear of making the wrong choices led to hesitation, and the team started doubting their initial ideas and strategies, further delaying the campaign's launch.

Shifting to Rational Thinking

1. **Establishing Clear Objectives:**

- The team leader decided to hold a meeting to reset the focus. They revisited the campaign's core objectives, emphasizing the importance of timely delivery and brand messaging. By grounding the conversation in their primary goals, the team regained perspective on what truly mattered.

- They established a clear timeline with specific milestones, ensuring that everyone was aligned on deadlines and responsibilities.

2. **Simplifying Decision-Making:**

- To counteract overthinking, the team adopted a simplified decision-making process. Instead of striving for perfection in every detail, they decided to prioritize the key elements that would resonate most with their target audience.

- For instance, they quickly agreed on a bold color scheme that aligned with their brand identity rather than getting bogged down in minor variations. They set a deadline for decisions, allowing for a quick consensus without unnecessary debates.

3. **Focusing on Action:**

- The team shifted their focus from analysis to action. They implemented a "good enough" principle, recognizing that they could always adjust and optimize elements of the campaign after launch based on real-time feedback.

- They initiated the campaign rollout with a limited social media teaser, allowing them to gauge audience reactions and adapt their strategy as needed. This approach fostered a culture of experimentation rather than fear of failure.

Outcomes of Rational Thinking

1. **Successful Campaign Launch:**

- By prioritizing rational thinking over overthinking, TrendyWear successfully launched their marketing campaign on schedule. The clear objectives and streamlined decision-making process enabled the team to execute their ideas efficiently.

- The campaign resonated well with their target audience, garnering positive engagement and strong sales for the fall collection.

2. **Increased Team Morale:**

- The shift from overthinking to rationality had a positive impact on team morale. Team members felt empowered to contribute their ideas without fear of prolonged debates, leading to a more collaborative atmosphere.

- They celebrated the successful launch together, reinforcing a sense of accomplishment and teamwork.

3. **Lessons Learned:**

- The experience taught the marketing team valuable lessons about the dangers of overthinking and the benefits of rational decision-making. They adopted new practices for future projects, emphasizing clarity, simplicity, and timely action.

- TrendyWear's leadership recognized the importance of fostering a culture that encourages quick decision-making and adaptability, which would enhance future project delivery.

SmartTech's Approach to Customer Engagement

Background: SmartTech, a tech company specializing in innovative home automation products, faced challenges in engaging customers effectively. Despite having high-quality products, they noticed a decline in customer satisfaction and retention rates. To address this issue, the marketing team decided to apply critical thinking strategies to understand customer needs better and enhance their engagement efforts.

Identifying the Problem

1. **Analyzing Customer Feedback:**

- The team started by analyzing customer feedback collected through surveys, reviews, and social media interactions. While many customers praised the technology and features of SmartTech's products, there were consistent complaints regarding the complexity of setup and use.

- The marketing team engaged in critical thinking by asking probing questions: "Why do customers find our products difficult to use?" and "What specific features are causing frustration?"

2. **Identifying Patterns:**

- By synthesizing the feedback, the team identified patterns indicating that many customers were overwhelmed by the product's advanced features and user interface. This insight prompted them to delve deeper into the root causes of these issues rather than merely addressing surface-level complaints.

Developing Solutions Through Critical Thinking

1. **Collaborative Brainstorming:**

- The marketing team organized a brainstorming session, encouraging diverse perspectives from various departments, including product development, customer support, and sales. This collaborative effort aimed to develop a comprehensive understanding of the customer experience.

- They applied critical thinking to evaluate existing solutions and explore new ideas, asking questions like, "How can we simplify the setup process?" and "What resources can we provide to assist customers better?"

2. **Creating Customer Personas:**

- The team developed detailed customer personas based on demographics, preferences, and pain points. They utilized critical thinking to analyze how different segments of their customer base interacted with the product and what barriers they faced.

- For instance, they identified that tech-savvy users appreciated advanced features, while less experienced users struggled. This realization led them to tailor their marketing and support efforts to meet the varying needs of different personas.

Implementing Changes

1. **Enhanced User Guides and Support:**

   - Based on their findings, SmartTech redesigned their user guides to be more intuitive and user-friendly. They created step-by-step video tutorials and interactive support features to assist customers during the setup process.

   - They also implemented a live chat support option on their website, allowing customers to seek help in real-time when facing difficulties.

2. **Targeted Marketing Campaigns:**

   - SmartTech launched targeted marketing campaigns that highlighted the ease of use of their products, focusing on the benefits of simplified features for less tech-savvy customers. They also provided tips and tricks through blog posts and newsletters to enhance customer experience.

   - By using critical thinking to evaluate market segmentation, they tailored their messaging to resonate with the specific concerns of each customer group.

Outcomes of Critical Thinking

1. **Increased Customer Satisfaction:**

   - After implementing the changes, SmartTech experienced a significant improvement in customer satisfaction scores. Customers reported that the enhanced user guides and support resources made it easier to set up and enjoy their products.

   - Positive reviews surged, and many customers expressed appreciation for the company's efforts to listen and respond to their needs.

2. **Higher Retention Rates:**

   - With increased satisfaction came higher customer retention rates. Customers who had previously been hesitant to continue using SmartTech products now felt more confident in their purchase decisions.

- The company saw an increase in repeat purchases, with many customers recommending SmartTech to friends and family, contributing to organic growth.

3. **Strengthened Brand Loyalty:**

- SmartTech's commitment to understanding and addressing customer concerns through critical thinking helped strengthen brand loyalty. Customers began to perceive the company as responsive and customer-centric, fostering long-term relationships.

- The company's reputation for excellent customer service became a key differentiator in the competitive tech market.

You are someone very special. You have got enormous unlimited capabilities which are hidden and in sleeping mode. You are completely unaware of them. It is your responsibility to explore self discovery and expand your capabilities such that your performance will be beyond your dream. You dream it but not act and then your dream dies. It is your accountability to accomplish your dream by caring your dream and working for it until the outcome is achieved with your full satisfaction.

The concept of **"never stop dreaming"** highlights the power of ambition and imagination, but dreams alone aren't enough—they need to be nurtured, guided, and translated into action. When you actively work towards your dreams, you align your actions, thoughts, and mindset to bring them to life. Here's how to **guide your mind to work for your dream** with an example:

1. **Define Your Dream Clearly**

- It's important to have a well-defined dream. The more precise and clear your vision is, the easier it is to make actionable steps toward achieving it. Without clarity, your mind can become distracted, and you may lose focus.

Example:

Emma, a young entrepreneur, dreams of starting her own eco-friendly clothing brand. Instead of just dreaming about "owning a business," she creates a specific vision for her brand—sustainable fabrics, ethically sourced materials, and designs that promote environmental consciousness.

2. **Visualize Your Dream as Reality**

- Visualization is a powerful mental tool. By imagining yourself already achieving your dream, your mind starts working to make that vision come true. Visualization primes your brain to recognize opportunities and boosts your motivation.

Example:

Every day, Emma visualizes her brand's products being worn by customers, featured in stores, and making a positive impact on the environment. She imagines the feeling of success, seeing her dream business grow, and uses this image to stay motivated.

3. **Create a Step-by-Step Plan**

- Dreams need a roadmap. Break your dream into smaller, manageable tasks and set deadlines. This process turns abstract ideas into actionable steps that your mind can work towards. It also helps prevent overwhelm and procrastination.

Example:

Emma breaks her dream into phases:

- Phase 1: Research sustainable materials and manufacturers

- Phase 2: Develop a business plan and budget

- Phase 3: Design the first clothing line

- Phase 4: Launch an online store

- By doing this, she's not just daydreaming but actively working on specific goals that push her closer to realizing her dream.

4. **Stay Committed and Persistent**

- Achieving a dream requires consistent effort, even when faced with challenges. Many people give up too soon when the journey gets tough. However, if you stay committed, your mind will find ways to overcome obstacles.

Example:

Emma faces several setbacks—finding suppliers that meet her ethical standards is difficult, and the first prototypes don't meet her expectations. Despite this, she stays focused on her dream and remains persistent. She views failures as learning experiences and keeps moving forward, adapting her approach where necessary.

5. **Train Your Mind to Stay Positive and Focused**

- The mind often wanders, gets distracted, or fixates on negative outcomes. Mindfulness and self-discipline are essential tools to train your mind to stay on track. Practice gratitude, affirmations, and focusing techniques to keep your energy on your goal.

Example:

Emma uses daily affirmations like "I am capable of building a successful business" to keep her confidence high. She practices mindfulness to manage stress, reminding herself to focus on the progress she's made rather than worrying about potential failures. Whenever she feels overwhelmed, she reminds herself why she started and what her ultimate goal is.

6. **Take Action Every Day**

- Your dream will only work for you if you take action. Even small, consistent steps toward your dream will lead to success over time. The mind works best when you actively engage it through practical efforts.

Example:

Emma dedicates at least an hour every day to work on her business, even when her regular job gets demanding. Whether it's networking, product development, or marketing, she consistently takes actions that inch her closer to her dream.

7. **Surround Yourself with Support**

- Your environment influences your mindset. Surround yourself with people who support your dreams, and seek out mentors who have achieved similar goals. Avoid negativity or naysayers who drain your motivation.

Example:

Emma joins a network of sustainable fashion entrepreneurs who share advice and support each other. Being part of a positive, growth-focused community strengthens her belief in her dream. When she feels discouraged, the encouragement from her network helps her stay motivated.

8. **Measure Progress and Celebrate Small Wins**

- Celebrate milestones along the way. These small victories boost your confidence and fuel your motivation to keep going. Your mind thrives on positive reinforcement, and acknowledging progress keeps your energy high.

Example:

After months of hard work, Emma successfully launches her first product line. Even though her initial sales are modest, she celebrates the fact that her brand is officially up and running. This small win propels her forward, encouraging her to continue refining her business.

Conclusion:

Guide Your Mind to Work for Your Dream

To bring your dream to life, you must guide your mind with clarity, commitment, and action. Dreams without action remain fantasies, but when you actively pursue them, you create opportunities for success. Your mind becomes a powerful tool when you:

- Define your dream clearly.

- Visualize your dream as reality.

- Break it down into actionable steps.

- Stay committed and persistent through challenges.

- Take consistent action every day.

- Surround yourself with positive influences.

- Celebrate small wins to fuel motivation.

Example Recap:

Emma didn't just dream of owning a successful eco-friendly brand; she guided her mind to make it a reality by following a structured process. Her determination, planning, and continuous efforts helped her overcome obstacles and turn her dream into a growing business. Her journey teaches us that nurturing your dream through action is what turns aspirations into reality.

By committing to work for your dream, you ensure that it will work for you!

What are the 3 approaches you to add, change and remove from your life from today to improve your current state and uplift your position into next level?

Add:

____

____

____

Change:

Remove:

Chapter 13

Case Study: Mind Programming and Success

Positive Mind Programming and Brain Wave Improvement for Inner Peace, Calmness, and Leadership Behaviour:

1. **Positive Mind Programming:** Positive mind programming involves consciously and consistently feeding the mind with affirmations, positive thoughts, and visualization techniques to reshape negative belief systems and reinforce positive habits. It helps in building resilience, improving emotional control, and enhancing overall mental health.

   One key method of positive mind programming is **affirmations**. For example, if a leader wants to cultivate calmness in stressful situations, they can practice the affirmation: "I remain calm, focused, and balanced in every situation."

   Through repetition, the subconscious mind begins to accept these affirmations as truths, making it easier to access calmness and focus in high-stress environments.

2. **Correlation with Brain Waves:** The brain operates on different frequencies, called brain waves, which affect our mental and emotional states. The main types of brain waves include:

   - **Beta (12-30 Hz)** – Alert, conscious thinking, active problem-solving

   - **Alpha (8-12 Hz)** – Relaxed state, calm, creative flow

- **Theta (4-8 Hz)** – Deep relaxation, meditation, subconscious programming

- **Delta (0.5-4 Hz)** – Deep sleep, healing, and regeneration

Positive mind programming typically encourages a transition from the **Beta state** (active thinking) to the **Alpha and Theta states**, which are more relaxed and conducive to inner peace and calmness. These states enhance the brain's ability to access the subconscious mind, allowing deep emotional regulation and the internalization of positive beliefs.

Example: A leader regularly practices **mindfulness meditation** before the start of their workday. This practice involves deep breathing, visualization of positive outcomes, and repeating affirmations such as "I lead with clarity, calmness, and confidence." As the leader enters a calm **Alpha state**, their subconscious mind becomes more receptive to these affirmations.

Over time, this positive mind programming helps the leader respond to challenges with more maturity, rather than reacting impulsively. In stressful situations, their **Theta brain waves** are activated, helping them remain grounded, access creative solutions, and take measured, thoughtful action.

3. **Impact on Leadership Behaviour:** By reprogramming the mind and optimizing brain waves, the leader can experience the following improvements:

- **Inner Peace and Calmness:** Regular positive affirmations and meditations induce the **Alpha state**, allowing the leader to remain calm under pressure, think clearly, and make balanced decisions.

- **Emotional Regulation:** Positive mind programming strengthens emotional control by accessing the **Theta state**, where the subconscious mind can rewire negative emotional responses. This helps leaders stay emotionally intelligent and resilient during crises.

- **Matured Leadership Actions:** With the subconscious mind programmed for success, leaders will consistently act with confidence, empathy, and patience. Their **Alpha and Theta brain waves** improve their ability to remain composed and make mature decisions, even in challenging circumstances.

    Example of Leadership Behaviour: A CEO facing a sudden business crisis practices deep breathing and reminds themselves of the affirmation, "I handle challenges with calm, clarity, and wisdom." Their subconscious, trained through weeks of positive mind programming, activates a **Theta state**, allowing them to stay calm. Instead of reacting impulsively, they methodically gather information, consult the team, and lead with empathy, guiding the company to a successful resolution.

In summary, **positive mind programming** directly influences brain wave patterns, creating a foundation of inner peace and calmness. This fosters emotionally intelligent, thoughtful leadership, which is critical for making sound decisions and maintaining balance in high-pressure situations.

how positive mind programming can improve various parts of your body:

Body Part	Effect of Positive Mind Programming	Explanation
Brain	Improved cognitive function, clarity, focus, and emotional balance	Positive affirmations and visualization can enhance brainwave patterns, boosting concentration and calmness.
Heart	Better cardiovascular health, reduced stress, and lower blood pressure	Positive thinking reduces stress hormones like cortisol, improving heart health and promoting relaxation.

Body Part	Effect of Positive Mind Programming	Explanation
Lungs	Improved breathing, better oxygenation, and enhanced respiratory health	Mindfulness and meditation improve breathing techniques, leading to deeper, slower breaths and more oxygen.
Digestive System	Enhanced digestion, reduced bloating, and fewer gastrointestinal issues	Positive programming reduces stress and anxiety, which can help regulate digestive functions and reduce discomfort.
Immune System	Boosted immunity, faster recovery from illnesses	Positive thinking and reduced stress strengthen the immune system, making it more effective against infections.
Muscles	Increased relaxation, reduced tension, and improved muscle recovery	Mind programming helps reduce mental tension, leading to relaxed muscles and better recovery after strain.
Skin	Healthier skin, reduced acne, and a more youthful appearance	Stress reduction through mind programming improves skin health by reducing inflammation and promoting healing.
Eyes	Reduced strain and better vision	Mental relaxation reduces eye strain, especially for those working in front of screens, improving eye comfort.
Hormonal System	Balanced hormone levels, especially stress hormones like cortisol	Positive thinking helps regulate cortisol and adrenaline, promoting hormonal balance and reducing burnout.

Body Part	Effect of Positive Mind Programming	Explanation
Nervous System	Greater calm, reduced anxiety, and improved overall nervous system health	Regular mental programming helps calm the nervous system, leading to reduced stress and anxiety responses.

Positive mind programming strengthens the body by reducing stress, promoting relaxation, and creating a balanced mental environment, leading to improved physical health across all systems.

Story 1: Mind Programming for Stress Management in Healthcare Professionals

The Challenge:

Dr. **Emily**, a senior physician at a large urban hospital, was facing extreme stress and burnout. Like many healthcare professionals, Emily had to manage long hours, high patient loads, and the emotional toll of dealing with life-and-death situations daily. The constant pressure affected her performance, led to frequent exhaustion, and diminished her ability to make critical decisions quickly. She knew she had to make a change but wasn't sure how to manage the stress effectively.

The Mind Programming Solution:

Emily's hospital introduced a **mind programming technology** known as **neuro-linguistic programming (NLP)** and **guided visualization techniques** to help their staff cope with stress. Emily participated in a program that combined these techniques with **neuroscientific principles** to rewire the brain's response to stress.

Here's how it worked:

- **NLP Reframing**: Emily was taught how to identify and reframe her automatic negative thoughts. For example, instead of thinking "I can't handle this," she learned to reprogram her mind to think, "I've handled challenging situations before and can do it again." This simple mental shift reduced her sense of overwhelm.

- **Guided Visualization**: Every morning, she would engage in a 10-minute guided visualization session that mentally rehearsed a calm, productive day at the hospital. This primed her mind for success and reduced anxiety about potential stressors.

- **Breathing and Mindfulness Techniques**: Emily also used mindfulness-based breathing techniques to regulate her emotions during high-pressure moments. When stress peaked, she used her training to trigger a calm, focused state of mind.

The Result:

After just a few weeks, Emily noticed significant changes. She felt more in control of her emotions, had more mental clarity during tough decisions, and was no longer overwhelmed by her workload. The hospital even reported that staff who participated in the program had a **25% reduction in burnout** and showed enhanced focus and decision-making during critical moments.

Story 2: Mind Programming for Enhanced Creativity in Marketing Professionals

The Challenge:

Ethan, a creative director at a large advertising firm, was under intense pressure to come up with an innovative campaign for a high-profile client. However, his creative well had run dry due to the constant demand for fresh ideas. He was stuck in a creative rut, unable to think of anything unique, and time was running out. The pressure to deliver was creating a mental block, and his usual brainstorming methods weren't working.

The Mind Programming Solution:

Ethan turned to a **mind programming technology** called **brainwave entrainment** and **subconscious reprogramming** for creativity enhancement. He enrolled in a specialized program that used sound frequencies to alter brainwave states and unlock his creative potential.

Here's how it worked:

- **Brainwave Entrainment**: Ethan used **binaural beats**, a form of soundwave therapy, to guide his brain into an **alpha state**—the optimal state for creativity. This involved listening to audio tracks with specific frequencies designed to slow his brainwaves, helping him access deeper levels of thought and imagination.

- **Creative Visualization**: Ethan also practiced creative visualization exercises where he imagined himself generating bold, new ideas. This programmed his subconscious mind to be more receptive to novel concepts, helping him think outside the box.

- **Affirmation Programming**: He listened to subliminal messages that reinforced positive beliefs about his creativity, such as "I am a source of endless creativity" and "Ideas flow easily to me." These affirmations worked on a subconscious level to dismantle mental blocks and negative beliefs.

The Result:

Within days of starting the program, Ethan noticed a breakthrough. His mind felt clearer, and new ideas began to flow effortlessly. By combining brainwave entrainment with creative visualization, Ethan developed a campaign that not only impressed the client but also garnered industry recognition. His ability to access deep levels of creativity under pressure marked a turning point in his career.

Story 3: Mind Programming for Performance Optimization in Sports

The Challenge:

Sarah, a professional tennis player, was struggling with inconsistency in her performance. During practice, she excelled, but in high-stakes matches, she would freeze under pressure, lose focus, and make critical errors. This mental block was preventing her from advancing in her career, and she realized that her problem wasn't physical—it was psychological.

The Mind Programming Solution:

Sarah's coach introduced her to **mental conditioning techniques** based on **self-hypnosis** and **visualization**—two powerful mind programming technologies used by elite athletes.

Here's how it worked:

- **Self-Hypnosis for Confidence**: Sarah learned how to enter a state of self-hypnosis before matches to program her mind with positive outcomes. By visualizing her matches and mentally rehearsing her shots, Sarah's brain was conditioned to expect success, reducing performance anxiety.

- **Pre-Game Visualization**: She visualized every part of her game, from her first serve to her winning point. This practice not only built muscle memory but also **reduced anxiety** by making high-pressure situations feel familiar to her mind. The more Sarah practiced visualization, the more she trained her brain to focus and perform optimally under pressure.

- **Anchor Techniques**: Sarah also learned to create a **mental anchor**, a physical trigger (such as squeezing her fingers) that would instantly shift her mind into a focused, calm state. This allowed her to regain composure and focus mid-game when her mind started to wander or anxiety crept in.

The Result:

Sarah's mental programming transformed her performance. During her next high-stakes match, she remained calm, composed, and confident. When the pressure mounted, she used her anchor technique to re-centre her focus. Her improved mental conditioning helped her advance to the finals for the first time in her career. Sarah now considers mental training as essential as physical training for her ongoing success.

Story 4: Mind Programming for Problem-Solving in Engineering

The Challenge:

James, a lead engineer working on a large-scale infrastructure project, encountered a serious problem: an unexpected geological issue that threatened to derail the construction timeline. The team needed to come up with an innovative solution, but every proposed fix was costly and time-consuming. James and his team were stuck in a loop of traditional thinking, unable to find a way forward.

The Mind Programming Solution:

James turned to **mind mapping techniques** and **cognitive reprogramming** technologies to stimulate creative problem-solving. He joined a workshop focused on unlocking new patterns of thinking through **neural conditioning** and **meditative problem-solving**.

Here's how it worked:

- **Mind Mapping**: James used mind mapping software to visually lay out the problem and brainstorm potential solutions. This helped him and his team see connections between different factors that weren't immediately obvious, expanding their problem-solving scope.

- **Theta State Meditation**: James practiced **theta brainwave meditation**, which is known to enhance creativity and out-of-the-box thinking. This meditation helped him relax, clear his mind of stress, and access deeper levels of subconscious insight.

- **Subconscious Programming**: By using subconscious programming techniques, James began to focus on creating mental pathways that framed the challenge as an **opportunity for innovation** rather than an obstacle. He repeated mantras like "Every problem has a solution" to prime his brain to see new possibilities.

The Result:

Within a week, James had a breakthrough. During one of his theta state meditations, he visualized an alternative engineering solution that dramatically reduced costs and construction delays. By reprogramming his mind to approach the issue from new angles, James was able to come up with a creative solution that saved the project. His use of mind programming techniques became a case study for problem-solving within the company.

Story 5: Mind Programming for Leadership and Decision-Making in Business

The Challenge:

Rachel, the CEO of a growing tech startup, was facing a crisis. Her company was at a critical juncture, needing to decide between two very different strategic directions. One choice involved scaling the business rapidly through aggressive expansion, while the other required a more conservative, steady growth approach. With stakeholders divided and no clear answer in sight, Rachel was overwhelmed with doubt and analysis paralysis.

The Mind Programming Solution:

Rachel enlisted the help of a **cognitive-behavioural reprogramming coach** who specialized in leadership development through mind programming. The coach introduced her to **neuroscience-backed decision-making techniques** and **executive mindfulness** practices.

Here's how it worked:

- **Mindfulness and Clarity**: Rachel practiced mindfulness exercises that helped her clear her mental clutter and access **clarity in decision-making**. These practices helped her step back from the emotional turmoil and make decisions from a place of calm and focus.

- **Mental Modelling**: She also worked with her coach to create mental models, visualizing both strategic paths in detail. This gave her a **holistic view** of potential outcomes and helped her make more informed choices by mentally rehearsing each scenario's consequences.

- **Self-Belief Affirmations**: To reduce self-doubt, Rachel incorporated daily affirmations to reinforce her confidence as a leader. Phrases like "I trust my judgment" and "I am decisive and clear" helped reprogram her subconscious mind to approach decisions with conviction.

The Result:

Rachel's decision-making improved dramatically. She chose the steady growth strategy after gaining mental clarity and visualizing its long-term success. Not only did the company thrive under her leadership, but Rachel's new decision-making framework became a part of her ongoing leadership strategy. She attributed her newfound decisiveness and clarity to the mental programming techniques she adopted

Story 6: Mind Programming for Corporate Professionals: Overcoming Imposter Syndrome

The Challenge:

Sophia was recently promoted to a senior management position at a global corporation. Despite her qualifications, she constantly felt like an imposter. Sophia feared that at any moment, her colleagues would realize she wasn't competent enough for the job. This lack of confidence affected her ability to lead, make decisions, and communicate effectively with her team.

The Mind Programming Solution:

Sophia turned to **cognitive-behavioural programming** and **affirmation-based reconditioning** to overcome imposter syndrome. She enrolled in a corporate wellness program that combined **positive affirmations, visualization, and NLP** techniques to rewire her subconscious beliefs about herself.

Here's how it worked:

- **Affirmations and Visualization**: Every morning, Sophia recited affirmations like "I am capable and deserving of success." She paired this with visualization techniques where she saw herself confidently leading meetings, making strategic decisions, and earning respect from her colleagues.

- **NLP Anchoring Techniques**: During moments of self-doubt, she used **NLP anchoring** to create a positive emotional state. By linking a specific physical action (like touching her wrist) to a feeling of confidence, she could instantly trigger that positive state during meetings and presentations.

- **Reprogramming Limiting Beliefs**: Sophia also worked with a coach to identify and reprogram her limiting beliefs around success and failure. She learned to reframe thoughts like "I'm not good enough" into empowering beliefs like "I have all the skills I need to succeed."

The Result:

Within months, Sophia's confidence soared. She no longer doubted her abilities and felt comfortable in her role. Her improved self-esteem led to better decision-making and stronger relationships with her colleagues. By using mind programming, she successfully overcame imposter syndrome and became a more effective leader.

Story 7: Mind Programming for Students: Enhancing Focus and Retention

The Challenge:

Ethan, a college student, struggled with concentration and retention during his studies. With multiple assignments, exams, and distractions from social media, he found it difficult to stay focused. As a result, his grades began to slip, and he became anxious about failing his courses.

The Mind Programming Solution:

Ethan discovered **brainwave entrainment technology** and **focus-based meditation** to improve his concentration and retention abilities. He started using **alpha and theta brainwave frequencies** to optimize his study sessions.

Here's how it worked:

- **Brainwave Entrainment**: Ethan listened to **binaural beats** designed to induce alpha and theta brainwave states, which are known to enhance focus, memory retention, and learning. He used these sound frequencies while studying to improve his ability to concentrate for longer periods.

- **Focused Attention Meditation**: Before study sessions, Ethan practiced focused attention meditation, where he trained his mind to block out distractions and remain laser-focused on his material for 20-30 minutes at a time.

- **Subliminal Learning**: He also used subliminal audio recordings with embedded affirmations like "I retain information easily" and "I am focused and disciplined." These helped reprogram his subconscious to reinforce positive learning habits.

The Result:

Ethan noticed significant improvements in his ability to focus and retain information. His study sessions became more productive, allowing him to absorb and recall material more effectively. As a result, his grades improved, and he regained confidence in his academic abilities.

Story 8: Mind Programming for Teachers: Boosting Classroom Engagement and Reducing Burnout

The Challenge:

Ms. Jane, a high school teacher, was feeling burnt out from the daily demands of managing a classroom. She found it challenging to keep her students engaged, and her stress levels were affecting her enthusiasm for teaching. The pressure to meet curriculum standards, manage student behaviour, and maintain a positive classroom atmosphere was overwhelming.

The Mind Programming Solution:

Ms. Jane adopted **mindfulness-based stress reduction (MBSR)** and **visualization techniques** to improve classroom management and reduce burnout. These mind programming techniques helped her reset her mindset and approach teaching with renewed energy.

Here's how it worked:

- **Mindfulness Meditation**: Every morning, Ms. Jane practiced a 10-minute mindfulness meditation to clear her mind of stress and start her day with a calm and focused mindset. This allowed her to respond to classroom challenges more patiently and with greater clarity.

- **Positive Visualization**: Before stepping into the classroom, she visualized herself engaging students in meaningful ways, seeing them actively participate and respond positively to her lessons. This mental rehearsal helped her stay confident and calm during the actual teaching process.

- **Stress Resilience Programming**: She also used **self-hypnosis techniques** to program her mind to stay composed during difficult moments, such as handling disruptive students or unexpected challenges. Through this, Ms. Jane conditioned her mind to stay resilient under pressure.

The Result:

Ms. Jane's energy and enthusiasm for teaching were restored. Her students responded better to her positive attitude, and engagement levels improved. The use of mindfulness and stress reduction techniques also reduced her feelings of burnout, allowing her to enjoy her work again and maintain a healthy work-life balance.

Story 9: Mind Programming for Entrepreneurs: Overcoming Fear of Failure

The Challenge:

Mark, an entrepreneur launching his first tech startup, was paralyzed by the fear of failure. Every decision he made felt heavy with the risk of his venture failing, and this fear stopped him from taking bold, necessary steps to grow his business. Mark found himself procrastinating on key actions, avoiding investor meetings, and doubting his vision.

The Mind Programming Solution:

Mark sought help through **self-hypnosis** and **fear-reconditioning techniques**. He learned how to use **visualization, affirmation programming, and mental rehearsal** to overcome his fear of failure and build his resilience as an entrepreneur.

Here's how it worked:

- **Self-Hypnosis for Confidence**: Mark used self-hypnosis audio sessions where he was guided into a deeply relaxed state, then programmed his subconscious mind with affirmations like "I am capable of success" and "Failure is just a step toward growth."

- **Mental Rehearsal for Success**: He practiced mental rehearsal by vividly imagining himself pitching to investors, negotiating deals, and successfully launching his product. This created a mental blueprint that made these actions feel more familiar and achievable.

- **Fear-Reconditioning Techniques**: Mark also worked with a coach to reframe his fear of failure. He learned to view failures as learning opportunities rather than catastrophic events. By continuously reinforcing this belief, he diminished the emotional weight of failure.

The Result:

Mark overcame his fear of failure and began taking decisive actions to grow his business. He successfully pitched to investors, secured funding, and launched his product within months. His ability to confront challenges with a fearless mindset allowed him to thrive in the fast-paced entrepreneurial world.

Story 10: Mind Programming for Researchers: Enhancing Focus and Problem-Solving Skills

The Challenge:

Dr. Elena, a research scientist working on a complex project in biotechnology, was struggling to stay focused and solve a critical problem in her research. The data wasn't aligning with her hypothesis, and she felt stuck. She needed a breakthrough, but mental fatigue and frustration were clouding her ability to think clearly.

The Mind Programming Solution:

Dr. Elena turned to **theta brainwave meditation** and **creative visualization techniques** to unlock deeper cognitive abilities and problem-solving skills. These methods helped her access creative solutions and boost her focus.

Here's how it worked:

- **Theta Brainwave Meditation**: Dr. Elena practiced **theta state meditation**, which is known for enhancing creativity, insight, and problem-solving abilities. During these sessions, her brain entered a relaxed state that allowed for deep, intuitive thinking.

- **Creative Visualization**: Before and after her research sessions, Dr. Elena visualized herself solving the problem and uncovering key insights. This mentally rehearsed success primed her brain to think more creatively when reviewing data.

- **Focus Training**: She also used **neural reconditioning** techniques, where she conditioned her mind to stay focused during long research sessions. This involved breaking down tasks into smaller, more manageable goals and rewarding herself mentally for each accomplishment.

The Result:

Within weeks, Dr. Elena had a breakthrough in her research. By using theta meditation to access deeper levels of thinking, she was able to see the problem from a new angle and develop a creative solution that advanced her project. Her ability to focus and approach the problem with a fresh perspective led to significant progress in her research and a published paper.

Story 11: Mind Programming for Effective Strategy making in Problem Solving and Decision Making

Lets assume you are in a leadership position in your organization. Your organization is adapting AI based technological solution to gain competitive advantage in the market as early adapter. But your middle level managers are becoming fearful for losing control and even their job as they are completely unaware of AI.

You being in the leadership role, how can you define effective strategy to normalize the solution? Lets assume you are practitioner of Neuro Linguistic Programming and Quantum Leadership Style. How can you use both the approaches ?

NLP Approach: Programming Your Mind for Effective Strategy

Step 1: Identify Your Own Beliefs and Reframe Them

Before leading others, it's important to examine your own internal beliefs about AI and the fears of your team. Use NLP to identify and challenge any limiting beliefs that may be affecting your approach. For example, ask yourself:

- **What do I believe about AI technology and its impact on jobs?**

- **Do I harbour any fear or uncertainty about this technology?**

If you find any limiting beliefs, reframe them using NLP. For example, if you believe, "AI might create too much disruption and resistance," reframe it to, "AI will enable us to automate routine tasks, freeing up human creativity for strategic growth."

NLP Reframing Process:

1. Identify the limiting belief: "My managers fear AI will replace them."

2. Reframe: "AI will help my managers evolve their roles into more strategic positions, enhancing their value."

Step 2: Use NLP for Empathy and Communication

Next, focus on empathizing with your managers using NLP techniques to build rapport and communicate effectively. Understand that their fear comes from uncertainty about the future. By applying **Mirroring and Matching** techniques, you can align with their body language, tone, and communication style, creating trust.

Effective Communication with NLP:

- **Reframing fears:** Instead of saying, "AI is inevitable," reframe the conversation to, "AI will help you focus on higher-level tasks where your leadership and creativity are most needed."

- **Anchoring positivity:** Anchor moments of past success when they adapted to other changes. For instance, remind them of a time they overcame a challenge and succeeded.

Step 3: Goal Setting and Visualizing Success

In NLP, visualization is a powerful tool. Program your mind to visualize your team thriving in this new environment, using AI as a tool to augment their roles rather than replace them. Visualize the end goal where the middle managers have mastered the new technology, their leadership is stronger, and the company is thriving.

Goal-setting: Set SMART goals for your middle managers, focusing on milestones like, "In 6 months, our team will have successfully integrated AI into our operations, and managers will be leading with greater efficiency."

NLP Meditation for Motivating Middle-Level Managers

[Step 1: Relaxation and Reframing]

Find a quiet place to sit and close your eyes. Take a deep breath in, and as you exhale, release any tension in your body. Breathe in again, and as you breathe out, let go of any doubts or worries. You are here in this moment, safe and open to new possibilities.

Now, bring to mind any fear or concern you may have about the upcoming AI technology. Maybe you feel uncertain about how it will affect your role, or perhaps you worry about losing control over the work you do. Acknowledge these feelings—it's okay to feel them.

Now, gently, imagine these concerns as clouds in the sky. You are watching them pass by, knowing they are temporary. As each cloud passes, see if you can reframe the thought. Instead of thinking, "AI will replace me," imagine yourself saying, "AI will help me become more strategic and valuable to my team."

[Step 2: Anchoring Positive Experiences]

Take a deep breath, and now recall a time when you successfully adapted to a major change. Maybe it was when you learned a new skill, or when you led your team through a challenging project. Feel the confidence and strength from that experience, knowing you are capable of growth and evolution.

As you hold onto that positive feeling, anchor it by pressing your thumb and forefinger together. Know that any time you feel doubt, you can return to this anchor, reminding yourself of your ability to thrive in change.

[Step 3: Visualizing Success with AI]

Now, imagine yourself six months from now. Picture yourself confidently using the new AI technology to streamline your work. See how it has freed up your time, allowing you to focus on the bigger picture. You're leading with more clarity, your team respects your new skills, and you're contributing even more to the company's success.

As you visualize this, notice how it feels. You are not being replaced by AI—you are empowered by it. Hold onto that feeling of empowerment as you take one more deep breath in... and slowly exhale.

When you're ready, open your eyes, feeling confident and ready to embrace this new technology as an ally in your leadership journey.

Quantum Leadership Approach: Programming Your Mind for Effective Strategy

Step 1: Embrace Uncertainty and Complexity

Quantum Leadership is about recognizing that the AI transition is part of a larger, interconnected system. Begin by programming your mind to embrace complexity rather than resist it. Instead of seeing the AI shift as a challenge that might cause resistance, understand it as part of a broader, evolving system that includes employee concerns, technological shifts, and market changes.

Quantum Thinking Process:

- **Ask yourself:** How does this AI change fit into the bigger picture of the organization's evolution? How can I leverage this complexity to foster innovation and growth?

- **Shift from control to facilitation:** Recognize that your role as a leader is to facilitate co-creation, guiding the organization through the AI transition by embracing the collective intelligence of your team.

Step 2: Use Collective Intelligence and Co-Creation

Program your mind to move away from hierarchical thinking and toward a collaborative approach. Quantum Leadership is about co-creating solutions with your team, especially your middle managers who are directly impacted. You are not the sole decision-maker; instead, you facilitate a process that involves everyone in shaping the future.

Quantum Leadership Strategy:

- **Create dialogue spaces:** Host open discussions where middle managers can express their concerns and ideas about AI. Encourage them to view AI as a tool they can shape to fit their needs.

- **Co-create the future:** Involve your team in designing how AI will be implemented. This makes them feel empowered and part of the change rather than victims of it.

Step 3: Embrace Potential Futures

In Quantum Leadership, the future is not fixed. Program your mind to see the AI transformation as a space of multiple potential futures. This flexibility allows you to adapt and lead through uncertainty. Visualize not one outcome, but several, and stay open to evolving strategies as the AI technology takes shape.

Quantum Leadership Thinking:

- **Explore different scenarios:** Imagine best-case, worst-case, and multiple middle scenarios for how the AI transition might unfold. Stay flexible, knowing that you can pivot and adapt based on feedback and real-world outcomes.

- **Focus on resilience:** Your role is to guide the organization through the uncertainties of the AI transition, building resilience rather than simply achieving fixed goals.

Quantum Leadership Meditation for Motivating Middle-Level Managers

[Step 1: Grounding and Connection]

Close your eyes and take a deep breath in, feeling your feet firmly planted on the ground. As you breathe out, feel the weight of the world lifting off your shoulders. You are here, connected to your surroundings, part of a larger whole.

With each breath, feel the interconnectedness of your team, your organization, and the AI technology. This is not something happening to you; it is happening with you. You are a vital part of this interconnected system.

[Step 2: Embracing Complexity and Multiple Futures]

Now, imagine the AI technology as a wave of potential flowing into your organization. It is not a rigid or fixed event—it is fluid, adaptable, and full of possibilities. Picture this wave moving through your team, your processes, and your leadership. Notice that it brings both challenges and opportunities, but in every challenge, there is a chance for growth.

Imagine several different futures ahead of you. In one, you and your team struggle with the new AI system. In another, you successfully integrate it, and in yet another, you discover entirely new ways of working that you hadn't imagined before. Take a moment to explore each of these futures.

Know that none of them is set in stone. The future will be shaped by how you and your team respond. Trust in your ability to adapt and co-create with your colleagues.

[Step 3: Co-Creation and Collective Leadership]

Now, visualize yourself sitting with your middle managers in a collaborative discussion. You are not leading from the top, but from within. You are co-creating solutions, asking for their ideas, and working together to shape how AI will fit into your organization.

See how their energy shifts as they realize they are part of the process. They are not losing control—they are gaining a new opportunity to shape the future alongside you. Breathe in the feeling of collective intelligence at work.

[Step 4: Navigating Change with Grace]

Finally, picture yourself leading your team through the next few months. You are calm, adaptable, and open to change. You don't need all the answers right now, because you trust that the solutions will emerge as you and your team move forward together. The AI transition is not an endpoint—it is part of an ongoing journey of growth and evolution.

*As you breathe deeply, feel a sense of confidence, knowing that you can navigate this change with grace, flexibility, and the support.

Story 12: let's say you are working in a high performing team. But few of your team members have great ego, they try to establish "they are the best" and reject your ideas. In that case how can you program your mind to define strategy using quantum leadership approach to cope up with such situations instead of feeling bad?

Using **Quantum Leadership** to handle colleagues with high ego who reject your ideas and fail to appreciate your hard work requires a shift in how you approach leadership and team dynamics. Quantum leadership embraces complexity, interconnectedness, and collective intelligence. It focuses on transforming challenges into opportunities for co-creation and collaboration. Here's how you can apply this approach:

1. **Shift Your Mindset: Embrace Complexity and Interconnectedness**

   In Quantum Leadership, you recognize that each member of your team, even those with high egos, is part of a larger, interconnected system. Their behaviour might stem from various factors such as insecurities, personal motivations, or external pressures. Instead of seeing their ego-driven actions as barriers, view them as part of the complexity that can be navigated with collaboration and openness.

- **Mindset Shift:** Instead of thinking, "They are blocking my ideas," shift to, "Their resistance offers an opportunity to understand underlying concerns and foster deeper collaboration."

Action: Begin by reflecting on your own response to their behaviour. Are you approaching the situation with openness, or are you reacting to their ego with resistance of your own? Quantum leadership encourages self-awareness and the ability to see every interaction as part of a larger system.

2. **Create Space for Dialogue and Co-Creation**

In quantum thinking, the goal is not to impose your ideas or control the outcome. Instead, it's about co-creating solutions. Invite your colleagues into a space where they can express their ideas, and you can work together to find common ground. When people feel heard and valued, their resistance often diminishes.

- **Approach with curiosity, not competition:** Instead of viewing their rejection of your ideas as a challenge to your authority, invite them into a conversation where their perspectives are heard. For example, you could say, "I see you have strong opinions on this project, and I'd love to hear your thoughts on how we can create the best solution together."

Action: Host a team meeting or one-on-one discussion where the focus is on collaboration. Ask open-ended questions like, "How do you see this project contributing to our overall goals?" or "What do you think would make our approach more successful?" This shifts the dynamic from a competition of ideas to collective problem-solving.

3. **Leverage Collective Intelligence**

Quantum leadership is about tapping into the collective intelligence of the group. Even though your colleagues have high egos, they likely bring valuable insights and skills to the table. By creating a space where all contributions are valued, including your own, you can shift the dynamic from individualism to a shared sense of purpose.

- **Focus on the bigger picture:** Remind the team that the ultimate goal is not about proving who is the best, but about achieving collective success. You can say something like, "Each of us brings unique strengths to this project. Let's find a way to combine our expertise to make this work great."

Action: Use facilitation techniques that encourage everyone's input. For example, during meetings, employ round-robin discussion formats where each person is given equal time to share their views. This ensures that all voices are heard, not just the loudest ones.

4. **Depersonalize Conflict: See Resistance as Feedback**

Quantum leadership views conflict as part of the natural dynamics of a team, not as a personal attack. If your ideas are being rejected, it might reflect concerns or different perspectives that haven't been addressed yet. Instead of taking it personally, treat the resistance as feedback to refine your approach.

- **Embrace feedback:** When colleagues reject your ideas, don't react with defensiveness. Instead, ask for more details about their concerns. For instance, "I'm curious to know what part of my proposal didn't resonate with you. I'd love to get your feedback so we can move forward effectively."

Action: After receiving feedback, incorporate their input into your work where appropriate. By doing this, you show that you value their opinions, which may reduce their need to assert dominance or prove superiority.

5. **Foster a Culture of Appreciation and Recognition**

People with high egos often seek validation. Quantum leadership teaches us to foster a culture of mutual appreciation. You can set an example by acknowledging the contributions of your colleagues, even if they haven't done the same for you. Over time, this can create an environment where recognition flows freely between all team members.

- **Recognize their strengths:** Instead of focusing on the lack of appreciation from your colleagues, look for opportunities to genuinely praise their work. For instance, say, "I really appreciate the way you handled the client's feedback last week. It brought a lot of clarity to our approach."

Action: At the beginning of team meetings, take a few moments to highlight achievements or contributions from various team members. This models the behaviour you want to see, encouraging others to follow suit and creating a culture of mutual appreciation.

6. **Engage in Adaptive Leadership: Be Flexible**

Quantum leadership is adaptive. It recognizes that rigid control and fixed mindsets won't work in complex environments. Be willing to adapt your strategies, shift your communication style, and explore new ways of engaging your colleagues. Sometimes, letting go of the need to have your ideas accepted right away allows space for creative solutions to emerge.

- **Practice flexibility:** If you sense strong resistance, be willing to adapt your approach. Instead of insisting on your idea, ask, "What aspects of my proposal do you think could be adjusted to fit our goals better?"

Action: Show flexibility by being open to different solutions. When your colleagues see that you are adaptable and not overly attached to your own ideas, they may begin to reciprocate and become more open to collaboration.

7. **Lead with Presence and Emotional Intelligence**

Quantum leadership emphasizes **presence** and **emotional intelligence**. Being fully present means being mindful of your reactions and emotions, while staying attuned to the emotions of your colleagues. High-ego colleagues may often react based on their own insecurities or need for control. By staying calm and cantered, you can de-escalate situations and guide the conversation toward collaboration.

- **Manage emotions mindfully:** When faced with rejection or ego-driven behaviours, take a deep breath and remain present. Acknowledge your own feelings but don't let them control your response. Maintain a calm and constructive demeanour.

Action: Practice mindfulness before meetings with difficult colleagues. Take a few minutes to centre yourself, focusing on your breath and preparing to engage with an open, calm mindset. During the meeting, observe your emotions and responses, making a conscious choice to remain non-reactive and solution-focused.

Quantum Leadership Meditation: Navigating Ego and Encouraging Collaboration

[Step 1: Grounding in Presence]

Find a comfortable place to sit, and close your eyes. Take a deep breath in, and as you exhale, let go of any tension or stress. Allow your breath to guide you into a state of calm presence. With each inhale, feel your body becoming more grounded, and with each exhale, release any need to control or prove yourself.

In this space, you are open, adaptable, and connected to the larger system around you. You are part of a collective whole, and your role is to guide and facilitate, not control.

[Step 2: Embracing Complexity and Interconnectedness]

Now, imagine the colleagues with whom you have experienced challenges. Visualize their faces, and instead of seeing them as competitors or obstacles, see them as part of the interconnected system that you are leading. They bring their own strengths, perspectives, and, yes, their own fears and insecurities. Understand that their actions are not directed at you personally—they are part of the complexity of this system.

As you breathe, embrace the complexity. Allow yourself to feel compassion for your colleagues, recognizing that their resistance is a natural response to change or fear. Breathe in acceptance and understanding.

[Step 3: Co-Creation and Collective Intelligence]

Now, picture yourself in a meeting with your team. Instead of trying to push your ideas or assert control, imagine yourself facilitating a conversation. You are listening deeply, encouraging everyone to share their perspectives. Notice how the energy in the room shifts as your colleagues realize that their voices are valued and heard.

You are co-creating solutions together. Feel the sense of collaboration and connection. You are not alone in solving these challenges—you are part of a collective intelligence that is greater than the sum of its parts.

[Step 4: Letting Go of Ego and Embracing Flexibility]

Finally, imagine letting go of your own ego. Feel the release as you no longer need to have the best idea or prove yourself. Instead, you are open to whatever emerges from the collective wisdom of the team. Visualize yourself leading with grace, flexibility, and openness, adapting to whatever comes your way.

Take one more deep breath in, and as you exhale, feel a sense of calm confidence. You are ready to lead your team through complexity, knowing that together, you will find the best path forward.

When you're ready, open your eyes and return to the present moment, carrying with you a sense of clarity, openness, and connection.

Conclusion

In Quantum Leadership, handling colleagues with high egos isn't about competing or forcing your ideas through. It's about embracing the complexity of team dynamics, creating space for collaboration, and leveraging the collective intelligence of everyone involved. By being flexible, emotionally intelligent, and fostering a culture of appreciation, you can guide your team toward a more harmonious, productive future where everyone's contributions are valued.

Story 13. Let's assume you work in a company where salary is only motivation. Your hard work is taken for granted and you are not recognized or appreciated. What will be your mind programming strategy to stay focused and internally motivated though the external environment is not awarding as you need money. also add reference point how you can creatively add value to get award in such tough working environment?

In a company where salary is the only motivation, and your hard work goes unnoticed and unappreciated, staying internally motivated requires a strategic shift in mindset and creative thinking. This kind of environment can be demoralizing, but with the right **mind programming strategy**, you can remain focused, find fulfilment in your work, and even creatively add value to gain recognition, despite the external conditions. Here's a **step-by-step approach** to programming your mind to stay motivated and adding value:

Mind Programming Strategy for Internal Motivation:

1. **Reframe Your Mindset Towards Intrinsic Goals**

   When external rewards (recognition, appreciation) are lacking, you must focus on **intrinsic motivators**—goals and values that you control and that personally fulfill you.

   - **Reframe Work as Personal Growth:** Instead of viewing work solely as a paycheck, shift your focus toward how your role contributes to your personal development, skill-building, or long-term career goals. Think of each task as an opportunity to become better at your craft, build resilience, or gain experience that will benefit you in the future.

- **Example:** "While I'm not being recognized now, every project I complete is making me more skilled and valuable for my future career. I am investing in my future self."

Action: Set personal goals unrelated to external validation. For example, aim to improve a specific skill or complete tasks with efficiency and quality that you can be proud of.

2. **Practice Gratitude for What the Job Provides**

   In tough environments, shifting focus from what's missing to what you have can help you stay motivated.

   - **Gratitude for Salary:** The salary, while not sufficient as a sole motivator, is enabling you to meet financial obligations, take care of personal responsibilities, or invest in future goals (such as savings, education, etc.).

   - **Gratitude for Opportunities:** Even if your work is taken for granted, each project or task allows you to develop expertise and experience, and the job might offer you stability or access to certain resources that can be valuable in the future.

   Action: Each day, write down at least three things you are grateful for in your current job. This helps shift your focus away from the lack of recognition and toward the aspects of your work that contribute positively to your life.

3. **Use Visualization to Reconnect with Long-Term Goals**

   Visualization is a powerful tool to keep you connected with your future aspirations, especially when day-to-day motivation is hard to find. By mentally picturing the rewards and success you want to achieve long-term, you build emotional resilience.

   - **Example:** Visualize yourself a few years down the line in a job where your efforts are recognized, or where you have built enough financial stability to pursue passions or interests outside of work. Imagine the skills and experiences you're gaining now being the key to unlocking future opportunities.

Action: Spend a few minutes daily visualizing your future self in a better, more rewarding situation. This helps you frame your current challenges as temporary and keeps you focused on the bigger picture.

4. **Anchor Motivation in Personal Values**

   One way to stay internally driven is to connect your work with your core values—such as dedication, mastery, or discipline. If your value is excellence, then completing work to the best of your ability becomes fulfilling, regardless of external rewards.

   - **Example:** If you value continuous learning, each project or challenge is an opportunity to hone your skills, regardless of whether others appreciate it.

   Action: Write down 2-3 core values that matter to you, such as growth, responsibility, or integrity. Regularly remind yourself how your work reflects these values.

Creative Strategies to Add Value and Stand Out in a Tough Environment:

Now, beyond staying motivated, you can **proactively add value** in ways that make you stand out creatively, which can lead to recognition or even awards in the future. Here's how you can approach this:

1. **Identify and Solve Unaddressed Problems**

   Look for inefficiencies, gaps, or unaddressed problems in your workplace. By using creativity to propose and implement solutions, you can demonstrate initiative and innovation.

   - **Example:** If there's a process that slows down team productivity, design a new system or tool that optimizes workflow. Propose automation or suggest better communication strategies that save time and resources.

Action: Conduct an informal audit of your work environment. Identify 2-3 areas where improvements can be made, and creatively propose solutions that could benefit the company. This can show your leadership that you're proactive and forward-thinking, even in tough environments.

2. **Focus on Cross-Departmental Collaboration**

Collaborating outside your usual team or department can expose you to new perspectives and help you gain visibility within the organization. Often, collaborating with different departments can lead to fresh ideas or innovative solutions that set you apart.

- **Example:** If you're in marketing, offer to assist with a customer service initiative that could improve client satisfaction. If you're in finance, collaborate with HR to find creative solutions for budgeting or resource allocation that benefits the entire company.

Action: Propose a cross-departmental project where different teams can work together to solve a company-wide challenge. This can build relationships and show your ability to innovate across roles.

3. **Innovate Within Limited Resources**

A hallmark of creativity is being able to do more with less. If your company is limited in resources (time, budget, manpower), find innovative ways to optimize what's available. This could mean streamlining workflows, using technology to automate mundane tasks, or implementing cost-effective solutions.

- **Example:** Introduce tools or platforms (such as free project management tools or AI-based solutions) that can help your team work more efficiently with fewer resources. If there's no budget for formal recognition programs, start an informal team appreciation system that boosts morale.

Action: Research cost-effective tools or systems that your team can adopt to increase productivity or enhance collaboration. Implement these solutions and track their impact to showcase your initiative.

4. **Develop Personal Creative Projects**

Sometimes, the best way to stand out creatively is by working on **personal projects** within the company. Even if formal recognition is absent, taking ownership of a passion project that aligns with your skills can help you stand out.

- **Example:** Start a company blog or newsletter where you share insights, trends, or innovations relevant to your field. Or, initiate a professional development group within the company, where employees can share ideas and learn new skills.

Action: Identify a personal project you can start within the company that aligns with your skills and passion. It could be as simple as creating an internal resource hub or organizing a workshop that benefits your colleagues.

5. **Showcase Data-Driven Results**

To win awards or recognition, it's important to demonstrate the **impact** of your work. Focus on creating value that can be quantified, as measurable results often speak louder than words.

- **Example:** If you develop a new system or improve a process, track its effectiveness through data. Show how your solution increased productivity by 20% or saved the company a certain amount of money. Presenting data-backed results positions you as a results-oriented professional.

Action: After implementing a creative solution, collect data to show its impact. Prepare a presentation or report that highlights the value of your contribution, making it easier to gain recognition or submit your work for awards.

6. **Actively Seek External Recognition**

If internal recognition is lacking, look for **external opportunities** to showcase your creativity and hard work. Many industries offer innovation awards, contests, or platforms to submit creative projects.

- **Example:** Submit your work to industry competitions, innovation challenges, or conferences where you can gain visibility. Winning an external award can often lead to greater recognition within your company, even if internal recognition is absent.

Action: Research industry-specific awards, innovation challenges, or conferences. Select projects you've worked on that could be entered for external recognition, and submit them to these platforms.

Conclusion: Blending Motivation with Creativity

Staying focused and internally motivated in an environment where your hard work is not appreciated can be challenging, but with the right **mind programming strategy**, it's possible to maintain motivation and even thrive creatively. By reframing your mindset, setting personal goals, practicing gratitude, and visualizing long-term success, you can stay resilient. Furthermore, by applying creative strategies—such as solving unaddressed problems, collaborating cross-departmentally, and innovating with limited resources—you can add value in ways that stand out, increasing your chances of earning recognition and possibly winning awards.

This dual approach of **internal motivation** and **external value creation** helps you stay grounded and continue making impactful contributions, even in a difficult work environment.

Story 14. Let's assume your manager and manager's manager are very tough, result oriented and does not accept any delay or mistake or quality deviations. What will be your mind

programming to define your strategy to work effectively to satisfy their requirement and make them satisfied?

When working in an environment where your manager and their superior are very tough, results-oriented, and intolerant of delays, mistakes, or quality deviations, it's crucial to adjust both your **mindset** and **strategic approach** to meet their expectations while maintaining your own well-being. Here's a detailed **mind programming strategy** and a **work strategy** to ensure you satisfy their demands and exceed expectations:

Mind Programming Strategy to Stay Focused and Meet Tough Demands:

1. **Adopt a High-Performance Mindset**

   - In a high-pressure environment, it's essential to embrace a **high-performance mindset**, which involves staying calm under pressure, setting clear priorities, and maintaining a strong commitment to excellence. Instead of seeing the strictness as overwhelming, reframe it as an opportunity to demonstrate your ability to perform at a high level.

   - **Reframe:** Think of each project or task as an opportunity to sharpen your skills, demonstrate your capacity to handle pressure, and refine your attention to detail.

   Affirmation: "I thrive under pressure and use challenges to grow. I meet expectations with confidence and precision."

2. **Focus on Precision and Efficiency**

   - Given that your managers are intolerant of mistakes, your mindset should be geared towards **accuracy and efficiency**. Program your mind to develop meticulous attention to detail while optimizing your workflow for speed.

   - **Mantra:** "I work with precision and efficiency, and I continuously improve my processes to deliver excellent results without errors."

Action: Before submitting any work, review it multiple times to catch potential errors. Create checklists or workflows that help you complete tasks more systematically, ensuring nothing is overlooked.

3. **Embrace Accountability and Ownership**

   - Take full **ownership** of your tasks and projects. Program yourself to avoid blame-shifting or excuses, and instead, take responsibility for outcomes. This mindset builds trust and credibility with demanding managers.

   - **Mental Shift:** Shift your perspective to see each task as your personal responsibility. By owning the outcome, you'll naturally be more proactive in preventing issues.

   Affirmation: "I take full ownership of my work. I anticipate challenges and take proactive steps to ensure success."

4. **Visualize Successful Outcomes**

   - Use visualization techniques to mentally rehearse delivering high-quality work that meets or exceeds expectations. By envisioning the process from start to finish, you prepare yourself for success.

   - **Example Visualization:** Picture yourself submitting a flawless project, receiving positive feedback, and knowing that your work meets the strict standards. Imagine the satisfaction you'll feel knowing you've exceeded their expectations.

   Daily Practice: Spend 5 minutes each day visualizing successful task completion, where you deliver error-free, timely results.

5. **Set Internal Standards Higher Than External Demands**

   - To handle tough managers, mentally program yourself to set standards for yourself that are **higher than those expected by your managers**. By raising the bar internally, external demands will feel more manageable and aligned with your own standards of excellence.

- **Mantra:** "My standards for quality and performance are even higher than what is expected of me. I consistently surpass external demands."

Action: Set personal benchmarks for quality and deadlines that are tighter than your managers' expectations. For instance, if a deadline is in a week, aim to complete the task in five days with a buffer for review and revision.

Strategic Approach to Work Effectively and Satisfy Tough Managers:

1. **Clarify Expectations Early and Often**

   - Start every project by clarifying the exact expectations from your managers. Ask for specific guidelines on timelines, quality levels, and any non-negotiable aspects. This way, you'll understand their criteria clearly and avoid misalignment.

   - **Key Questions to Ask:**

     - What are the key priorities for this project?

     - What constitutes acceptable quality for you?

     - Are there any potential risks or areas of concern I should focus on to prevent mistakes?

   Action: Keep communication channels open and confirm expectations at each project milestone. Summarize and send a recap of discussions to ensure alignment.

2. **Use Proactive Communication**

   - In high-pressure environments, **proactive communication** is key to managing relationships with demanding managers. Provide regular updates on your progress, inform them of potential risks early, and involve them in key decision points before problems arise.

- **Example of Proactive Update:** "We're currently at 60% completion on the project, and I've identified a potential delay in the supplier chain. I'm addressing this by switching to an alternative supplier. I'll keep you posted on any further developments."

Action: Schedule regular check-ins or progress reports to give visibility into your work and anticipate concerns before they escalate.

3. **Focus on Time Management and Prioritization**

- Tough managers often demand strict adherence to deadlines, so your ability to manage time effectively is critical. Use **time-blocking** or the **Eisenhower Matrix** to prioritize urgent and important tasks first, ensuring you meet all deadlines with room for unexpected issues.

- **Time Management Tip:** Break down large projects into smaller, manageable chunks and set mini-deadlines for each segment. This not only keeps you on track but also allows for course correction if needed.

Action: At the start of each day, prioritize 3-5 key tasks and allocate specific time slots for each. Set deadlines ahead of the actual ones to build in review time.

4. **Pre-Emptively Mitigate Risks and Quality Issues**

- Since your managers have a zero-tolerance approach to errors, you need to develop a **risk mitigation strategy**. Proactively identify areas where mistakes are likely to occur and take steps to prevent them.

- **Example:** If there's a high risk of data errors in your work, double-check or have a peer review your work before submission. Implement quality control steps at each stage of a project.

Action: At the start of any task, list potential risks or common mistakes and create a preventive checklist to mitigate them. Regularly review this checklist as you work through the task.

5. **Learn from Mistakes to Avoid Repetition**

- In a strict work environment, mistakes can have significant consequences. If errors occur, take them as learning experiences to implement stronger controls and avoid similar issues in the future. Use a **feedback loop** to continuously improve.

- **Mindset Shift:** Rather than being demoralized by mistakes, view them as opportunities to create systems that prevent future errors.

Action: After any mistake or deviation, conduct a self-assessment to understand why it happened, what control measures were missing, and how you can prevent a repeat. Present this improvement plan to your manager as a sign of accountability and growth.

6. **Deliver Ahead of Schedule and Over-Deliver on Quality**

- Exceeding expectations is the best way to stand out in a tough work environment. If you can, aim to **deliver your work ahead of deadlines** and ensure it meets the highest standards of quality. Over-delivering will not only satisfy your managers but also build trust.

- **Example:** If your manager expects a report in one week, deliver it in five days with additional insights or suggestions for improvement that go beyond the scope.

Action: Always build buffer time into your schedule to allow for review and refinement. Consider ways you can add extra value, whether through additional data, insights, or recommendations.

Mind Programming Visualization for Success in a Tough Environment:

1. **Daily Visualization:** Each morning, take a few minutes to **visualize yourself successfully completing projects** that meet or exceed expectations. Picture yourself handing in

high-quality work that is error-free and on time. Imagine receiving positive feedback from your managers for your precision, efficiency, and initiative.

2. **Breathing and Focus Meditation:** Before starting a challenging task or presentation, take a few moments for a simple **breathing exercise**:

   - Close your eyes and take a deep breath in, focusing on the feeling of calm and control.

   - As you breathe out, imagine releasing any stress or anxiety.

   - Visualize yourself working methodically and completing each task with attention to detail. Repeat an affirmation like, "I am capable and in control. I deliver high-quality work on time."

3. **End-of-Day Reflection:** Reflect on your progress at the end of each day. What did you achieve? What went well? What can be improved tomorrow? Acknowledge small victories and make adjustments for the next day's tasks to continuously improve.

Conclusion: Excellence Through Mind Programming and Strategic Focus

By adopting a mindset of **accountability, precision, and continuous improvement**, and pairing it with a well-structured work strategy, you can not only meet but exceed the expectations of tough, results-oriented managers. Program your mind to embrace high performance, efficiency, and ownership, while strategically managing time, mitigating risks, and communicating proactively. With consistent effort, attention to detail, and a growth mindset, you will deliver high-quality results and build trust with even the most demanding leaders.

Story 15. Let's assume you have joined in a company as strategic leader where their product and service along with market reputation is very bad in the recent past due to quality and timely servicing issue. How can you define your strategy and

act mindfully to make the company successfully growing in all aspect internal motivation, quality enhancement and customer satisfaction?

Joining a company with a bad market reputation, poor product and service quality, and issues with timely servicing is a challenging but rewarding opportunity to implement transformative changes. As a strategic leader, you'll need to define a **multi-dimensional strategy** that not only addresses the **external** issues (like customer satisfaction and market perception) but also focuses on **internal factors** (like employee motivation and quality improvement).

Here's a detailed strategy to revive the company and promote sustainable growth, focusing on **internal motivation, quality enhancement, and customer satisfaction**, while acting **mindfully** as a leader.

1. **Strategic Assessment: Understanding the Current Situation**

   Key Actions:

   - **Internal Audit:** Begin with a thorough assessment of the company's current state—examine quality processes, customer service protocols, employee engagement, and market performance. Identify specific reasons for poor quality and late deliveries.

   - **Customer Feedback:** Collect detailed customer feedback to understand where the company is falling short. This can be done through surveys, interviews, or by analyzing online reviews and complaints.

   - **Employee Sentiment:** Meet with employees at all levels, especially those in frontline roles, to understand internal challenges. Identify the bottlenecks they face in delivering high-quality and timely services.

   Mindful Leadership Approach:

   - Be **non-judgmental** and maintain an **open mindset** during the assessment phase. Approach this with curiosity rather than blame. Mindfulness here means being present and listening deeply to employees, customers, and other stakeholders without preconceived notions.

2. **Building Internal Motivation and Ownership**

Key Focus:

- A key element of the turnaround will be improving **employee morale** and fostering a sense of **ownership** over their work. Disengaged employees can lead to quality and service issues. Start by aligning the team with a **renewed vision**.

Steps to Build Motivation:

- **Create a Vision and Purpose:** Clearly communicate a **revitalized company vision** that emphasizes quality, customer satisfaction, and employee well-being. When employees feel they are part of a meaningful mission, their motivation rises.

Example: "We are committed to becoming a leader in the industry by delivering exceptional quality products on time, while fostering a work culture of innovation and responsibility."

- **Empower Employees:** Give employees more **autonomy** and **responsibility** in decision-making processes related to quality and service. This increases ownership and accountability.

Action: Create **cross-functional teams** to identify solutions for specific quality and service problems. Employees are more motivated when they are trusted to contribute solutions, not just execute orders.

- **Recognize and Reward Effort:** Recognize and celebrate small wins along the path to improvement. Employee recognition programs can significantly boost morale.

Action: Set up a **monthly rewards program** to recognize teams or individuals who improve quality metrics or customer service.

Mindful Leadership Approach:

- Practice **compassionate leadership** by acknowledging the challenges employees have faced. Be present, actively listen, and offer **support** rather than pressure. Implement **stress-reduction practices** (like mindfulness or meditation sessions) to help teams stay calm and focused under pressure.

3. **Quality Enhancement Strategy**

Key Focus:

- **Quality control and process optimization** should be at the heart of the turnaround strategy. Poor quality products or services are likely rooted in either flawed processes, insufficient training, or poor resource allocation.

Steps to Improve Quality:

- **Root Cause Analysis (RCA):** Conduct an in-depth RCA to identify why the quality issues are occurring. Is it due to poor materials, lack of quality checks, outdated processes, or insufficient training?

Action: Implement RCA tools like **Fishbone Diagrams** or **5 Whys** to systematically identify the root causes of quality failures.

- **Process Redesign and Standardization:** Based on your RCA findings, redesign critical processes to improve product quality and reduce errors. Standardize quality control checkpoints across the production or service delivery process.

Action: Introduce **Six Sigma** or **Lean methodologies** to streamline processes, eliminate waste, and improve efficiency.

- **Training and Development:** Ensure that employees receive ongoing **training** on new quality standards, best practices, and the use of updated tools and technologies.

Action: Develop a **continuous improvement training program** focused on quality assurance, customer service excellence, and cross-functional collaboration.

- **Introduce Technology for Quality Monitoring:** Leverage **AI-based tools** or other **quality management software** to monitor product quality in real-time, detect defects early, and ensure that products meet customer expectations before they leave the facility.

Mindful Leadership Approach:

- Approach quality improvement from a place of **non-reactivity**. Instead of reacting to every quality issue with urgency and blame, respond thoughtfully by identifying systemic fixes. Lead with a mindset of **continuous improvement**, understanding that quality is a process, not a one-time fix.

4. **Customer Satisfaction Strategy**

Key Focus:

- Address the external impact of poor service and product quality through a strategic focus on **improving customer experience**. This will help rebuild trust and reputation in the market.

Steps to Improve Customer Satisfaction:

- **Listen and Act on Feedback:** Actively engage with customers through feedback loops. Use surveys, customer interviews, and feedback forms to gather insights and **act on complaints** and suggestions.

Action: Develop a **customer feedback task force** that regularly reviews customer feedback and implements changes based on common complaints.

- **Improve Communication and Transparency:** Customers value transparency, especially when things go wrong. Be proactive in your communication regarding product delays, service issues, or quality concerns.

Action: Send **real-time updates** to customers about the status of their orders and services. Use **personalized communication** to address their concerns and reassure them of your commitment to improvement.

- **Offer Value-Added Services:** To differentiate the company from competitors, offer **value-added services** that enhance customer experience. This could include extended warranties, faster delivery options, or personalized customer service.

Action: Introduce a **VIP customer program** offering special privileges like priority servicing or product customization.

Mindful Leadership Approach:

- Lead the customer service transformation with **empathy**. Understand the frustrations of your customers and communicate your solutions with a calm and authentic presence. Show that you truly care about their experience and are personally invested in their satisfaction.

5. **Enhancing Market Reputation**

Key Focus:

- A key part of your strategy will involve **rebuilding the company's reputation** in the market. This requires both **internal quality improvements** and **external communication strategies**.

Steps to Rebuild Market Reputation:

- **Brand Reinvention Campaign:** Once internal improvements are underway, launch a **rebranding** campaign that highlights the company's renewed focus on quality, customer satisfaction, and timely delivery.

Action: Work with the marketing team to develop a **content strategy** that showcases customer testimonials, case studies of successful projects, and quality certifications or improvements.

- **Leverage Social Proof:** Engage with loyal customers and incentivize them to leave **positive reviews** or refer new customers. Social proof is one of the most effective ways to rebuild a brand's market perception.

Action: Launch a **referral program** that rewards customers for recommending the company. Encourage satisfied clients to share their experiences on review platforms.

- **Focus on Key Performance Metrics (KPIs):** Track KPIs related to quality (defect rates, customer complaints), customer satisfaction (Net Promoter Score, customer retention), and market performance (sales growth, brand engagement).

Action: Publish **quarterly reports** that highlight the progress made in these areas, showing that the company is on an upward trajectory.

Mindful Leadership Approach:

- Approach reputation management mindfully by ensuring that the **external messaging** matches the **internal improvements**. Be authentic in your communications—don't overpromise or inflate the reality of the changes taking place. Consistency between actions and words will rebuild trust with both customers and the market.

Conclusion: A Holistic Strategy for Sustainable Growth

To turn around a company with a poor market reputation and operational inefficiencies, you need a multi-layered strategy that addresses **internal motivation**, **quality enhancement**, and

customer satisfaction—all while remaining grounded in mindful leadership. The keys to success are:

1. **Inspiring Internal Motivation** through a renewed vision, employee empowerment, and a recognition of achievements.

2. **Enhancing Product and Service Quality** by implementing process improvements, leveraging technology, and fostering a culture of continuous learning.

3. **Improving Customer Satisfaction** by listening to feedback, improving transparency, and offering value-added services.

4. **Rebuilding Market Reputation** through honest communication, a focus on key metrics, and leveraging customer testimonials.

By leading with empathy, precision, and transparency, you can successfully guide the company towards sustainable growth, improved reputation, and a culture of excellence.

Story 16. Finding best strategy for Relationship Enhancement – NLP vs Quantum Leadership Top of Form

Let's explore a real-life scenario in the **relationship management sector**, specifically addressing **communication breakdown** in personal or professional relationships, and compare how this issue can be tackled using **Neuro-Linguistic Programming (NLP)** versus **Quantum Leadership**.

Scenario: Communication Breakdown and Conflict

A team in a company, or a couple in a personal relationship, is struggling with a communication breakdown. Misunderstandings, assumptions, and emotional triggers have led to conflicts, mistrust, and a lack of effective communication. Both parties feel unheard and unappreciated, which is affecting productivity, teamwork, or emotional intimacy.

Addressing the Problem: NLP vs. Quantum Leadership

Aspect	NLP Approach	Quantum Leadership Approach
Understanding the Problem	**Focus on communication models and internal filters**: NLP views the communication breakdown as a result of **different internal representations** and **filters**. Each person has a unique way of processing information based on past experiences, beliefs, and values, leading to misunderstandings. NLP helps identify the communication styles of each party, including their **sensory preferences** (visual, auditory, kinaesthetic) and **language patterns**. The goal is to align communication so that each party feels understood.	**Focus on energetic misalignment and disharmony**: In Quantum Leadership, the breakdown is seen as a result of **energetic disharmony** between individuals. Both parties are out of sync with their **authentic energy** and the flow of the relationship. Quantum Leadership looks at the relationship as an energetic field where **coherence** is lost, and the goal is to restore harmony by realigning the individual and collective energy within the relationship.
Resolving Conflicts	**Reframing and pattern interrupts**: NLP focuses on changing how both parties **frame** the conflict. The coach uses **reframing** techniques to help each individual see the situation from the other person's perspective. For instance, if one person believes "They never listen to me," the NLP practitioner helps them reframe this belief into something like, "Maybe they don't understand the way I express myself." NLP also uses **pattern interrupts** to break negative communication cycles and introduce new, positive ways of interacting.	**Shifting consciousness and energy fields**: Quantum Leadership seeks to **shift the energy** of both individuals to a higher, more coherent level. The coach facilitates **energy healing** or **mindfulness practices** that help both parties release emotional blocks and reestablish a connection to their higher selves. By addressing the **energetic imbalances** between them, the coach helps the individuals achieve a state of **coherence** where their communication flows naturally, without the interference of ego or negative emotions.

Aspect	NLP Approach	Quantum Leadership Approach
Improving Communication	**Mirroring and rapport-building**: NLP emphasizes the importance of **building rapport** through **mirroring** (matching the other person's body language, tone of voice, and language patterns). By doing this, both parties begin to feel more connected and understood, which improves communication. The NLP practitioner also teaches **active listening** techniques, helping both individuals become more aware of each other's communication styles and needs. This builds **trust** and reduces misunderstandings.	**Restoring energetic alignment and trust**: In Quantum Leadership, communication is improved by focusing on **energetic alignment**. The coach encourages both parties to engage in **meditation**, **visualization**, or **mindfulness** practices that raise their vibrational energy and help them reconnect to their **authentic selves**. As individuals restore their internal energy alignment, they become more open and present in their communication, fostering **trust and openness** naturally, without forcing connection through verbal strategies alone.
Dealing with Emotional Triggers	**Anchoring and state management**: NLP teaches both parties how to manage their emotional triggers through **anchoring** techniques. For example, when one person feels angry or hurt during communication, the coach can help them anchor a **calm emotional state** (using a gesture or word) to prevent them from reacting impulsively. This allows individuals to remain calm and present, even when faced with emotionally charged situations. NLP also teaches **dissociation techniques** to help individuals step back from their emotional responses and observe the situation more objectively.	**Releasing emotional blocks and raising vibrational energy**: Quantum Leadership addresses emotional triggers as **energetic blocks** that prevent harmony and flow in the relationship. The coach helps both parties release these blocks through **energy healing** practices such as **breathwork, chakra alignment**, or **emotional release techniques**. As these blocks are removed, both individuals experience emotional healing, which naturally reduces their emotional reactivity and enables them to engage in more **compassionate and mindful communication**.

Aspect	NLP Approach	Quantum Leadership Approach
Handling Negative Patterns	**Breaking negative communication loops**: NLP uses techniques like **pattern interrupts** to break the cycle of negative communication patterns. For example, if both individuals tend to escalate conflicts through harsh words or defensiveness, the NLP coach can introduce new communication patterns, such as using positive language or taking a break when emotions run high. The idea is to replace destructive patterns with constructive ones, creating new **neurological pathways** for healthier communication.	**Quantum leaps in relational growth**: Quantum Leadership sees negative patterns as **low-vibrational energy** that keeps the relationship stuck in an unhealthy state. The coach helps individuals take a **quantum leap** in their relational growth by aligning them with a **higher vibrational frequency**. Through **consciousness expansion** practices like **meditation** or **visualization**, both parties are guided to a new state of **awareness and growth**, where the old negative patterns dissolve and new, higher-frequency interactions emerge.
Rebuilding Trust	**Future pacing and belief change**: NLP uses **future pacing** to help both parties envision a future where trust is restored and communication flows smoothly. The coach guides both individuals through exercises that allow them to mentally rehearse future interactions, focusing on how they would feel and act if they trusted each other fully. NLP also works on **changing limiting beliefs** about trust, such as "I can't trust anyone" to "Trust is built through open, honest communication, and I am capable of that."	**Energetic coherence and mutual growth**: Quantum Leadership approaches trust as an energetic state of **coherence** between individuals. The coach helps both parties reestablish trust by aligning their energy fields and encouraging mutual growth through **shared meditative** or **mindfulness practices**. When individuals are energetically aligned, trust becomes a natural outcome because both parties are in sync at a deeper level of **universal connection**, rather than just relying on verbal promises or past actions.

Aspect	NLP Approach	Quantum Leadership Approach
Sustaining Long-Term Harmony	**Habituating positive communication patterns**: NLP teaches both individuals how to build long-term harmony by habituating **positive communication patterns** through repetition. The coach works with both parties to create **daily or weekly routines** that reinforce good communication habits, such as regular check-ins, expressing appreciation, and managing emotions. The focus is on creating lasting change in their neurological wiring so that healthy communication becomes second nature.	**Maintaining energetic coherence**: In Quantum Leadership, long-term harmony is sustained by ensuring that both individuals remain energetically coherent. The coach encourages both parties to engage in **ongoing practices** like **group meditation, energy alignment**, or **mindfulness**, where they can maintain a high level of vibrational energy. By staying aligned at an energetic level, harmony in the relationship is naturally sustained without the need for continuous effort or forced communication strategies.

Summary

- **NLP Approach**: In the relationship management sector, NLP focuses on **identifying communication styles**, **reframing limiting beliefs**, and **breaking negative communication patterns**. Techniques like **mirroring, anchoring**, and **pattern interrupts** help individuals understand each other better, manage emotional triggers, and build rapport. NLP aims to reprogram mental and emotional patterns that lead to conflict, ensuring that communication is clear, productive, and supportive.

- **Quantum Leadership Approach**: Quantum Leadership addresses relationship issues by focusing on **energetic alignment** and **coherence** between individuals. Communication breakdowns and conflicts are seen as a result of **misaligned energy fields** and emotional blocks. The approach uses practices like **meditation**, **energy healing**, and **consciousness expansion** to help both individuals release negative energy, reconnect with their higher selves, and restore a state of **energetic harmony** in the relationship. Trust, communication, and connection flow naturally once the energy fields are aligned.

In this **relationship management scenario**, NLP provides practical tools for improving communication, managing emotional triggers, and resolving conflicts through **behavioural and cognitive shifts**, while Quantum Leadership offers a more holistic and **energetic approach**, where the focus is on realigning the individuals' energy to restore harmony and build a deep, lasting connection. Both approaches can be powerful depending on the needs and dynamics of the relationship.

Story 17. Defining Effective Strategies on Wellness using NLP vs Quantum Leadership Method

Real-Life Scenario: Wellness Sector

In the wellness sector, let's consider a situation where individuals are facing **chronic stress and burnout** due to work pressures, lifestyle imbalances, and emotional exhaustion. This problem is common in high-demand work environments, where the focus on productivity and results leads to neglect of self-care and emotional well-being.

Both **Neuro-Linguistic Programming (NLP)** and **Quantum Leadership** offer different approaches to addressing this issue.

Addressing the Problem: NLP vs. Quantum Leadership

Aspect	NLP Approach	Quantum Leadership Approach
Understanding the Problem	**Focus on mental patterns and stress triggers**: NLP views stress and burnout as resulting from **internal mental processes** and beliefs. The way individuals interpret external events or pressures creates the emotional experience of stress. For instance, believing "I have to be perfect" or "I can't say no" can trigger stress. The goal is to identify and change the **unconscious mental patterns** that lead to stress.	**Focus on energy misalignment and disconnection**: Quantum Leadership sees chronic stress and burnout as signs of being **disconnected** from one's **authentic self** and from the larger universal energy. The issue is a result of not being aligned with one's inner purpose and energy flow. Quantum Leadership emphasizes creating **energetic coherence** between mind, body, and spirit to restore balance and vitality.
Root Cause Exploration	**Limiting beliefs and emotional triggers**: NLP helps individuals explore the root causes of their stress by identifying **limiting beliefs** (e.g., "I have to do everything myself" or "I'm not allowed to relax") and emotional triggers. Using NLP techniques such as **reframing** and **pattern interrupts**, individuals learn how to change their mental and emotional reactions to stress-inducing situations.	**Energy flow and lack of coherence**: Quantum Leadership encourages individuals to explore the **energetic root** of their burnout. The coach guides participants to look beyond the surface stressors and identify **where their energy is blocked** or out of alignment with their higher self. Practices like **mindfulness** and **meditation** help individuals reconnect with their authentic purpose and restore **energetic flow**.

Aspect	NLP Approach	Quantum Leadership Approach
Managing Stress	**Anchoring relaxation and calm**: NLP techniques like **anchoring** are used to help individuals access states of **calm and relaxation** on demand. For instance, the coach helps the individual associate a specific **gesture** or **word** with a feeling of calm, allowing them to activate that feeling whenever they feel stressed. By anchoring positive emotional states, participants can manage stress more effectively in high-pressure situations.	**Restoring energetic balance**: Quantum Leadership uses practices like **energy alignment**, **meditation**, and **visualization** to help individuals restore balance and coherence in their energy field. The coach guides participants through meditative practices that help them **release stress** and **recharge their energy** by connecting to the universal flow. Stress is viewed as a disruption in energy, so restoring balance at an energetic level resolves the issue more holistically.
Handling Burnout	**Changing internal representations**: NLP helps individuals reframe how they mentally represent their workload and responsibilities. For example, instead of viewing work as overwhelming, individuals are guided to mentally break tasks into **manageable chunks** and **reframe** work challenges as opportunities for growth. Techniques like **timeline therapy** can be used to revisit and change the emotional charge of past stressful events, which may be contributing to burnout.	**Shifting consciousness and energy fields**: Quantum Leadership sees burnout as a sign that the individual is not living in alignment with their **authentic self**. The approach involves guiding participants through **consciousness-shifting practices** to raise their vibration and align with their higher potential. Individuals are encouraged to **let go of rigid expectations** and adopt a **non-linear growth mindset**, where they are attuned to their intuitive energy and the flow of life. By **elevating consciousness**, burnout naturally dissipates as individuals reconnect with their inner vitality.

Aspect	NLP Approach	Quantum Leadership Approach
Sustaining Wellness	**Goal setting and habit formation**: NLP helps individuals set **wellness goals** that are clear, achievable, and aligned with their values. The coach guides participants to create new, positive habits that support long-term wellness, such as regular exercise, relaxation routines, and time management strategies. By breaking down larger wellness goals into **actionable steps**, individuals can create sustainable change without feeling overwhelmed.	**Sustaining high-vibrational energy**: Quantum Leadership encourages individuals to maintain wellness by staying in a state of **energetic coherence**. The coach emphasizes the importance of daily practices like **meditation, breathwork, and mindfulness** to keep the energy field in balance. Wellness is not just about physical health but about staying aligned with **one's true essence** and the universal flow. By maintaining a high vibrational state, wellness becomes a natural and sustained part of life.
Reframing Work-Life Balance	**Balancing priorities through reframing**: NLP helps individuals reframe how they view work-life balance. For instance, if someone feels guilty for taking time for themselves, NLP techniques help them reframe this as "self-care is necessary for me to be my best at work and home." NLP also teaches techniques like **chunking** to help individuals manage time more effectively, ensuring they allocate enough time to both personal well-being and professional responsibilities.	**Integrating work-life flow**: Quantum Leadership views work-life balance not as a strict division of time but as a **holistic integration** of life's energy flow. The coach guides participants to align their energy at work and home, so there is **coherence and flow** in all aspects of life. Rather than focusing on balance as a linear equation, participants are encouraged to live in **alignment with purpose** and **flow with universal energy**, where work and personal life can coexist in harmony.

Aspect	NLP Approach	Quantum Leadership Approach
Preventing Relapse into Burnout	**Future pacing and anchoring**: NLP uses **future pacing** to help individuals imagine themselves successfully managing stress and avoiding burnout in the future. By visualizing a future where they consistently handle work pressures with ease, participants program their minds to stay calm and focused. Anchoring positive states also ensures that individuals can tap into feelings of calm whenever they sense burnout creeping back.	**Consciousness expansion and energy field maintenance**: Quantum Leadership encourages individuals to maintain long-term wellness by regularly engaging in practices that **expand consciousness** and **align energy**. Participants are taught to remain aware of any **shifts in their energy field** and to address imbalances before they lead to burnout. By staying connected to their higher purpose and the universal flow, individuals prevent stress and burnout from reoccurring.

Summary

- **NLP Approach**: In the wellness sector, NLP addresses stress and burnout by focusing on changing mental patterns, limiting beliefs, and emotional responses. Techniques like **reframing**, **anchoring**, and **timeline therapy** are used to help individuals manage stress, reprogram their internal representations of work pressures, and develop sustainable wellness habits.

- **Quantum Leadership Approach**: Quantum Leadership focuses on **energy alignment** and **consciousness shifts** to address burnout at an energetic level. Stress and burnout are viewed as signs of **energetic misalignment** with one's true self, and practices like **meditation, energy coherence**, and **consciousness expansion** are used to restore balance. The approach emphasizes long-term wellness through alignment with **universal flow** and higher purpose.

In this **wellness sector scenario**, NLP provides practical tools to manage stress by changing thought patterns and emotional responses, while Quantum Leadership offers a deeper, more holistic approach focused on **energy alignment** and raising **vibrational frequency** to create lasting wellness. Both approaches can be highly effective depending on the individual's needs and the wellness goals of the organization or program.

Story 18. How can you define your best strategy in Training and coaching sector? Using NLP vs Quantum leadership.

Let's explore a real-life scenario in the **training and coaching sector**, specifically in **personality development**, and compare how it can be addressed using **Neuro-Linguistic Programming (NLP)** versus **Quantum Leadership**.

Scenario: Low Confidence and Limiting Beliefs in Participants

A personal development coach is working with a group of individuals who struggle with **low confidence** and **self-limiting beliefs**. Many of the participants are stuck in their careers, personal lives, or relationships because they believe they are not capable of achieving more or stepping outside their comfort zone. The coach needs to help these participants break through these barriers, build confidence, and develop a more empowered self-image to achieve personal and professional success.

Addressing the Problem: NLP vs. Quantum Leadership

Aspect	NLP Approach	Quantum Leadership Approach
Understanding the Problem	**Focus on internal mental models and belief systems**: NLP views the participants' low confidence as a result of **limiting beliefs** and negative mental patterns they have built over time. The coach helps participants identify the root causes of their self-doubt, such as beliefs like "I'm not good enough" or "I always fail." These beliefs are often internalized from past experiences, and NLP focuses on reprogramming these **internal mental models** by changing how participants represent their reality.	**Focus on energy misalignment and collective consciousness**: In Quantum Leadership, the participants' low confidence is seen as an **energetic misalignment** with their higher potential. The participants are not in tune with their **true energetic frequency**—the field of possibility where they are empowered, confident, and capable of achieving great things. Quantum Leadership views the coach's role as a facilitator of **collective and individual energy alignment**, helping participants tap into their **higher self** and the infinite possibilities around them.
Changing Limiting Beliefs	**Reframing and belief change techniques**: In NLP, the coach uses **reframing** techniques to help participants see their self-limiting beliefs in a new light. For example, if a participant believes "I'm not smart enough to succeed," the coach can guide them to **reframe** this belief to "I am constantly learning and growing, and I can achieve success through effort and persistence." NLP also employs **belief change patterns** that allow participants to substitute limiting beliefs with more empowering ones, reprogramming their minds for success.	**Shifting consciousness and energy fields**: Quantum Leadership views limiting beliefs as **vibrational patterns** that no longer serve the individual. The coach helps participants raise their energy levels and **shift consciousness** to align with their **highest self**. This process involves creating a space of **coherence** where participants can release old energetic patterns (limiting beliefs) and access higher vibrational states of empowerment, confidence, and possibility. Practices like **meditation**, **visualization**, and **energy alignment** are used to help participants shift into this new state of being.

Aspect	NLP Approach	Quantum Leadership Approach
Building Confidence	**Anchoring positive emotional states**: NLP uses **anchoring** techniques to help participants access states of confidence whenever needed. The coach works with participants to create physical or mental "anchors" that trigger positive emotions. For example, the coach might help a participant recall a moment when they felt confident and ask them to associate that feeling with a specific gesture or word. Whenever the participant faces a challenging situation, they can use that anchor to instantly recall the confidence they felt before, boosting their emotional state.	**Creating a resonant energy field of confidence**: Quantum Leadership focuses on **raising the collective energy** of the group, creating a resonant field where confidence and empowerment naturally emerge. The coach encourages participants to engage in **group meditations or visualizations** where they align their energy with their **highest potential**. The idea is that as each individual raises their energy and aligns with confidence, the collective energy of the group amplifies, helping everyone become more confident. The coach emphasizes a sense of **oneness**, where the participants can support each other in maintaining high energy and confidence.
Overcoming Past Failures	**Perceptual shifts and timeline therapy**: NLP practitioners use techniques like **timeline therapy** to help participants overcome past failures and negative experiences that are holding them back. The coach guides participants to revisit past failures, reframe them, and extract positive lessons. This allows participants to change their relationship with failure, seeing it not as a permanent mark of inadequacy but as a stepping stone to growth. **Perceptual shifts** also help participants view past experiences from new perspectives, such as seeing failure as an opportunity for learning rather than defeat.	**Transcending time and embracing non-linear growth**: Quantum Leadership encourages participants to see past failures not as fixed points in time but as part of a larger, **non-linear growth** process. The coach guides participants to step out of linear thinking, where past failures limit future success, and instead embrace the idea that success can happen in **quantum leaps**. Through **energy alignment** and mindfulness, participants are encouraged to let go of their attachment to past failures and step into the **field of infinite possibilities**, where the past does not define their future.

Aspect	NLP Approach	Quantum Leadership Approach
Motivation and Drive	**Outcome-oriented goal setting**: In NLP, the coach helps participants set **clear, specific, and achievable goals** that align with their values and desires. By setting well-defined outcomes, participants can focus their energy and attention on reaching these goals, increasing their motivation and drive. NLP techniques like **future pacing** are used, where participants imagine their desired future in vivid detail, helping them stay motivated by connecting emotionally to their future success.	**Aligning with purpose and universal flow**: Quantum Leadership shifts the focus from individual, outcome-oriented motivation to a larger sense of **purpose and alignment** with the universal flow. The coach encourages participants to connect with their **higher purpose**—the reason why they want to achieve success, beyond material goals. This creates a sense of **intrinsic motivation**, where participants are driven by a deep connection to their purpose and feel guided by the **universal energy** toward fulfilling that purpose. Motivation comes from being in alignment with the **flow of life**, rather than pushing toward external goals.
Handling Fear of Failure	**Reframing and fear dissociation**: NLP practitioners use **reframing** techniques to help participants dissociate from the fear of failure. The coach helps participants reframe fear as a **natural part of growth**. For instance, instead of seeing fear as a sign of impending failure, participants can reframe it as "an indicator that I'm pushing my boundaries and growing." NLP also uses techniques like **chunking down** fears, breaking them into smaller, more manageable concerns, and addressing them step by step.	**Embracing uncertainty and non-duality**: Quantum Leadership teaches participants to **embrace uncertainty** and let go of the dualistic thinking that frames success and failure as opposites. The coach encourages participants to see all experiences as part of the **quantum field of possibility**, where fear no longer has a limiting role. Instead of fearing failure, participants are taught to trust in the **non-linear nature** of growth and the idea that even perceived failures are part of their energetic expansion. By raising their vibration and aligning with their purpose, fear of failure naturally dissipates.

Aspect	NLP Approach	Quantum Leadership Approach
Sustaining Long-Term Confidence	**Anchoring and future pacing**: NLP focuses on sustaining confidence through regular use of **anchors** and **future pacing** exercises. The coach teaches participants how to continually reinforce positive mental states by anchoring confidence to specific physical gestures, words, or thoughts. Participants also engage in **visualizing future success**, allowing them to keep their long-term vision in mind, which fuels sustained confidence and motivation.	**Maintaining energetic coherence**: In Quantum Leadership, sustaining confidence comes from maintaining **energetic coherence** within oneself and the group. The coach encourages participants to regularly engage in practices like **meditation, energy alignment**, and **mindfulness** to stay connected to their **higher energy frequency**. By staying in a state of energetic alignment, participants naturally feel more confident and empowered over the long term, as they are consistently connected to their inner strength and universal flow.

Summary

- **NLP Approach**: Focuses on identifying and reprogramming limiting beliefs, building confidence through practical techniques like **anchoring**, and reframing challenges to see them as opportunities. NLP is rooted in understanding how internal thought patterns influence behaviour, with an emphasis on goal-setting, overcoming past failures, and sustaining motivation through **future pacing**.

- **Quantum Leadership Approach**: Views personality development from an energetic and holistic perspective. The coach helps participants align with their **higher purpose and universal energy**, guiding them to release limiting beliefs by raising their energy field. Confidence and motivation come from being in a state of **energetic coherence** and connectedness to the **quantum field of possibilities**. Quantum Leadership encourages participants to embrace uncertainty and trust in non-linear, quantum leaps of growth.

In this **training and coaching scenario**, NLP provides specific techniques for **reprogramming beliefs** and sustaining confidence on a personal level, while Quantum Leadership focuses on **energetic alignment** and **collective consciousness**, helping participants access a state of **empowerment and infinite potential**. Both approaches offer valuable tools depending on the needs of the participants and the goals of the coaching program.

Story19. How you can make effective strategies to address your entrepreneurship issues where you have two tools NLP and Quantum leadership to be considered?

Here's a real-life scenario in the entrepreneurship sector, and how it can be addressed using **Neuro-Linguistic Programming (NLP)** versus **Quantum Leadership**:

Scenario: Entrepreneur Facing Stagnant Business Growth

An entrepreneur who runs a tech startup has seen stagnant growth over the past year. While the business initially gained traction, recent efforts to scale have fallen flat. Sales are plateauing, employees seem disengaged, and the entrepreneur feels stuck in a cycle of uncertainty and self-doubt. They struggle to find new ways to innovate, feeling that every effort doesn't deliver the desired results. The entrepreneur needs to find a way to break through the stagnation, reignite their creativity, and lead their team toward new growth.

Addressing the Problem: NLP vs. Quantum Leadership

Aspect	NLP Approach	Quantum Leadership Approach
Understanding the Problem	**Focus on internal beliefs and limitations**: In NLP, the entrepreneur's stagnation is seen as a result of limiting beliefs or internal conflicts that are blocking their ability to innovate and scale the business. NLP practitioners would focus on uncovering the entrepreneur's internal mental and emotional patterns (e.g., "I don't have what it takes" or "Innovation is too risky") that are preventing forward progress. Once identified, these beliefs are reprogrammed to more empowering ones.	**Focus on the interconnected field of possibilities**: Quantum leadership views the entrepreneur's stagnation as a reflection of an **energetic misalignment** between their vision and actions. The business's lack of growth is seen as a symptom of disconnection from the **field of potential** and collective consciousness within the company. The entrepreneur must realign their energy and the company's energy with **limitless possibilities** in the quantum field. Instead of focusing on fixing individual problems, the leader works on reconnecting with the company's highest potential.
Innovation and Creativity	**Modelling and reframing**: NLP helps the entrepreneur access **creativity and innovation** by modelling the behaviours and thought patterns of successful entrepreneurs or innovators. By observing and replicating how others have succeeded in overcoming similar challenges, the entrepreneur can unlock new pathways. Additionally, **reframing** the problem from "stagnation" to "an opportunity for creative solutions" can help change the entrepreneur's approach, opening up new ideas and strategies. NLP encourages a shift in thinking to perceive challenges as **stepping stones** rather than obstacles.	**Quantum leap thinking and coherence**: Quantum leadership doesn't view innovation as a step-by-step process but as a **quantum leap**—a sudden, transformative shift in consciousness and action. The leader encourages the entrepreneur to tap into **non-linear possibilities**, exploring ideas that may seem radical or outside traditional business models. By meditating on and visualizing the business as thriving, connected to an infinite field of innovation, the entrepreneur can manifest creative breakthroughs. Quantum leadership also fosters a sense of **coherence** within the team, helping to unify collective creative energy toward a shared goal.

Aspect	NLP Approach	Quantum Leadership Approach
Overcoming Self-Doubt	**Changing limiting beliefs**: NLP addresses the entrepreneur's **self-doubt** by using techniques like **belief change patterns**. The leader helps the entrepreneur identify the limiting belief (e.g., "I'm not good enough to scale this business") and rewire it to a more empowering belief (e.g., "I am capable of taking this business to the next level"). Techniques like **visualization** and **future pacing** allow the entrepreneur to vividly experience success in their mind, helping to build confidence and remove self-doubt.	**Tapping into infinite potential**: Quantum leadership approaches self-doubt not as a personal limitation but as a result of disconnecting from the **infinite potential** in the quantum field. The entrepreneur is encouraged to shift their energy from fear and doubt to **trust and openness**, recognizing that they are part of a limitless flow of creativity and success. The leader facilitates practices like **visualization** and **collective intention-setting** to help the entrepreneur see themselves as part of a larger cosmic flow of abundance, where self-doubt no longer has a place.
Engaging the Team	**Rapport-building and anchoring positive states**: NLP techniques can help the entrepreneur rebuild **rapport** with their team. By understanding each employee's communication style and needs, the entrepreneur can foster better relationships. **Anchoring positive states** like excitement, collaboration, and passion can also re-engage the team. The leader helps the entrepreneur create **positive emotional states** during meetings or creative sessions by anchoring key emotions, which fosters a collaborative, motivated atmosphere. For example, celebrating small wins could serve as a positive anchor to motivate the team.	**Creating a collective field of energy and vision**: Quantum leadership focuses on **unifying the energy field** of the team. Rather than focusing on individuals' motivation through traditional methods, the leader taps into the collective energy of the team, aligning them toward a **shared vision**. Through practices like **collective meditation**, visioning exercises, or group mindfulness, the entrepreneur helps the team connect to a higher sense of purpose. This creates a sense of **shared coherence**, where each team member feels part of something larger, boosting intrinsic motivation and engagement.

Aspect	NLP Approach	Quantum Leadership Approach
Customer Relations and Market Positioning	**Perceptual shifts and reframing customer needs**: NLP helps the entrepreneur and team use **perceptual positions** to see their product or service from multiple perspectives, including that of the customer. This technique allows the business to gain new insights into how customers perceive the product and why growth might have stalled. **Reframing** can also be applied to customer feedback, viewing it as valuable information for improvement rather than criticism. NLP helps shift the mindset from "reacting to the market" to "anticipating customer needs."	**Attracting customers through resonance**: Quantum leadership sees customers not just as transactional entities but as part of the **energy field** the business operates in. The leader encourages the entrepreneur to create an energetic resonance that naturally attracts the right customers. This could involve aligning the product, marketing, and customer service with the business's **core energy** and purpose. By fostering an energetic alignment within the business, the leader helps the entrepreneur attract customers who resonate with the company's vision, creating growth through natural **resonance and attraction** rather than forceful strategies.
Growth Strategy	**Outcome setting and modelling success**: NLP emphasizes clear **outcome-setting** and identifying **specific, measurable goals** that align with the entrepreneur's vision. By setting clear, future-oriented outcomes (e.g., doubling revenue in 12 months, expanding to new markets), the entrepreneur can model their behaviour and strategies based on other successful business models. NLP techniques like **chunking** help the entrepreneur break down complex growth goals into smaller, actionable steps, making the process less overwhelming.	**Quantum leaps and systemic transformation**: Quantum leadership approaches growth as a **non-linear process**, where transformation happens through **quantum leaps** rather than incremental changes. The entrepreneur is encouraged to focus on the **energy and consciousness** of the business, aligning it with expansive growth. Instead of traditional planning, the entrepreneur taps into the **field of possibilities** and allows for sudden, exponential growth through **intuitive insights** and creative breakthroughs. This approach encourages the entrepreneur to step into bold, visionary leadership, trusting in **synchronicity** and the larger universal flow to guide growth.

Aspect	NLP Approach	Quantum Leadership Approach
Sustaining Long-Term Motivation	**Anchoring motivation and future pacing**: In NLP, the leader helps the entrepreneur create **long-term motivation** by anchoring positive emotional states to their vision of success. The leader guides the entrepreneur to **future pace** and vividly imagine the future success of the business, anchoring that vision to daily practices. By regularly accessing this **positive future state**, the entrepreneur stays motivated and energized to take action.	**Maintaining collective coherence and purpose**: Quantum leadership sustains long-term motivation by ensuring that the entire organization is **aligned with a collective purpose**. The entrepreneur fosters a culture where innovation, success, and growth are seen as **collective achievements**, driven by the team's shared vision and energy. This creates a self-sustaining environment where employees and leaders stay motivated because they feel deeply connected to the **collective energy** of the business. Long-term motivation is maintained through regular reflection, visioning, and alignment with universal principles of growth and abundance.

Summary

- **NLP Approach**: Focuses on identifying and changing limiting beliefs, reframing problems, and using practical tools to increase innovation and motivation. NLP is based on understanding how internal mental frameworks and communication patterns influence behaviour and business success. Techniques like anchoring, modelling, and future pacing are key to re-energizing the entrepreneur and team.

- **Quantum Leadership Approach**: Views the entrepreneur's challenges as symptoms of energetic misalignment with the field of potential. Quantum leadership focuses on creating **coherence**, aligning the entrepreneur and team with **universal energies** of abundance and innovation. It emphasizes **collective consciousness, shared vision, and**

non-linear growth, using practices like meditation, energy alignment, and intuitive leadership to create breakthroughs and success.

In the entrepreneurship sector, NLP provides practical tools for personal and team-level change, while quantum leadership taps into a deeper, more systemic transformation that aligns with **limitless possibilities** and **collective growth**. Both approaches offer powerful strategies depending on the context and goals of the entrepreneur.

Story 20. How NLP and Quantum leadership techniques can help you in defining effective strategies by reprograming your mind to address healthcare sector issues ?

Let's explore a real-life scenario in the healthcare sector and compare how it can be addressed using **Neuro-Linguistic Programming (NLP)** and **Quantum Leadership**.

Scenario: Burnout Among Healthcare Workers

A hospital is experiencing significant burnout among its healthcare workers. Nurses and doctors are reporting stress, exhaustion, and emotional fatigue due to long working hours, emotionally demanding work, and insufficient breaks. As a result, the quality of patient care is declining, and staff morale is low. The leadership team needs to address this problem urgently to ensure the well-being of the staff and the quality of patient care.

Addressing the Problem: NLP vs. Quantum Leadership

Aspect	NLP Approach	Quantum Leadership Approach
Understanding the Problem	**Focus on individual mental states and patterns**: NLP practitioners view burnout as a result of accumulated stress and negative mental patterns. The leader focuses on identifying the **internal representations** (how staff perceive their work, stress, and responsibilities) and uncovering limiting beliefs (e.g., "I must be perfect" or "I can't handle this pressure"). By understanding these patterns, the leader can help healthcare workers reframe their mindset and address their emotional exhaustion.	**Focus on the interconnected energy field and collective consciousness**: Quantum leadership views burnout not as an individual problem but as a symptom of a **misalignment** in the energy field of the organization. The stress, exhaustion, and emotional fatigue experienced by staff are seen as disruptions in the hospital's overall energy and coherence. The leader focuses on creating an environment where **collective well-being** is prioritized, and the flow of energy is harmonized throughout the organization.
Staff Well-Being and Resilience	**Anchoring positive emotional states**: The leader can use NLP techniques like **anchoring** to help staff regain control over their emotional states. By anchoring positive emotional experiences (e.g., times when they felt calm, in control, or successful) to specific physical gestures or words, staff members can access these states during stressful situations. For example, before starting a shift, staff can anchor feelings of relaxation and confidence to reset their mindset.	**Creating a resonant field of well-being**: Quantum leadership seeks to enhance the **collective emotional and energetic environment** of the hospital. The leader might encourage group meditations, mindfulness practices, or reflective pauses during shifts to create moments of collective **energy coherence**. By focusing on the **unified field of well-being**, the leader helps staff members align their energy and resilience with the collective goal of patient care. This creates a culture of emotional support, where everyone feels connected and supported.

Aspect	NLP Approach	Quantum Leadership Approach
Addressing Stress	**Reframing and perceptual shifts**: NLP helps individuals reframe their **internal dialogue** about stressful situations. The leader teaches staff to reframe negative thoughts, such as "I can't handle the pressure," into more empowering beliefs like "I am capable of handling this moment." Additionally, using **perceptual positions**, the leader encourages staff to step into the shoes of others (e.g., colleagues or patients) to gain new perspectives, reducing the personal burden and stress through empathy and understanding.	**Embracing uncertainty and flow**: In quantum leadership, stress is viewed as part of the **dynamic uncertainty** inherent in healthcare. The leader encourages staff to embrace **uncertainty** and stay present in the flow of each moment rather than resist it. By fostering **mindfulness and presence**, the leader helps staff navigate the complexities of healthcare without becoming overwhelmed. The focus is on staying aligned with the **bigger purpose** (patient care) and not getting lost in individual stressful moments.
Improving Patient Care	**Modelling excellence and changing behaviour patterns**: The leader applies **modelling** techniques from NLP, where staff are encouraged to observe and replicate the behaviour of high-performing colleagues who manage stress well and provide exceptional patient care. This allows the leader to identify **patterns of excellence** in the workplace and help others adopt these patterns. Additionally, by breaking negative behavioural patterns, such as reactive responses, staff can improve patient care through **calm, responsive communication**.	**Co-creating a healing environment**: Quantum leadership sees the hospital not only as a place where patient care happens but as a **collective healing environment** where both staff and patients contribute to the healing process. The leader facilitates a shift in collective consciousness, where staff see themselves as co-creators of a compassionate, healing energy field. This means focusing not only on physical care but also on the **energetic and emotional** environment. By aligning the team's intention toward healing and well-being, staff naturally provide better care, creating a ripple effect that benefits both patients and caregivers.

Aspect	NLP Approach	Quantum Leadership Approach
Reducing Burnout and Fatigue	**Break state and anchoring relaxation**: NLP techniques like **state breaks** help interrupt cycles of stress. The leader encourages staff to take **micro-breaks** where they use physical gestures or techniques to break the pattern of stress. Anchoring techniques can also be applied to relax during brief breaks. For example, a nurse can use an anchoring gesture (such as deep breathing or stretching) to instantly calm their mind and body between patient interactions.	**Energy management and collective resilience**: Quantum leadership addresses burnout by focusing on **energy management** rather than just time management. The leader encourages staff to manage their **personal and collective energy** consciously, using regular energy-balancing techniques (such as grounding exercises or energy alignment practices). Additionally, the leader fosters **collective resilience** by building a culture where staff support each other energetically, sharing moments of renewal and creating a **resilient, high-vibration workplace**.
Motivation and Engagement	**Future pacing and goal alignment**: In NLP, **future pacing** is used to motivate staff by helping them visualize a positive future where they feel engaged, empowered, and fulfilled in their work. The leader encourages staff to set **positive, outcome-oriented goals** that resonate with their personal values and align with the hospital's mission. This forward-focused thinking re-energizes the staff and provides them with a clear sense of purpose.	**Collective visioning and shared purpose**: Quantum leadership taps into the collective energy of the hospital, where motivation and engagement come from the **shared vision** of healing and transformation. The leader regularly engages staff in **collective visioning exercises**, where they co-create a future where the hospital is thriving, patient care is exemplary, and staff well-being is prioritized. This shared sense of purpose inspires motivation and engagement as staff feel connected to something larger than themselves.

Summary

- **NLP Approach**: Focuses on changing individual mental states, emotional responses, and behaviour patterns. Techniques like anchoring, reframing, and perceptual shifts help healthcare workers manage stress and burnout, improve communication, and increase motivation. NLP is grounded in understanding how people's internal representations influence their external behaviour.

- **Quantum Leadership Approach**: Takes a holistic, systemic view of the hospital environment, treating burnout and stress as disruptions in the collective energy field. It emphasizes coherence, energy alignment, and conscious co-creation, helping the healthcare team align with a shared purpose and vision. Quantum leadership encourages mindfulness, presence, and fostering a collective atmosphere of well-being and resilience.

In this healthcare scenario, NLP helps address individual stress and emotional states, while quantum leadership works on transforming the collective energy of the team, creating a supportive, harmonious environment that can enhance patient care and staff well-being. Both approaches provide valuable tools depending on the context and desired outcomes.

Story 21. Defining strategies combining NLP and Quantum leadership tool for issues in Education sector. Highlighting the differences.

Here's another real-life scenario in the education sector, comparing how it can be addressed using **Neuro-Linguistic Programming (NLP)** versus **Quantum Leadership**:

Scenario: Low Student Engagement and Motivation

A high school has been experiencing a significant drop in student engagement. Many students are disengaged during lessons, showing low motivation, poor performance, and minimal participation in class discussions. Teachers are frustrated, feeling that their efforts are not yielding the desired results. The school leader is tasked with addressing this issue, motivating students, and helping teachers reconnect with their passion for education.

Addressing the Problem: NLP vs. Quantum Leadership

Aspect	NLP Approach	Quantum Leadership Approach
Understanding the Problem	**Focus on individual mindsets and language patterns**: NLP practitioners would view the problem as being rooted in the individual beliefs, perceptions, and internal representations of both students and teachers. By observing students' behaviour, body language, and the language used in the classroom, the leader can identify limiting beliefs (e.g., "I'm not good enough" or "This is boring") and the negative language patterns that reinforce disengagement.	**Understanding the collective energy field**: Quantum leadership takes a broader view, looking at the school as a dynamic system of interconnected relationships and energies. The problem of student disengagement is seen as a symptom of a misaligned or fragmented collective consciousness in the school. Rather than focusing solely on individuals, the leader perceives the energy of the whole environment and how it affects motivation.

Aspect	NLP Approach	Quantum Leadership Approach
Teacher-Student Communication	**Rapport building and reframing**: The NLP approach focuses on improving the **communication patterns** between teachers and students. The leader can train teachers to build **rapport** with students by mirroring their body language, matching their communication styles, and using language that resonates with them. Additionally, **reframing** can help teachers and students view challenges as opportunities for growth (e.g., reframing failures as steps toward learning). This could involve shifting a negative conversation like "Math is too hard" to "Math helps us solve real-world problems."	**Creating coherence and alignment**: From a quantum perspective, the leader fosters **coherence** in the classroom, helping both teachers and students align with a shared vision of education. Instead of focusing on changing individual language or behavior, the leader works to create an environment where the **energy of learning** becomes contagious. They encourage mindfulness practices, group reflection sessions, or collective visioning to create a resonant atmosphere where engagement and passion naturally flow. The leader might ask, "What energy do we want to create together in this school?" and guide teachers and students in co-creating that shared intention.
Addressing Student Beliefs	**Changing limiting beliefs and anchoring positive states**: NLP techniques like **belief change patterns** help students shift from negative, disempowering beliefs to empowering ones. For instance, if students believe they are not capable of success, the leader might use a **sub modalities shift** exercise, where students visualize their success vividly, and then help them "anchor" those positive feelings. Anchoring could be applied in a way that students experience **confidence** whenever they face challenges.	**Embracing the field of infinite potential**: Quantum leadership operates on the understanding that each student has **limitless potential**, waiting to be unlocked. The leader encourages students to **expand their consciousness** and envision themselves as creators of their own learning experiences. Through activities like guided group meditations or reflective journaling, students are encouraged to tap into their inner creativity and explore new possibilities for their education. The leader fosters a mindset of **abundance**, where students believe that their potential is not limited by past failures or current difficulties, but by what they collectively choose to create.

Aspect	NLP Approach	Quantum Leadership Approach
Teacher Motivation and Burnout	**Anchoring and perceptual positions**: The NLP approach also works well for teachers who are facing burnout or frustration. By using techniques like **anchoring**, teachers can reconnect to their original passion for teaching by associating it with specific stimuli (e.g., remembering the first successful class they taught and anchoring those feelings to a hand gesture). Additionally, using **perceptual positions**, the leader can guide teachers to see situations from multiple perspectives, including the viewpoint of their students and colleagues, to foster empathy and new insights into their teaching methods.	**Building collective awareness and intention**: Quantum leadership views burnout not as an individual issue, but as a result of disconnection from the **collective energy** of purpose and passion. The leader holds space for teachers to rediscover their **higher purpose** as educators by engaging in **collective visioning exercises** or deep reflective practices. Teachers are encouraged to tap into the energy of the school's collective mission, understanding that their individual well-being contributes to the school's overall vibrational energy. The focus is on **conscious co-creation**: the teachers and the leader co-create a nurturing, energizing learning space together.
Learning and Performance	**Setting outcomes and modelling excellence**: NLP emphasizes the importance of setting clear, achievable **outcomes**. The leader works with teachers and students to set specific learning goals that are framed in positive, outcome-oriented language. The leader also introduces the idea of **modelling excellence**, where students and teachers identify role models (either real or imagined) whose behaviours and attitudes they can replicate to achieve success. For example, a struggling student might model the behaviour of a high-performing classmate.	**Seeing learning as a quantum leap**: Quantum leadership sees learning as a **non-linear process**, where growth happens through leaps of understanding and breakthroughs in consciousness. Instead of focusing on gradual, step-by-step improvement, the leader encourages teachers and students to be open to sudden **quantum leaps** in learning. This could involve unconventional approaches, like cross-disciplinary learning, project-based inquiry, or experiential learning, where students are empowered to explore and co-create knowledge in new and expansive ways. The goal is to unlock **creative intelligence** and allow students to experience transformative, exponential growth.

Aspect	NLP Approach	Quantum Leadership Approach
Sustaining Long-Term Motivation	**Future pacing and visualizing success**: NLP encourages students to engage in **future pacing** exercises, where they imagine themselves succeeding in the future (graduating, excelling in college, or mastering a subject). By visualizing their future success, students create a **mental map** of what they want, which helps to guide their present actions. This reinforces motivation by making the desired outcomes seem real and achievable.	**Sustaining collective resonance and innovation**: In quantum leadership, long-term motivation is maintained by keeping the team connected to a constantly evolving vision of what's possible. The leader cultivates a learning culture where **innovation** is continuous, and where the group is always exploring new possibilities for growth. This culture of **innovation** helps students and teachers feel like they are part of something larger than themselves, tapping into the endless potential of learning.

Summary

- **NLP Approach**: Focuses on specific, practical techniques like reframing, anchoring, and rapport building to address individual behaviour, beliefs, and communication patterns. It targets the mental and emotional frameworks that drive motivation and engagement.

- **Quantum Leadership Approach**: Looks at the school environment as an interconnected whole, working with the collective energy, intention, and consciousness of the students and teachers. It emphasizes coherence, alignment, and the power of collective potential to transform engagement and learning.

In the education sector, NLP tends to address individual cognitive and behavioural changes, while quantum leadership fosters a shift in collective energy and systemic transformation. Both approaches offer valuable tools for motivating and engaging students and teachers.

Story 22. How industry aspirant will define effective strategy to crack interview and ground discussion using NLP, Mindfulness, Quantum Leadership tools

efining an Effective Strategy to Crack Interviews and Ground Discussions Using NLP, Mindfulness, and Quantum Leadership Tools

For an industry aspirant preparing to crack interviews and ground discussions, blending **NLP**, **Mindfulness**, and **Quantum Leadership** can provide a powerful framework to not only prepare mentally but also project confidence, clarity, and authenticity. Here's how each tool can be leveraged to form a strategy:

1. **Neuro-Linguistic Programming (NLP): Mastering Communication, Confidence, and Influence**

   NLP can be used to optimize mindset, communication skills, and emotional state to succeed in interviews.

NLP Technique	Application for Interviews
Anchoring	Anchor positive emotional states (like confidence, calmness, and focus) using physical cues. For example, you can associate a calm feeling with a specific gesture (like touching your thumb and forefinger together) to trigger a relaxed and confident state when facing tough questions.
Reframing	Reframe anxiety about failure into excitement about learning. Shift your perspective from "What if I mess up?" to "What can I learn from this opportunity, regardless of the outcome?" This helps reduce pressure.
Rapport Building	Use **mirroring** and **matching** techniques to build rapport with the interviewer. This means subtly aligning your body language, tone of voice, and language patterns with theirs to create a subconscious connection.

NLP Technique	Application for Interviews
Visualization	Practice **future pacing**, where you visualize the interview going well, answering questions with confidence, and seeing the interviewer respond positively. Visualizing success makes the brain more familiar with it, increasing actual success in the real scenario.
Chunking Down	Break complex questions or challenges into smaller, more manageable parts. If you face a difficult question, mentally break it down and answer one part at a time, ensuring a structured and confident response.
Perceptual Positions	Use this technique to gain different perspectives. Think from three positions: 1) your perspective, 2) the interviewer's perspective, and 3) an objective observer's perspective. This allows you to prepare better by understanding what the interviewer is likely looking for.

NLP Strategy for Interviews:

- **Before the interview**: Practice anchoring positive emotions, use visualization to mentally rehearse the interview, and reframe any limiting beliefs.

- **During the interview**: Use rapport-building techniques, manage emotional state with anchoring, and chunk down complex questions.

- **Post-interview reflection**: Use perceptual positions to evaluate how the interview went from multiple viewpoints and learn for future discussions.

2. **Mindfulness: Cultivating Presence, Calm, and Clarity**

Mindfulness is about staying fully present, grounded, and centered in the moment, which is crucial during interviews.

Mindfulness Technique	Application for Interviews
Breath Awareness	Use deep, mindful breathing before and during the interview to stay calm and grounded. This prevents anxiety from overwhelming you and helps regulate your nervous system.
Body Scan	Practice a quick body scan before the interview to release any tension or nervous energy, allowing you to walk into the room with relaxed confidence.
Non-Judgmental Awareness	Adopt a mindset of non-judgmental awareness. During the interview, if you make a mistake, don't let it derail you. Acknowledge it without judgment and bring your focus back to the next question.
Present Moment Focus	Stay fully present with each question instead of worrying about future questions or overanalysing past answers. By being fully engaged with what is being asked, you can respond thoughtfully and authentically.
Compassion for Self	Cultivate self-compassion to manage pressure. Instead of being harsh on yourself for any perceived mistakes, acknowledge your effort and stay positive. This helps maintain inner calm throughout the interview process.

Mindfulness Strategy for Interviews:

- **Before the interview**: Practice mindful breathing and body scanning to release stress and centre your energy.

- **During the interview**: Stay present and engaged with each question, using breath awareness to calm any nerves.

- **After the interview**: Practice non-judgmental awareness to reflect calmly on the interview experience and learn from it, rather than getting bogged down in self-criticism.

3. **Quantum Leadership: Aligning Energy, Intuition, and Authenticity**

Quantum Leadership encourages you to approach the interview from a state of alignment with your **authentic self** and a higher **energetic coherence**. It integrates intuitive insight and holistic thinking.

Quantum Leadership Technique	Application for Interviews
Energetic Alignment	Align your energy with your higher purpose before the interview. Ask yourself, "What value do I bring to this role?" and connect with the deeper reason why you're pursuing this opportunity. This creates a strong, authentic presence that interviewers can sense.
Intuition and Inner Knowing	Tune into your intuition during the interview process. Often, you'll know the right way to answer a question or the best way to handle a situation by trusting your gut feeling rather than overthinking.
Consciousness Expansion	See the interview as more than just a linear, question-and-answer process. Think of it as an opportunity to **expand consciousness**, where you and the interviewer exchange ideas, values, and energy. This shifts the perspective from performance anxiety to **co-creation** of possibilities.
Vibrational State Management	Focus on maintaining a **high vibrational state**. Engage in practices like **meditation** or **visualization** before the interview to raise your energy frequency, making you feel more empowered and connected to your authentic self. This state attracts positive outcomes and creates a magnetic presence during the interview.

Quantum Leadership Technique	Application for Interviews
Quantum Thinking	Think holistically about the interview process. Rather than seeing it as just a test of knowledge or skills, view it as an **energetic exchange** where you showcase not only what you know but who you are. Be open to seeing possibilities that may not be immediately obvious and trust the flow of the conversation.

Quantum Leadership Strategy for Interviews:

- **Before the interview**: Align your energy with your purpose, meditate to raise your vibrational state, and connect with your intuition to stay grounded in authenticity.

- **During the interview**: Stay aligned with your purpose and be open to the flow of energy between you and the interviewer. Trust your intuition to guide you in answering questions confidently.

- **After the interview**: Reflect on the energetic exchange and how you contributed to the conversation, regardless of the immediate outcome.

Integration of NLP, Mindfulness, and Quantum Leadership

By combining these three tools, you can develop a **holistic strategy** for cracking interviews and ground discussions that goes beyond traditional preparation methods.

Step-by-Step Strategy:

1. **Pre-Interview Preparation**:

   - **NLP**: Visualize the interview, anchor positive emotions, and rehearse key responses.

- **Mindfulness**: Practice mindful breathing and body scanning to stay calm.

- **Quantum Leadership**: Meditate on your purpose, align your energy with your goals, and set a high vibrational state.

2. **During the Interview**:

- **NLP**: Build rapport through mirroring, reframe difficult questions, and manage emotions with anchoring.

- **Mindfulness**: Stay present with each question and engage deeply in the conversation.

- **Quantum Leadership**: Trust your intuition and view the interview as an energetic exchange, not just a test.

3. **Post-Interview Reflection**:

- **NLP**: Use perceptual positions to evaluate how it went and identify improvements.

- **Mindfulness**: Practice non-judgmental awareness to avoid harsh self-criticism.

- **Quantum Leadership**: Reflect on how well you aligned with your authentic self and stayed in flow.

By mastering these tools, the industry aspirant becomes **mentally resilient, emotionally intelligent, and energetically aligned**, making them a strong contender for any role they seek. This comprehensive approach ensures that they **stand out** not just for their skills but for their **presence, confidence, and authenticity** in any interview or discussion.

Chapter 14

Financial Sustainability & Wealth Creation

Successful people with rich mindset has got different belief and perception about money. They care about money, invest money and focus on optimization of expenses such that for them money grows automatically for them while they are not working or rather sleeping. They keep on creating wealth such that their financial sustainability becomes stronger over the period of time.

The interesting object is, money requires to keep you fit and healthy. Money requires for your skill development. Money is the fuel for your success. Money helps for your business which brings success and success also helps your money growing. So Devi Laxmi is the integral part of our life. We need to get rid of all of the old negative emotions regarding money and need to get associated with money, start living with abundant flow of money such that law of attraction will expand our mental richness.

Since money makes money growing and people will only pay you when with your unique contribution you start adding value to their life in problem solving or quality enhancement, it is important to wisely select / adjust your domain of operation ensuring you grow financially. Have financial expert working with you to make your wealth build up in a consolidated way and start your passive income and necessary insurance which will provide security and safety in your life and family for long term benefit.

Achieving financial sustainability and creating consolidated wealth involves strategic planning, disciplined financial management, and wise investment decisions. Here are examples across different scenarios that illustrate how individuals and organizations can attain these goals:

Example 1: Personal Financial Sustainability

Background: Emily, a young professional, aims to achieve financial sustainability to ensure a secure future while building wealth.

1. **Budgeting and Saving:**

   - Emily creates a detailed budget that outlines her monthly income and expenses. By tracking her spending, she identifies areas where she can cut back, such as dining out and subscription services.

   - She allocates a portion of her income to an emergency fund and retirement savings. Emily sets a goal to save at least 20% of her monthly income, ensuring she has a safety net for unforeseen circumstances.

2. **Investing Wisely:**

   - With her savings, Emily explores investment options that align with her risk tolerance and financial goals. She starts by investing in low-cost index funds and considers opening a tax-advantaged retirement account (like a 401(k) or IRA).

   - Emily also educates herself about compound interest and the importance of starting early, leading her to appreciate the long-term benefits of consistent investing.

3. **Generating Passive Income:**

   - To further enhance her financial sustainability, Emily begins exploring passive income streams. She decides to invest in rental property, leveraging her savings for a down payment.

   - By carefully selecting a property in a desirable location and managing it effectively, Emily generates consistent rental income that contributes to her overall wealth.

Outcome:

By following disciplined budgeting, investing wisely, and creating passive income, Emily achieves financial sustainability. Over time, her investments grow, her emergency fund provides peace of mind, and her rental property adds to her wealth, allowing her to pursue her passions without financial stress.

Example 2: Small Business Financial Sustainability

Background: Jake runs a small coffee shop and wants to ensure its financial sustainability while creating consolidated wealth for future growth.

1. **Cost Management:**

   - Jake analyses his business expenses and identifies areas to reduce costs without compromising quality. He renegotiates supplier contracts and implements inventory management practices to minimize waste.

   - By controlling costs, Jake increases his profit margins, allowing more funds to be reinvested into the business.

2. **Diversifying Revenue Streams:**

   - To achieve greater financial sustainability, Jake diversifies his offerings by adding catering services and selling branded merchandise. This diversification attracts new customers and generates additional revenue.

   - He also considers hosting events and workshops, further expanding his customer base and creating community engagement.

3. **Strategic Investments:**

   - With the increased revenue, Jake invests in upgrading equipment for efficiency and enhancing the customer experience. He also allocates funds for marketing efforts, using social media to reach a broader audience.

- By reinvesting profits strategically, Jake positions his coffee shop for growth and consolidation in the local market.

Outcome:

Through careful cost management, revenue diversification, and strategic investments, Jake achieves financial sustainability for his coffee shop. The business thrives, allowing Jake to consolidate wealth, explore new opportunities, and potentially open additional locations.

Example 3: Corporate Financial Sustainability

Background: A medium-sized technology firm, TechInnovate, seeks to enhance its financial sustainability and create consolidated wealth for its shareholders.

1. **Sustainable Business Practices:**

   - TechInnovate adopts sustainable business practices, such as reducing energy consumption and minimizing waste. These practices lower operational costs and enhance the company's brand reputation.

   - The firm invests in sustainable technologies that improve efficiency and attract environmentally conscious clients, increasing revenue potential.

2. **Financial Planning and Analysis:**

   - The finance team conducts thorough financial planning and analysis to forecast revenue, expenses, and cash flow. By using data-driven insights, TechInnovate can make informed decisions about investments and resource allocation.

   - The company sets clear financial targets and regularly reviews performance against these targets to ensure financial health.

3. **Shareholder Engagement:**

   - TechInnovate prioritizes transparent communication with shareholders about its financial performance and long-term strategy. By engaging with stakeholders, the company builds trust and loyalty, leading to increased investment and support.

- They offer regular dividends to shareholders as a reward for their investment, creating a sense of shared success and incentivizing long-term holding.

Outcome:

By integrating sustainable practices, conducting thorough financial planning, and engaging shareholders, TechInnovate achieves financial sustainability and creates consolidated wealth. The company experiences steady growth, increasing its market share and establishing itself as a leader in the tech industry.

Conclusion

Achieving financial sustainability and creating consolidated wealth requires strategic planning and disciplined financial management, whether at a personal level, in small businesses, or within large corporations. The examples of Emily, Jake, and TechInnovate demonstrate that by prioritizing budgeting, diversifying revenue streams, investing wisely, and maintaining transparent communication, individuals and organizations can establish a strong financial foundation for long-term success.

The journey to **financial sustainability and wealth creation** involves cultivating a **rich mindset**, which focuses on long-term growth, smart investments, and a disciplined approach to managing money. This mindset, unlike a scarcity mindset, sees money as a tool for creating opportunities rather than something to be feared or hoarded. Below is an explanation of the hidden secrets of a rich mindset, using an example to show how it can lead to wealth creation.

Key Secrets of a Rich Mindset:

1. **Focus on Assets Over Income**

2. **Invest for the Long Term**

3. **Discipline in Spending and Saving**

4. **Create Multiple Streams of Income**

5. **Leverage Opportunities and Networks**

6. **Continuous Learning and Growth**

Let's break each of these down with a detailed story example.

Example: Sarah's Journey from Financial Struggle to Wealth Creation

Sarah started her career as a graphic designer, earning a modest salary. Like many people, she found herself living paycheck to paycheck, barely able to save anything at the end of each month. While she was diligent in her work, her focus was on increasing her income, thinking that earning more would eventually solve her financial problems. However, despite raises and freelance gigs, she still struggled to build wealth.

One day, Sarah came across a financial mentor who introduced her to the **rich mindset**, explaining that wealth is not built by just earning more money but by how you manage, invest, and multiply what you earn. This opened Sarah's eyes to a new way of thinking about money.

1. **Focus on Assets Over Income**

   - **Secret**: People with a rich mindset prioritize buying assets that generate income over focusing solely on increasing their salary.

Shift in Sarah's Thinking:

Instead of only thinking about how much she earns, Sarah learned to focus on building assets—things that put money in her pocket over time, such as investments, real estate, or businesses. She started small by setting aside a portion of her income every month to invest in stocks and mutual funds.

Example:

Sarah invested in a low-cost index fund. Although it was a small amount initially, the power of compound interest started working in her favor. Over the next few years, her investments grew, and the dividends she earned were reinvested, creating a snowball effect. Her focus shifted from trying to make more money at her job to building wealth through smart investments.

2. **Invest for the Long Term**

   - **Secret**: Wealthy individuals think long-term and make decisions that will benefit them years or even decades down the line. They don't look for quick wins; instead, they focus on sustainable growth.

Shift in Sarah's Thinking:

Sarah understood the importance of delayed gratification. Instead of spending money on instant luxuries like a new car or vacations, she opted to invest in opportunities that would yield greater returns in the future.

Example:

Sarah researched real estate and bought a small rental property using her savings and a loan. The rental income helped cover the mortgage payments, and over time, the property's value appreciated. While it didn't make her rich overnight, her patience paid off as her real estate investment grew in value and provided a steady passive income.

3. **Discipline in Spending and Saving**

   - **Secret**: The rich mindset emphasizes financial discipline—spending less than you earn, avoiding unnecessary debt, and consistently saving a portion of your income.

Shift in Sarah's Thinking:

Sarah became much more intentional with her spending. She created a budget that prioritized her savings and investments over lifestyle inflation. Every time she received extra income, whether through a raise or a freelance gig, she saved and invested most of it.

Example:

Instead of upgrading her lifestyle every time she earned more money, Sarah continued to live below her means. She avoided lifestyle creep and focused on funneling extra income into her savings and investments. Over time, these small sacrifices helped her build a significant financial cushion.

4. **Create Multiple Streams of Income**

   - **Secret**: The wealthy don't rely on a single source of income. They diversify their income streams through investments, side businesses, or passive income sources.

Shift in Sarah's Thinking:

Sarah realized the importance of diversifying her income streams. While her graphic design job was her primary income, she started working on a side project—designing and selling digital products online. This opened up a new stream of income for her.

Example:

Sarah created digital assets like design templates, which she sold on platforms like Etsy and Creative Market. Once she uploaded the products, they continued to generate passive income without much additional effort. Soon, she was earning extra income each month, which she reinvested in her stock portfolio and real estate.

5. **Leverage Opportunities and Networks**

   - **Secret**: Wealthy individuals often leverage their networks and opportunities. They understand the value of collaboration and know that the right connections can lead to great financial gains.

Shift in Sarah's Thinking:

Sarah started networking with other entrepreneurs and investors in her community. By surrounding herself with like-minded people, she gained valuable insights, advice, and even investment opportunities that she wouldn't have encountered otherwise.

Example:

Through her network, Sarah was introduced to a partnership opportunity with a startup that needed design work. Instead of charging her usual fee, she negotiated equity in the company. As the startup grew, her equity stake increased in value, providing her with an additional wealth-building asset.

6. **Continuous Learning and Growth**

   - **Secret**: A rich mindset requires constant learning. Wealthy people stay informed, read about finance and investments, and are open to new strategies for wealth creation.

Shift in Sarah's Thinking:

Sarah committed to continuously educating herself about personal finance, investing, and wealth-building strategies. She read books on financial independence, took online courses, and sought mentorship from successful investors.

Example:

Through her learning, Sarah discovered new investment opportunities, such as peer-to-peer lending and cryptocurrency, and diversified her portfolio further. This constant learning allowed her to stay ahead of financial trends and make informed decisions.

Conclusion:

Sarah's journey from financial struggle to wealth creation is a testament to the power of adopting a **rich mindset**. By focusing on building assets, practicing financial discipline, creating multiple income streams, and investing in long-term opportunities, she transformed her financial situation. The key secrets to her success included:

- Focusing on **assets over income**.
- Investing for the **long term**.
- Practicing **financial discipline**.
- Creating **multiple streams of income**.
- **Leveraging networks** and opportunities.
- Committing to **continuous learning**.

The rich mindset is not about making money quickly—it's about nurturing wealth steadily over time through smart decisions, patience, and consistent effort. **Wealth is a result of how you think about and manage money**, not just how much you earn.

By following this mindset, anyone can work towards financial sustainability and wealth creation, regardless of their starting point.

Dos	Don'ts
Create a Budget	**Neglect Budgeting**
Regularly track income and expenses to understand your financial situation.	Avoid tracking expenses, leading to overspending.
Save Consistently	**Live Pay check to Pay check**
Set aside a percentage of your income for savings each month.	Spend all your income without saving for emergencies.
Invest Wisely	**Avoid Investing**
Research and invest in assets that can grow over time, such as stocks or mutual funds.	Keep all your money in low-interest accounts or cash.
Diversify Income Streams	**Rely on a Single Source of Income**
Explore side hustles or passive income opportunities to reduce risk.	Depend solely on one job or income source.

Dos	Don'ts
Educate Yourself About Finances	**Ignore Financial Education**
Continuously learn about personal finance, investing, and market trends.	Remain uninformed about financial matters.
Review and Adjust Financial Goals Regularly	**Set It and Forget It**
Regularly assess and adjust your financial goals based on changing circumstances.	Ignore your financial goals after setting them.
Seek Professional Advice When Needed	**Avoid Asking for Help**
Consult financial advisors for personalized guidance.	Hesitate to seek help, leading to poor financial decisions.
Maintain an Emergency Fund	**Ignore Emergency Savings**
Build and maintain a fund to cover unexpected expenses.	Rely on credit cards or loans for emergencies.
Practice Frugality	**Overspend on Non-Essentials**
Make informed decisions on spending and prioritize needs over wants.	Indulge in unnecessary expenses without consideration.

This table outlines key practices to follow and pitfalls to avoid on the path to achieving good financial sustainability.

Law of attraction and relevant matured, focused, mindful action creates magic:

The **Law of Attraction**, when paired with **conscious, mature action**, can create powerful transformations in people's lives, whether they are starting from a place of financial struggle or already have wealth. Here's a unique story that highlights how the **right mindset** and **deliberate actions** can help poor people become wealthy, and how wealthy individuals can achieve even greater success.

A Tale of Two Paths: From Poverty to Wealth and from Wealth to Greater Riches

Part 1: The Journey from Poverty to Wealth

Meet Maria, a single mother living in a small, impoverished village. She worked long hours as a seamstress, barely making enough to support her children. Despite her difficult circumstances, Maria believed there had to be more to life than just surviving. She had heard about the **Law of Attraction** but had always been sceptical. One day, a friend introduced her to the concept more deeply, explaining how it wasn't just about "wishful thinking" but about **aligning thoughts with actions**.

Maria decided to take control of her mindset. She started by writing down her **financial goals**: she wanted to build a sustainable clothing business that would allow her to support her family comfortably. Instead of focusing on what she lacked, Maria shifted her thoughts to what she **desired**: a thriving business, financial freedom, and the ability to provide for her children without worry.

She began practicing **visualization** every morning. Maria would close her eyes and **imagine herself running a successful business**, seeing herself confidently meeting clients, making sales, and managing a growing enterprise. She didn't just visualize money but pictured the **emotions** that came with her success: the relief of no longer worrying about rent, the joy of sending her children to good schools, and the pride in building something meaningful.

However, Maria knew that **visualization alone** would not transform her life. Inspired by her vision, she **took deliberate, mature action**:

- **Learning New Skills**: Maria invested her limited free time in learning new sewing techniques and business skills. She watched free online tutorials and read books about entrepreneurship. By improving her craft, she could offer higher-quality products.

- **Expanding Her Network**: She began networking with other local business owners, finding out where she could source cheaper yet higher-quality materials. She also reached out to a nearby city's market vendors to see if they could stock her clothing.

- **Setting Small, Achievable Goals**: Rather than feeling overwhelmed by the idea of becoming wealthy, Maria broke her vision into smaller, actionable steps. Her first goal was to double her income in six months. She worked tirelessly, but with **purpose** and **focus** on this tangible outcome.

Within a year, Maria's efforts paid off. She started attracting more clients, and her income doubled as planned. Her mindset of **abundance** and **possibility** helped her spot opportunities she would have missed when she was focused on scarcity. Eventually, Maria's clothing line gained popularity beyond her village, and she opened her own small shop in the city.

As she continued to **believe in her vision**, visualize her success, and pair those thoughts with **consistent, conscious action**, Maria's business grew into a local success story. She not only lifted herself and her children out of poverty but began employing other women from her village, helping them also achieve financial independence.

Part 2: From Wealth to Greater Riches

On the other side of the story is **David**, a successful tech entrepreneur who already enjoyed financial wealth. However, David had plateaued in his career. He had built a solid business, but growth had slowed, and he felt like he was stuck. While David was already wealthy, he had an inner desire to make a **bigger impact**, create new wealth, and innovate beyond his current business model.

David, like Maria, was familiar with the **Law of Attraction**, but his mindset had started to shift toward **complacency**. He had achieved comfort, and his thoughts began to revolve around maintaining what he had rather than expanding his horizons.

One evening, while attending a leadership retreat, David was reminded of the **power of the mind** and how his **thought patterns** directly influenced his reality. He realized that while his earlier success was driven by a hunger for innovation and growth, his current thinking was holding him back from new possibilities. He committed to **reframing his mindset**.

David began to visualize **new opportunities** for his business, focusing on **expansion, innovation, and impact**. He imagined:

- His company being at the forefront of new technological breakthroughs.

- Expanding globally into untapped markets.

- Partnering with other visionary leaders to create products that transformed industries.

But visualization wasn't enough. David knew he had to take **mature, conscious action** to bring these new ideas to life.

- **Reinvesting in Innovation**: David reallocated a significant portion of his profits into research and development, something he had hesitated to do for years out of fear of risk. This bold move allowed his company to start developing cutting-edge technology that set them apart from competitors.

- **Creating a Visionary Team**: He began recruiting **forward-thinking individuals** who were passionate about innovation and weren't afraid to challenge the status quo. Surrounding himself with a more dynamic and creative team reignited his own passion for growth.

- **Entering New Markets**: David expanded his company's reach by exploring **international markets** that were underserved in his industry. This required a great deal of learning and adaptation, but he embraced the challenge.

As a result of these conscious actions, David's company not only recovered from its stagnation but went on to achieve **unprecedented success**. His new innovations disrupted the tech industry, attracting partnerships, media attention, and ultimately, enormous profits. David was no longer just maintaining his wealth—he was expanding it exponentially.

Key Lessons from the Story: Law of Attraction + Conscious Action

1. **The Power of Belief and Mindset**:

   - Both Maria and David started their journeys by changing their **mindsets**. Maria shifted from a focus on scarcity to a focus on **possibility**, while David moved from complacency to **expansion**. The **Law of Attraction** begins with believing that **abundance is possible**, regardless of your starting point. When you **envision success**, you start aligning your thoughts and emotions with that future reality, drawing opportunities into your life.

2. **Visualization Paired with Action**:

   - Visualization alone isn't enough to create lasting change. Maria and David both **took deliberate actions** based on their vision. Maria learned new skills and networked, while David reinvested in innovation and expanded into new markets. **Mature action** bridges the gap between imagination and reality.

3. **Consistency and Patience**:

   - Transformation doesn't happen overnight. Maria's journey out of poverty took time, just as David's move from stagnation to greater success required consistent effort. The **Law of Attraction** works best when paired with **persistent, conscious actions** that align with long-term goals.

4. **Mindful Awareness and Adaptation**:

   - Both characters remained **mindfully aware** of their environment and opportunities. Maria recognized that staying focused on scarcity would keep her stuck, while David realized his complacency was limiting his potential. In both cases, the ability to **self-reflect** and adapt their strategies was key to their transformation.

Conclusion: A Mindset of Abundance with Conscious Action

The **Law of Attraction** teaches us that our **thoughts create our reality**, but for that reality to take shape, we must follow up with **conscious, mature action**. Whether you're coming from a place of financial struggle or you're already wealthy but seeking greater heights, success begins in the mind. **Belief**, paired with **strategic action**, can lead to remarkable transformations, helping poor people rise to wealth and wealthy people achieve even greater success. Both paths require a commitment to **personal growth**, **learning**, and **taking bold steps** outside of comfort zones.

Transformation is possible for anyone who is willing to believe in their vision and take deliberate steps toward that future.

Chapter 15

Digital transformation and Cyber Psychology

In your personal and professional growth, growing with technological advancement is the only way. AI, Automation. Robotics, Virtual Reality, Metaverse. IoT will bring huge difference in way of working in human life. You need to adapt the technology fast in your work front to stay relevant with positive mindset fearlessly and you need to invest on your learning development wisely to uplift your technological skill set. You need to make sure your knowledge should always better than knowledge of your customer otherwise blackhole will make you in a position where you will start losing your customers sadly. Always try to be integral part of your customer's technology enabler to keep growing tother.

This is how human intelligence, and artificial intelligence can be complementary to each other for success. It is the mind game; you always have a choice to become fearful of losing job or quickly adapt the technology to use effectively for your growth. Couple of real-life examples that can be referenced:

Example 1: Human Intelligence and AI in Personal Growth:

Background: James is a freelance graphic designer who wants to improve his skills and manage his workload more efficiently. He decides to use artificial intelligence tools to help streamline his personal and professional tasks while focusing on creative growth.

How Human Intelligence and AI Complement Each Other for Personal Success:

1. **AI for Efficiency, Human Intelligence for Creativity:**

   - **AI Automation Tools:**

     - James uses AI-powered design tools like **Canva's Magic Design** or **Adobe Sensei** to automate repetitive tasks such as resizing images, enhancing photo quality, or creating basic templates.

     - These AI tools allow him to spend less time on technical details and more time on creative, conceptual design work, where his human intelligence and intuition shine.

   - **Human Creativity:**

     - While AI helps with efficiency, it is James' creative vision, understanding of aesthetics, and ability to empathize with his clients' needs that set him apart. He creates unique designs, customized logos, and branding that reflect a client's identity—something AI can assist with but cannot fully conceptualize.

2. **AI for Learning, Human Intelligence for Adaptation:**

   - **AI-Assisted Learning Platforms:**

     - James uses **AI-driven learning platforms** like **Skillshare** or **Udemy** that personalize course recommendations based on his past learning behaviour. These platforms help him quickly learn new design trends, software techniques, and industry best practices.

   - **Human Adaptation:**

     - James applies this knowledge by adapting it to real-world client projects. While AI helps him gain knowledge efficiently, it is his ability to adapt and apply these skills creatively and contextually in different projects that helps him succeed.

Outcome:

James becomes a more efficient and well-rounded designer by combining AI's ability to automate tasks and accelerate learning with his human creative thinking and adaptability. He can deliver better-quality designs to clients faster, improving his professional reputation and allowing him to pursue personal projects.

Example 2: Human Intelligence and AI in a Professional Environment:

Background: Maria is a project manager at a large consulting firm. She oversees multiple projects simultaneously and is responsible for delivering them on time and within budget. She decides to integrate AI into her project management workflow to improve decision-making and resource management.

How Human Intelligence and AI Complement Each Other for Professional Success:

1. **AI for Data-Driven Insights, Human Intelligence for Decision-Making:**

   - **AI for Predictive Analytics:**

     - Maria uses AI-powered project management tools like **Monday.com** or **Trello** with **AI-driven analytics** to analyse project timelines, resource allocation, and potential risks. The AI identifies patterns in project data and predicts delays or bottlenecks, allowing Maria to act proactively.

   - **Human Intelligence for Strategic Decisions:**

     - While the AI provides valuable insights and predictions, it is Maria's human intelligence—her understanding of her team's dynamics, client relationships, and strategic objectives—that informs her final decisions. She uses AI data as a guide but makes judgment calls based on her experience and intuition.

2. **AI for Routine Task Management, Human Intelligence for Team Leadership:**

   - **AI for Automating Routine Tasks:**

     - Maria uses AI-powered chatbots and workflow automation tools like **Slackbots** or **Zapier** to automate routine tasks such as scheduling meetings, sending project reminders, and tracking task completion. This reduces her administrative workload.

   - **Human Leadership for Motivation and Teamwork:**

     - By offloading routine tasks to AI, Maria has more time to focus on leading her team, motivating them, and resolving interpersonal conflicts—areas where emotional intelligence and leadership skills are crucial. AI handles the mechanics, but Maria ensures team cohesion and morale remain high.

3. **AI for Risk Mitigation, Human Intelligence for Creativity and Flexibility:**

   - **AI for Risk Management:**

     - Maria uses **AI-driven risk management tools** to identify potential project risks, such as budget overruns or missed deadlines, by analyzing historical data and current project conditions. The AI flags high-risk areas early, enabling her to take corrective action.

   - **Human Intelligence for Creativity and Problem-Solving:**

     - When the AI identifies a risk, it is up to Maria to think creatively and come up with flexible solutions. For example, if AI predicts a delay in project delivery, Maria might reorganize resources or come up with alternative workarounds that AI algorithms cannot generate on their own.

Outcome:

Maria's use of AI in project management enables her to handle larger, more complex projects with higher accuracy and efficiency. AI takes care of data processing and task automation, while Maria uses her human intelligence to make strategic decisions, lead her team effectively, and creatively solve problems. This complementary relationship helps her deliver successful projects, gain client trust, and build her reputation as a highly effective project manager.

Example 3: Human Intelligence and AI in Business Decision-Making for Entrepreneurs:

Background: Anil is the founder of a startup that specializes in sustainable consumer goods. As an entrepreneur, he needs to make strategic business decisions, from marketing to product development, while keeping his budget in check. He integrates AI to help him gain insights into the market, manage his operations, and grow his business efficiently.

How Human Intelligence and AI Complement Each Other for Business Success:

1. **AI for Market Analysis, Human Intelligence for Strategic Business Vision:**

   - **AI for Consumer Insights:**

     - Anil uses AI tools like **Google Analytics** and **AI-powered CRM systems** to analyse consumer behaviour and market trends. These tools provide him with insights into what products are most popular, customer preferences, and where his business could expand.

   - **Human Business Vision:**

     - While AI helps Anil identify opportunities, it is his business vision that defines the company's direction. He uses these insights to make strategic decisions about which products to develop and where to focus his marketing efforts, considering the broader picture of his company's goals.

2. **AI for Automating Operations, Human Intelligence for Innovation:**

- **AI for Supply Chain and Inventory Management:**

  - Anil implements AI-based supply chain management software that predicts demand and optimizes inventory levels. The AI ensures that his stock meets customer demand without over- or under-ordering products.

- **Human Innovation:**

  - While AI optimizes operations, Anil focuses on innovating his product line, testing new eco-friendly materials, and designing products that stand out in the market. AI helps his business run smoothly, while his human creativity drives innovation and product differentiation.

Outcome:

Anil's use of AI allows him to focus on strategic growth and product innovation while automating the more operational aspects of his business. The combination of AI for efficiency and human intelligence for vision and creativity ensures his startup is both agile and competitive in the market, resulting in steady growth and customer satisfaction.

One area of concern, you need to focus on. As technologies are evolving fast, hackers are becoming smarter, and they are creating organized strategy to get financial gain with their skill. You need to be aware of the vulnerabilities and stay secure by matured action. Every device should be updated and unnecessary clicking on unknown URL or attachment (document) will help to stay away from Phishing or ransomware attacks. Remember you are smart human being, smarter than your smart device, you need to operate and act wisely to get technological advancement rather than becoming victim of cyber-attack.

Since all business are on Internet platform and online presence is no more optional, Cyber Psychology truly add value in your success for business growth. You need to learn a quick how to and define your cyber strategy to stay secure and performing excellent online business with the domain knowledge.

Mark's Journey to Success through Cyber Psychology

Background: Mark, a recent college graduate, started his career as a digital marketing specialist at a tech startup. He quickly realized that understanding consumer behaviour online was critical to his success in the competitive landscape. To gain a deeper insight into how people interact with technology, Mark decided to explore the field of cyber psychology.

The Role of Cyber Psychology in Mark's Success

1. **Understanding User Behaviour:**

   - Mark utilized principles of cyber psychology to analyse how users interacted with his company's website and social media platforms. By studying user engagement metrics, he learned about patterns in user behaviour, such as peak activity times and content preferences.

   - He discovered that users were more engaged with visual content and short video clips rather than lengthy articles. This insight allowed him to recommend changes to the content strategy, leading to increased user engagement.

2. **Enhancing User Experience:**

   - By applying cyber psychological concepts, Mark recognized the importance of user experience (UX) design. He collaborated with the UX team to improve the website's navigation and layout, ensuring it was intuitive and visually appealing.

   - Understanding concepts like the "Hick-Hyman Law," which states that as the number of choices increases, the time taken to make a decision also increases, he advocated for simplifying navigation options. This led to a smoother user experience and reduced bounce rates on the website.

3. **Leveraging Social Proof:**

   - Mark learned about the concept of social proof, which suggests that people are influenced by the actions and opinions of others. He implemented strategies to showcase customer testimonials and reviews prominently on the website and social media platforms.

   - By highlighting positive feedback from existing customers, Mark effectively built trust and credibility, which significantly improved conversion rates. Potential customers felt more confident making a purchase decision, knowing that others had positive experiences.

4. **Effective Communication and Engagement:**

   - Understanding the psychological triggers that motivate users, Mark crafted targeted marketing campaigns that resonated with the audience's emotions. He utilized storytelling techniques to create relatable content that connected with users on a personal level.

   - By incorporating elements like urgency (limited-time offers) and exclusivity (special member discounts), he increased customer engagement and conversion rates. Mark's campaigns received positive feedback and drove significant sales growth.

5. **Analysing and Adapting Strategies:**

   - Mark used tools and analytics to monitor the effectiveness of his campaigns. By continually analysing user behaviour and feedback, he adapted his strategies in real time, ensuring that they remained relevant and effective.

   - When he noticed a decline in engagement with certain posts, he investigated further and adjusted the content to align with current trends and user interests.

Outcomes of Applying Cyber Psychology

1. **Increased Engagement and Sales:**

   - By applying cyber psychology principles, Mark's recommendations led to a substantial increase in website traffic and social media engagement. The company saw a 30% rise in online sales within six months.

   - Customers reported a more enjoyable shopping experience, citing the website's improved navigation and engaging content as reasons for their satisfaction.

2. **Career Advancement:**

   - Mark's understanding of cyber psychology set him apart from his peers. His ability to analyse consumer behaviour and implement effective marketing strategies caught the attention of his superiors.

   - Within a year, he was promoted to a senior digital marketing position, where he took on more responsibilities and led a team. His insights into user behaviour became a key asset for the company's marketing initiatives.

3. **Building a Positive Company Reputation:**

   - The successful implementation of cyber psychology strategies helped the startup build a strong brand presence and a positive reputation in the market. Satisfied customers became brand advocates, sharing their experiences with others and contributing to organic growth.

   - The company's increased visibility and customer satisfaction led to additional funding and opportunities for expansion.

Conclusion

Mark's journey illustrates how cyber psychology can significantly contribute to personal and professional success. By understanding user behaviour, enhancing user experience, leveraging social proof, and adapting strategies based on psychological principles, he was able to drive engagement, boost sales, and advance his career. This example highlights the value of integrating psychological insights into digital marketing and business strategies, demonstrating how cyber psychology can be a powerful tool for success in today's technology-driven landscape.

Sophie's E-Commerce Business and Cyber Psychology

Background: Sophie runs a successful e-commerce business that sells eco-friendly products. With the increasing number of cyber attacks targeting online businesses, she realized the importance of protecting her website and customer data. To enhance her security measures, Sophie decided to apply principles of cyber psychology to understand how to better protect her business and create a safe shopping environment for her customers.

How Cyber Psychology Helps in Cybersecurity

1. **Understanding User Behaviour:**

   - **Recognizing Phishing Vulnerabilities:**

     - Sophie studied common phishing techniques that cybercriminals use to exploit user behaviour, such as email scams and fake websites. By understanding how customers might fall prey to these tactics, she could develop strategies to educate them on recognizing and avoiding phishing attempts.

     - For example, Sophie created informative blog posts and videos that explained how to identify suspicious emails and the importance of checking website URLs before entering personal information.

2. **Designing User-Friendly Security Features:**

   - **Simplifying Password Management:**

     - Realizing that many users struggle with managing complex passwords, Sophie implemented a password manager recommendation on her website. This not only enhances security but also encourages customers to create stronger passwords.

- ○ She also added a password strength indicator during account creation, which guided users in creating secure passwords, reinforcing the importance of cybersecurity while making it user-friendly.

3. **Building Trust Through Transparency:**

- **Clear Communication of Security Measures:**

  - ○ Sophie understood that consumers are more likely to shop with businesses that demonstrate transparency regarding their security measures. She added a dedicated "Security" section on her website that explained how customer data is protected.

  - ○ This section included information on SSL certificates, data encryption, and privacy policies, which helped build trust with her customers. Users felt more secure knowing that their information was protected by robust security practices.

4. **Implementing Two-Factor Authentication (2FA):**

- **Encouraging Secure Login Practices:**

  - ○ To enhance security further, Sophie implemented two-factor authentication (2FA) for customer accounts. By requiring a second form of verification (like a code sent to their mobile devices), she significantly reduced the risk of unauthorized access.

  - ○ Sophie educated her customers about the importance of 2FA through email newsletters and social media, emphasizing how it protects their accounts from potential breaches.

5. **Creating a Safe Shopping Environment:**

- **Using Positive Reinforcement:**

  - ○ To encourage customers to report suspicious activity or potential security issues, Sophie employed a positive reinforcement strategy. She set up a reward system where customers who reported any fraudulent activity received discounts on future purchases.

- This not only incentivized customers to be vigilant but also created a collaborative approach to maintaining security, as customers felt empowered to contribute to the safety of the online shopping experience.

Outcomes of Applying Cyber Psychology

1. **Reduced Cybersecurity Incidents:**

   - By implementing educational initiatives and transparent communication, Sophie noticed a significant decrease in customer reports of phishing attempts and suspicious activity. Customers became more informed and vigilant about their online security.

   - The incorporation of 2FA led to a substantial reduction in unauthorized access attempts to customer accounts.

2. **Increased Customer Trust and Loyalty:**

   - Sophie's proactive approach to cybersecurity fostered trust among her customers. They appreciated the effort made to protect their data and felt more secure shopping on her site.

   - This trust translated into increased customer loyalty, with many customers returning for repeat purchases and recommending the store to friends and family.

3. **Positive Brand Reputation:**

   - By prioritizing cybersecurity and effectively communicating her efforts, Sophie established her business as a trusted brand in the eco-friendly product market. Positive reviews highlighted the secure shopping experience, further enhancing her reputation.

- The emphasis on security attracted new customers, as potential buyers were more likely to choose a brand that prioritized their safety.

Conclusion

Sophie's e-commerce business exemplifies how cyber psychology can be leveraged to enhance cybersecurity and create a secure online shopping environment. By understanding user behaviour, simplifying security features, fostering transparency, and encouraging proactive measures, she successfully protected her business from cyber-attacks while building customer trust and loyalty. This approach illustrates the vital role of cyber psychology in establishing a secure and thriving online business in today's digital landscape.

Common Situation	Behaviour with Cyber Psychological Awareness	Behaviour Without Knowledge of Cyber Psychology
Social Media Interaction	Engages thoughtfully, considering the emotional impact of posts.	Posts impulsively, often reacting emotionally without consideration.
Online Privacy Settings	Proactively manages privacy settings and understands risks.	Neglects privacy settings, exposing personal information.
Cyberbullying	Recognizes the signs of cyberbullying and intervenes appropriately.	Fails to identify or address bullying behaviors, potentially enabling them.
Digital Footprint Awareness	Considers the long-term effects of online actions and digital footprint.	Ignores the concept of a digital footprint, leading to careless online behaviour.
Information Sharing	Evaluates the reliability of information before sharing.	Shares information without verifying its source or accuracy.

Common Situation	Behaviour with Cyber Psychological Awareness	Behaviour Without Knowledge of Cyber Psychology
Emotional Regulation	Manages emotions when interacting online, recognizing triggers.	Reacts impulsively to online interactions, often escalating conflicts.
Understanding of Online Addiction	Recognizes signs of addiction and takes steps to limit screen time.	Engages excessively with technology, often unaware of potential addiction.
Response to Misinformation	Critically analyses and fact-checks information before reacting.	Spreads misinformation without verification, leading to confusion.
Communication Styles	Adapts communication based on audience and context for better clarity.	Communicates in a rigid manner, often leading to misunderstandings.
Empathy in Online Interactions	Demonstrates empathy, understanding the emotional states of others online.	Lacks awareness of others' feelings, leading to insensitivity in interactions.
Conflict Resolution	Uses constructive communication to resolve disagreements.	Engages in negative interactions, often escalating conflicts.

This table outlines the differences in behaviour influenced by cyber psychological awareness compared to behaviours exhibited without that knowledge in common online situations.

Key takeaways: Your Mind Programming is a must for your aspiring and bright future

- "Excellence begins in the mind; program it with positivity, and the body will follow."

- "When you consciously choose your thoughts, you set the stage for extraordinary achievements."

- "Transform your thoughts, and you'll transform your reality; the path to excellence starts within."

- "A well-programmed mind can turn obstacles into opportunities and dreams into reality."

- "Success is not a destination but a journey fueled by the power of a positively programmed mind."

- "Programming your mind for excellence means believing in your potential, even when the world tells you otherwise."

- "Every thought is a seed; cultivate the ones that lead to greatness and watch your life blossom."

- Your mind is a powerful tool; use it to sculpt your future and forge your path to excellence."

- "When negativity knocks at the door, a strong mindset will keep it at bay and pave the way for success."

- "Elevate your mindset, and you'll elevate your life; excellence is a reflection of your internal dialogue."

- "The mind is the architect of your destiny; program it wisely to build a life of excellence."

- "To achieve greatness, train your mind to see possibilities where others see limitations."

- "A positive mindset is the compass that guides you through the storms of doubt towards the shores of excellence."

- "By rewiring your subconscious beliefs, you unleash a reservoir of potential waiting to be realized."

- "Success is a mindset; nurture it with empowering thoughts and witness your world transform."

Mind Programming that influences your future as bright, compelling and improved

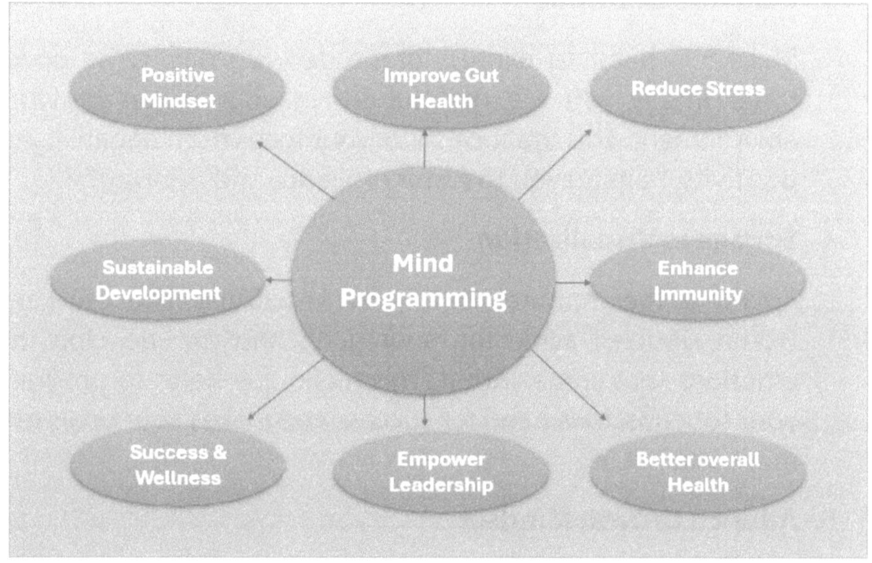

Summarizing Top 12 mind programming tips that you can incorporate into your daily routine to achieve remarkable career success. Thus these will become subconscious habit to create different outlook which will enable you to change the approach of doing things differently:

1. **Set Clear Intentions**

   Start each day by defining your intentions. Take a few moments to visualize what you want to achieve that day, whether it's completing a project, enhancing a skill, or improving a relationship at work. Setting clear intentions aligns your mindset with your goals and helps you stay focused.

2. **Practice Affirmations**

   Use positive affirmations to reshape your beliefs and boost your confidence. Create affirmations that resonate with your career goals, such as "I am capable of achieving great things" or "I attract success in my endeavours." Repeat them daily to reinforce a positive self-image.

3. **Cultivate Gratitude**

Make it a habit to express gratitude each day. Write down three things you are grateful for in your career or work environment. This practice shifts your focus from negativity to positivity, helping you to foster resilience and motivation.

4. **Engage in Visualization**

Spend a few minutes each day visualizing your success. Picture yourself achieving your goals and experiencing the emotions that come with it. This technique helps to program your subconscious mind for success and makes your goals feel more attainable.

5. **Adopt a Growth Mindset**

Embrace challenges as opportunities for growth. When faced with setbacks, remind yourself that every failure is a stepping stone to success. Adopt a mindset that values learning and resilience, which will empower you to face obstacles with confidence.

6. **Limit Negative Inputs**

Be mindful of the information you consume. Surround yourself with positive influences, whether it's uplifting podcasts, motivational books, or supportive colleagues. Limiting exposure to negativity helps to keep your mind focused on success.

7. **Establish a Daily Reflection Practice**

At the end of each day, take time to reflect on your accomplishments and areas for improvement. Write down what went well and what you can change moving forward. This practice fosters self-awareness and encourages continuous growth.

8. **Engage in Mindfulness or Meditation**

Incorporate mindfulness practices or meditation into your daily routine. Even just 10 minutes of focused breathing can help clear your mind, reduce stress, and enhance your ability to concentrate on your career objectives.

9. **Network and Build Relationships**

Make it a point to connect with colleagues and industry professionals regularly. Building a strong network opens doors to new opportunities and collaborations. Approach networking with a mindset of curiosity and willingness to learn from others.

10. **Take Consistent Action**

Break your goals into smaller, actionable steps and commit to taking consistent action every day. Establish a routine that includes these small tasks, and celebrate your progress. Consistency in action reinforces a success-oriented mindset and propels you toward your larger goals.

11. **Self Hypnosis**

Self-hypnosis is a powerful tool that can help you relax, reprogram your subconscious mind, and transform your life in various ways. Here's a step-by-step example of a self-hypnosis routine you can practice regularly before going to bed:

Example of Self-Hypnosis for Transformation

Preparation:

1. **Find a Quiet Space:** Choose a calm, quiet environment where you won't be disturbed. This could be your bedroom or a comfortable chair in your home.

2. **Set a Timer:** Decide how long you want to practice self-hypnosis (typically 15-30 minutes) and set a timer to avoid interruptions.

3. **Comfortable Position:** Sit or lie down comfortably. Ensure your body is relaxed, with your arms resting at your sides or on your lap.

Induction:

1. **Deep Breathing:** Close your eyes and take a few deep breaths. Inhale deeply through your nose, hold for a moment, and exhale slowly through your mouth. Repeat this three to five times to calm your mind and body.

2. **Progressive Relaxation:** Gradually relax each part of your body, starting from your toes and moving up to your head. Imagine each part of your body becoming heavy and relaxed. For example:

   - "Feel your toes relax… your feet… your ankles… your calves… your thighs…"

3. **Count Down:** Visualize yourself descending an elevator. With each step down, feel yourself sinking deeper into relaxation. Count down from 10 to 1, telling yourself that with each number, you are becoming more relaxed.

Suggestion Phase:

1. **Positive Affirmations:** Once you feel deeply relaxed, start repeating positive affirmations or suggestions related to your transformation goals. For example:

   - "I am confident and capable of achieving my goals."

   - "I attract positive energy and opportunities."

   - "I am worthy of love and success."

2. **Visualize Success:** Picture yourself achieving your goals. Imagine a specific scenario where you feel successful, confident, and happy. Engage all your senses in this visualization—see the colours, hear the sounds, feel the emotions associated with your success.

3. **Reinforce the Suggestions:** Repeat your affirmations mentally while visualizing success. You can say:

- "Every day, in every way, I am getting better and better."

- "I embrace change and welcome new opportunities."

Return to Awareness:

1. **Count Up:** To conclude your session, count up from 1 to 5, telling yourself that when you reach 5, you will feel refreshed, alert, and ready to sleep peacefully.

- "As I count to 5, I will awaken with energy and positivity."

2. **Open Your Eyes:** Gently open your eyes when you reach 5, and take a moment to notice how relaxed and calm you feel.

3. **Reflect:** Take a moment to reflect on your experience. Acknowledge any feelings or thoughts that came up during the process.

Tips for Practice:

- **Consistency:** Practice this self-hypnosis routine nightly for best results.

- **Record Your Affirmations:** Consider recording your affirmations in your voice and playing them during your session.

- **Stay Patient:** Transformation takes time; be patient with yourself and allow the process to unfold naturally.

By incorporating this self-hypnosis routine into your nightly routine, you can gradually reprogram your mind, reduce stress, and work toward your personal transformation effectively.

12. **One Minute As-If analysis**

Let's assume you became world's richest man for 1 minute. Write down what all will you do to remove pain of the society. Few examples that you can refer from following. See yourself that you are contributing on that area in one minute.

Immediate Actions to Remove Pain

1. **Allocate Resources for Emergency Relief:**

   - **Disaster Relief Fund:** I would immediately allocate a significant amount of funds to disaster relief efforts in areas affected by natural disasters, such as earthquakes, floods, or hurricanes. This would provide immediate assistance to those in dire need.

   - **Medical Aid:** Funds would be directed toward healthcare organizations to provide medical assistance, supplies, and vaccinations to underserved populations facing health crises.

2. **Invest in Education:**

   - **Scholarship Programs:** Establish scholarships for underprivileged children worldwide, ensuring they have access to quality education and the resources needed to thrive.

   - **Infrastructure Development:** Invest in building schools in remote or impoverished areas, providing children with a safe and nurturing environment to learn.

3. **Support Food Security Initiatives:**

   - **Food Banks:** Donate funds to food banks and organizations that provide meals to those experiencing hunger. I would aim to double their capacity to meet immediate needs.

   - **Sustainable Farming:** Invest in sustainable farming initiatives that empower local farmers and improve food production in food-insecure regions.

4. **Promote Clean Water Access:**

   - **Water Purification Projects:** Allocate funds for clean water initiatives, such as building wells and water purification systems in areas without access to clean drinking water.

- **Sanitation Facilities:** Invest in building sanitation facilities to promote hygiene and reduce waterborne diseases.

5. **Address Mental Health:**

- **Mental Health Support Programs:** Fund mental health organizations that provide counselling and support to those suffering from trauma, anxiety, or depression, particularly in conflict or disaster-stricken areas.

6. **Environmental Conservation:**

- **Tree Planting Campaigns:** Initiate global tree planting campaigns to combat climate change, improve air quality, and enhance biodiversity.

- **Renewable Energy Projects:** Invest in renewable energy projects to provide sustainable energy solutions to communities reliant on fossil fuels.

7. **Empower Local Communities:**

- **Microloans for Small Businesses:** Create a microloan program to help aspiring entrepreneurs in developing regions start their own businesses, fostering economic growth and self-sufficiency.

- **Skill Development Programs:** Fund skill development and vocational training programs to empower individuals with the skills needed to secure stable employment.

By integrating these mind programming tips into your daily routine, you can cultivate a mindset that fosters resilience, positivity, and a clear vision for your career success. Start small, remain committed, and watch how these practices transform your professional life!

Quick Reference: Mind Programming Tools vs Feature mapping

Mind Programming Technique	Description	Benefits for Subconscious Mind
Affirmations	Positive statements repeated regularly to install beliefs in the subconscious mind.	- Increases self-esteem - Shifts negative thought patterns - Encourages a positive mindset
Visualization	Creating mental images of desired outcomes to manifest goals and aspirations.	- Enhances motivation - Strengthens focus - Improves confidence in achieving goals
Meditation	A practice of focusing the mind to achieve a mentally clear and emotionally calm state.	- Reduces stress and anxiety - Enhances self-awareness - Promotes mental clarity
Self-Hypnosis	A state of focused attention where individuals can reprogram their subconscious thoughts and beliefs.	- Reduces negative beliefs - Increases relaxation - Aids in habit formation
Neuro-Linguistic Programming (NLP)	Techniques that explore the connection between neurological processes, language, and behavioural patterns.	- Improves communication skills - Enhances emotional intelligence - Breaks negative habits
Gratitude Journaling	Writing down things you are grateful for to shift focus from negativity to positivity.	- Boosts mood and happiness - Enhances perspective - Reinforces positive thinking

Mind Programming Technique	Description	Benefits for Subconscious Mind
Subliminal Messaging	Audio or visual messages presented below the threshold of conscious perception to influence behaviour.	- Installs positive beliefs subconsciously - Enhances motivation and confidence - Reduces anxiety levels
Mindfulness Practices	Techniques that promote awareness and focus on the present moment without judgment.	- Improves emotional regulation - Reduces stress and anxiety - Enhances overall well-being
Breathwork	Controlled breathing techniques to promote relaxation and focus.	- Reduces stress response - Increases mental clarity - Enhances emotional resilience
Vision Boards	A collage of images and affirmations representing goals and dreams.	- Clarifies goals - Increases motivation - Strengthens commitment to goals

With the mind programming your subconscious mind will be boosted enough to follow H5 Pathway as below to become the best and high performer to get consistent success in personal and professional life and to create positive vibes for others to follow and grow together. This will create positive impact on the development of Mind for better living for aspiring tomorrow.

Mind Map: Habit Formula for Success (H5 Pathway)

Central Idea: Happiness, High Aim, Hope, Hard Work, High Performance

1. **Happiness**

   - **Definition**: A state of well-being and contentment.

- **Key Aspects**:
  - Gratitude
  - Positive Relationships
  - Self-Care
- **Connections**:
  - Increases motivation
  - Boosts creativity
  - Enhances resilience

2. **High Aim**

   - **Definition**: Setting ambitious and challenging goals.
   - **Key Aspects**:
     - Vision and Purpose
     - Long-Term Planning
     - SMART Goals (Specific, Measurable, Achievable, Relevant, Time-bound)
   - **Connections**:
     - Provides direction
     - Fuels motivation
     - Aligns efforts with values

3. **Hope**

   - **Definition**: The belief in a positive outcome and the motivation to pursue goals.
   - **Key Aspects**:
     - Optimism
     - Positive Mindset
     - Resilience in Adversity

- **Connections**:
    - Drives persistence
    - Encourages problem-solving
    - Enhances emotional strength

4. **Hard Work**

   - **Definition**: Diligent effort and perseverance in pursuing goals.

   - **Key Aspects**:
       - Discipline
       - Time Management
       - Consistency

   - **Connections**:
       - Builds skills and experience
       - Increases confidence
       - Leads to mastery and success

5. **High Performance**

   - **Definition**: Achieving excellence and optimal results in activities.

   - **Key Aspects**:
       - Continuous Improvement
       - Feedback and Adaptation
       - Collaboration and Teamwork

   - **Connections**:
       - Enhances productivity
       - Drives innovation
       - Inspires others

Connecting Elements

- **Interdependencies**:
  - Happiness boosts motivation and resilience for hard work.
  - High aim sets the direction and purpose that fuels hope.
  - Hope encourages hard work, which leads to high performance.
  - High performance reinforces happiness through achievement.

Conclusion

By cultivating **Happiness**, setting **High Aims**, fostering **Hope**, committing to **Hard Work**, and striving for **High Performance**, individuals can create a powerful habit formula that leads to personal and professional success.

It is our moral duty and the key responsibility to make our world a better place for living. A must do positive affirmation before starting your work each day will help to align our every action harmless to the society and create ecological aspiration for daily living.

Morning Affirmation for Environmental Stewardship and Positive Impact

"Today, I commit to living in harmony with the Earth. Every choice I make contributes to a cleaner, greener world. I am mindful of the resources I use, the waste I create, and the impact I leave behind.

I choose sustainable actions, reducing harm to the environment with each step I take. I conserve energy, water, and materials, knowing that small actions lead to great change. My decisions today will positively influence future generations.

I am part of the solution. I will inspire others through my actions and lead by example. I breathe in the vitality of nature, and I breathe out love and respect for this planet. I choose to nurture the Earth, just as it nurtures me.

Together, we create a cleaner, healthier world. My heart is open to innovation and creativity for sustainability. My mind is focused on zero harm, and my spirit is aligned with the well-being of the planet. I am grateful for the Earth and dedicate my energy to protecting it.

Today, I am an environmental steward, contributing to a better, kinder, and greener planet."

Key Elements of the Affirmation:

- **Mindfulness**: Awareness of actions and their impact on the environment.

- **Sustainability**: Focus on conserving resources and choosing eco-friendly options.

- **Inspiration**: A commitment to lead by example and influence others positively.

- **Responsibility**: Personal accountability in protecting the environment and promoting zero harm.

- **Gratitude**: Appreciation for the Earth and a sense of duty to care for it.

The Life may throw you in a pond. you may be pushed hard and go completely into deep water. but you are unstoppable. it is your inner mind, skill, energy, strength, faith to inner ability, gratitude to almighty and blessings of well-wishers by which you will try in full force to sink again, rise again, swim again and come to the land being powerful and mindful. The key life lesson is not only to bounce back but to bounce forward again and again and show the life you are powerful enough to make something new from broken situation.

The Unstoppable Force Within: A Story of Resilience and Power

Once upon a time, in a small village surrounded by mountains and rivers, there lived a young man named **Arjun**. From an early age, Arjun was known for his **enthusiasm, determination, and**

kindness. He had big dreams of building a life full of purpose, success, and joy. Despite growing up in a humble background, he believed that with hard work and dedication, he could carve out a future that would make his family and village proud.

Arjun was also passionate about swimming, often seen practicing in the nearby river. His father had taught him to swim, saying, "Life is like this river, my son. Sometimes it will flow gently, and sometimes it will try to pull you under with its strong currents. But if you learn to swim with strength and faith, you will always reach the shore."

As the years passed, Arjun's dreams grew bigger. He moved to the city to pursue his studies and started a small business. But as life often does, it threw him into an unexpected **storm**.

The Fall into the Deep Waters of Life

One day, after months of hard work and pouring all his savings into his business, Arjun's dream came crashing down. A sudden economic downturn hit the city, and his small business collapsed. He lost everything—his savings, his reputation, and even his confidence. His debts piled up, and he felt like he had been tossed into a deep, dark pond where the currents were too strong to swim against. The weight of failure dragged him down, and despair began to cloud his once bright vision.

To make matters worse, he received a call that his father had fallen seriously ill. Arjun returned to his village, heartbroken and feeling defeated. He stood by the river where he had once practiced swimming as a child. The river's waters were calm, but Arjun felt nothing but chaos inside.

"Why me?" he thought. "Why do I always end up drowning in life's challenges? I gave everything I had, and it still wasn't enough."

The Turning Point: Faith and Inner Power

One evening, as Arjun sat by the riverbank, his elderly father, now weak but wise, came to sit beside him. Sensing his son's despair, the father spoke softly:

"Arjun, do you remember what I taught you about swimming? Life may throw you into deep waters, and it may even push you under, but you have something within you that will always bring you back to the surface. It's not just your skill—it's your **inner mind**, your **strength**, and your **faith**. You are unstoppable, my son. The river doesn't defeat you; it teaches you. And when you rise again, you don't just bounce back to where you were. You bounce forward—stronger, wiser, and more powerful."

His father's words echoed in his heart, and something inside him began to shift. Arjun realized that his failure, while painful, was not the end of his story. It was merely a lesson, a temporary dip in the waters of life. The more he thought about it, the more he felt a deep **determination** growing within him.

He remembered all the times he had struggled in the river, how the currents had tried to pull him under, and how he had used his strength, his technique, and his **faith** to rise above. Life was no different.

Arjun made a promise to himself that night. **He would rise.** Not just to where he had been before but far beyond it. He would use the experience of failure as a springboard to leap toward his future with even more vigor, skill, and wisdom.

Bouncing Forward: From Failure to Success

Arjun returned to the city, but this time he came back with a **different mindset**. He wasn't trying to rebuild what he had lost. Instead, he embraced the idea of **bouncing forward**—using every setback as an opportunity to grow, learn, and evolve.

He started a new business, this time in a field he was passionate about and more knowledgeable in. He applied the lessons he had learned from his first failure—managing his finances better, focusing on building relationships, and creating a solid foundation for long-term growth.

Along the way, Arjun faced new challenges, but each time, he remembered the words of his father. Instead of feeling defeated, he welcomed challenges as part of his journey. He would get knocked down at times, but he would **rise stronger each time**, armed with more experience, resilience, and the belief that he was **unstoppable**.

As the months went by, his business grew, and his reputation began to spread. People admired his perseverance and positive attitude, even in the face of adversity. Arjun didn't just build a successful business—he built a **life filled with purpose, gratitude, and power**.

His story of bouncing forward, not just back, became an inspiration to many. He shared his journey openly, teaching others that no matter how deep the waters of life may seem, with **inner strength, skill, and faith**, anyone can rise to the surface and swim to new shores.

Key Life Lessons: Bounce Forward, Not Just Back

1. **Life Will Throw You Into the Pond**:

   - Life is full of challenges, failures, and unexpected setbacks. Sometimes, we are pushed into the deep waters where we feel like we're drowning. But these moments are opportunities to grow, not reasons to give up.

2. **Inner Strength and Faith Are Your Lifeline**:

   - What allows you to rise from the depths is your **inner strength**, your **faith in your abilities**, and your belief that you can overcome any obstacle. These qualities are like the lifeline that keeps you afloat even when the current is strong.

3. **Bounce Forward, Not Just Back**:

   - When we face failure, the goal isn't just to recover and return to where we were before. True success comes from **bouncing forward**, using the setback as a springboard to reach even greater heights. Each failure is a lesson that can propel you toward a stronger and more fulfilled version of yourself.

4. **Action with Purpose**:

- Arjun didn't just rely on faith alone. He took **conscious, purposeful action** to build a better life. Similarly, when life challenges us, we need to take practical steps, learn from our experiences, and apply our wisdom to keep moving forward.

5. **Mindfulness and Gratitude**:

- Through all his struggles, Arjun remained **mindful** of the lessons he was learning. He practiced **gratitude** for the small wins and the growth that each challenge brought him. This mindset shift allowed him to embrace life's ups and downs with resilience.

Conclusion: You Are Unstoppable

Like Arjun, each of us has the power to rise above the deepest waters of life. We may be knocked down, thrown into the pond, or feel as if we're sinking, but our **inner strength, skill, and faith** can always bring us back to the surface. When we learn to **bounce forward**, rather than just back, we unlock our true potential and show life that we are truly **unstoppable**.

Remember, life is not about avoiding the storms—it's about learning to swim through them, grow stronger, and rise higher every time you face adversity. Your story is not defined by how many times you fall but by how many times you **rise** and move **forward** with more power and purpose.

You are a champion, you are a great player. one failure is not impacting you rather it is giving learning to contribute more to win again. You have a great spirit of winner.

The Champion's Mindset: A Story of Winning Against All Odds

Once upon a time, in a small town, there was a young athlete named **Ravi**. From an early age, he had shown a natural talent for **running**. He loved the feeling of wind rushing past him and the sound of his feet hitting the ground with rhythmic precision. His dream was to represent his country in the **100-meter sprint** at the national level and, one day, even in the Olympics.

Ravi trained relentlessly every day, waking up before dawn to practice at the local track. He was fast, and as he grew older, his speed improved, earning him a reputation as one of the top young runners in his region. With each race, his confidence soared. Everyone in the town believed he was destined for greatness.

However, life had its own plans. At the most important regional championship, the one that would determine if he would qualify for nationals, **Ravi stumbled**. As he was sprinting full-speed toward the finish line, he made a slight misstep, and before he knew it, he tripped and fell just a few meters away from victory. He hit the ground hard, watching helplessly as the other runners sped past him.

The crowd gasped in shock. Ravi's dream of qualifying for nationals had vanished in that split second. He lay there on the track, physically bruised and emotionally shattered. This was his moment, and he had lost it. His confidence, which had once been unshakable, now felt fragile. For the first time, doubt crept into his mind.

"Maybe I'm not as good as I thought," he said to himself. "Maybe I don't have what it takes to be a champion."

The Choice: Stay Down or Rise

For days after the race, Ravi couldn't bring himself to return to the track. He avoided his friends and teammates, ashamed of his failure. But deep down, he knew this wasn't who he was. **Winners don't give up.** Champions don't let one setback define them.

One evening, as Ravi sat in his room reflecting on his fall, his coach came to visit him. His coach had been with him through every win, every tough practice, and every struggle. Seeing Ravi so broken was difficult, but the coach knew this was an important moment in the young athlete's journey.

"Ravi," the coach said, "you may have fallen in that race, but what matters is how you rise from it. Champions aren't defined by how they win; they're defined by how they handle failure. **One failure does not define you.** It teaches you. You can either let this moment defeat you, or you can use it to make you stronger, faster, and more determined than ever. The real race, Ravi, isn't on the track—it's in your mind."

Ravi listened, and slowly, something stirred within him. He realized that the fall, while painful, was not the end of his story. It was a **lesson**—an opportunity to grow and become even better. He hadn't lost his ability to run. What he needed now was to rebuild his mindset.

The Rebuilding: Winning in the Mind

The next morning, Ravi woke up early, just like he always had, but this time there was something different. He wasn't chasing the victory he had lost—he was **chasing growth**. He knew that to win again, he first had to conquer his inner doubts.

- **Self-Belief**: Ravi began each day by reminding himself of his past successes and the hard work he had put in over the years. He told himself, "I am a champion, and one setback doesn't change that. Champions fall, but they rise again stronger."

- **Visualization**: He started practicing **visualization techniques**, imagining himself on the track, sprinting with perfect form, crossing the finish line with confidence. Every time he felt doubt creeping in, he would close his eyes and see himself succeeding, feeling the joy of victory.

- **Learning from Failure**: Instead of avoiding the memory of his fall, Ravi embraced it. He analysed what went wrong—not as a way to punish himself, but to learn. He worked on his footwork, his balance, and his reaction time so that the same mistake would never happen again.

- **Gratitude for the Process**: Ravi also shifted his mindset from focusing solely on the outcome to enjoying the **process**. He began to appreciate every practice session, every sprint, and every drop of sweat, knowing that each one was making him stronger.

The Comeback: Rising to Victory

Months later, Ravi had another chance to compete, this time in a smaller local event. But this race was special. It was the first time he would step back onto the track after his fall. As he stood at the starting line, he could feel the tension in his muscles, the anticipation in the air. His heart raced, but this time, it wasn't fear—it was **focus**.

The gunshot rang out, and Ravi launched himself forward with all the power and precision he had rebuilt over the months. His legs moved effortlessly, his breathing steady. He was not just running to win—he was running to prove to himself that he had risen above his failure.

As he neared the finish line, memories of his fall flashed in his mind, but he pushed them aside with a deep **sense of belief**. He crossed the line, this time upright, with the crowd cheering him on.

Ravi had won. Not just the race, but something far more important—he had won the battle within his own mind. He had learned that a **winning mindset** isn't about always being victorious; it's about how you respond to setbacks. It's about believing in yourself even when the world doubts you and using every failure as a stepping stone toward success.

The Champion's Mindset: Key Lessons

1. **One Failure Doesn't Define You:**

   - Every champion faces failure. The key is not to let that failure break your spirit but to use it as a **lesson** to come back stronger. Winning is not about never falling—it's about how quickly and effectively you get back up.

2. **Winning Begins in the Mind:**

   - Before you can win on the field, on the track, or in any endeavor, you must first win in your **mind. Self-belief,** visualization, and resilience are the cornerstones of a winning mindset. Ravi's journey taught him that no external victory is possible without first overcoming the internal battles.

3. **Embrace the Process, Not Just the Outcome**:

   - True champions love the **process** of growth and improvement. Ravi learned to appreciate every step of his journey—the practices, the pain, and even the failure—because they were all part of what made him stronger.

4. **Turn Setbacks into Comebacks**:

   - Every setback is an opportunity to come back even stronger. Ravi's fall could have ended his dreams, but instead, he used it to **bounce forward** with more power and determination than ever.

5. **Resilience is Key**:

   - Champions are not the ones who never experience difficulties. They are the ones who have the resilience to get back up every time they fall. The race is not to the swiftest, but to those who keep running no matter how many times they stumble.

Conclusion: The Spirit of a Winner

Ravi's story is a reminder that a **winning mindset** is not about always coming in first or never facing defeat. It's about having the courage to rise after every fall, the resilience to keep pushing forward, and the belief in your own ability to succeed.

When you embrace failure as a part of your journey and choose to learn from it rather than be defined by it, you tap into the true spirit of a champion. **You are a great player, and one failure does not impact you**—it makes you **stronger**, more capable, and more prepared to win again.

So, when life knocks you down, remember Ravi's story. Rise with **confidence**, run with **purpose**, and let your heart remind you that you are a **champion** in the making. Keep pushing forward—because the race is far from over, and the finish line of your dreams is within reach.

An architect never cries. Being student of Lord Biswakarma Mind architect only knows to explore the unlimited possibilities and create wow result.

The Mind Architect: Transforming Broken Dreams into Great Creations

In the heart of a bustling city, where towering skyscrapers kissed the clouds, lived an architect named **Nandini**. From a young age, she was captivated by the beauty of buildings and the stories they told. Her father often shared tales of **Lord Vishwakarma**, the divine architect of the universe, who crafted magnificent structures with an unwavering vision. Inspired by these stories, Nandini decided to dedicate her life to architecture, believing that she could create spaces that transformed lives.

The Broken Dream

After years of hard work, Nandini graduated at the top of her class from a prestigious architecture school. Her dreams soared as she joined a renowned architectural firm. However, the reality of her first project was far from what she had envisioned. Tasked with designing a community centre in a struggling neighbourhood, she faced countless challenges.

The budget was limited, and the community was sceptical. Many residents had lost hope after years of neglect and broken promises. When Nandini presented her initial designs, she was met with harsh criticism. "These plans don't reflect our needs," some community members said. Others were quick to point out that they had seen too many failed projects before.

Nandini felt shattered. For the first time, her confidence wavered. The voices of doubt echoed in her mind, and she began to question her abilities. In a moment of despair, she thought, "Maybe I'm not cut out for this. Maybe I can't make a difference."

The Turning Point: Rediscovering the Architect Within

One evening, feeling defeated, Nandini wandered through the city, searching for inspiration. As she strolled, she came across a dilapidated old building covered in vines and graffiti. Despite its broken state, it held an undeniable charm. She imagined the stories it had witnessed, the lives it had touched. In that moment, something sparked within her.

Nandini remembered the teachings of **Lord Vishwakarma**, who believed in exploring **unlimited possibilities**. She realized that to create something beautiful, she needed to see beyond the brokenness. Instead of viewing her project as a burden, she decided to approach it as an opportunity to **transform**.

The Process of Creation: Mind Power and Skilful Action

Nandini returned to her drafting table with a renewed spirit. She shifted her perspective and focused on the community's needs. Instead of imposing her vision, she began to **listen** to the residents. She held meetings, gathered ideas, and encouraged everyone to share their thoughts.

Empathy and Collaboration: By fostering an open dialogue, Nandini learned about the dreams and aspirations of the community. She discovered that they didn't just want a building; they wanted a space that reflected their **identity** and brought people together.

Visualization: Inspired by her conversations, she began to visualize a vibrant community centre. In her mind, it transformed from a mere structure into a **living space** where laughter, art, and connection thrived. She envisioned gardens, open areas for activities, and art installations that celebrated the community's culture.

Design and Planning: Armed with newfound knowledge and enthusiasm, Nandini crafted a new design that embraced sustainability and innovation. She incorporated **natural light, green spaces**, and **multifunctional areas** that could adapt to various community needs. Every decision was guided by the community's voice and her vision to create a haven of hope.

The Transformation: From Broken to Great Creation

Months of hard work and collaboration paid off. The day of the unveiling arrived, and the community centre stood tall, a testament to what could be achieved when minds and hearts aligned.

When Nandini presented her design, the residents marvelled at the transformation. The once broken land was now a vibrant space filled with colours, creativity, and energy. The community centre featured an **art gallery** showcasing local artists, a **theatre** for performances, and a **garden** for children to play and families to gather.

Tears of joy filled the eyes of the residents as they stepped inside, and Nandini felt a sense of fulfilment that she had never experienced before. The centre was not just a building; it was a **symbol of resilience**, creativity, and hope.

Key Lessons from Nandini's Journey

1. **See Beyond the Brokenness**: Just as Nandini transformed a broken community into a thriving space, we too can learn to see beyond our setbacks. Every challenge holds the potential for growth and change.

2. **Empathy is Powerful**: Understanding the needs and dreams of others can lead to innovative solutions. By listening and collaborating, we can create results that resonate with people and truly make a difference.

3. **Visualize Your Success**: Harness the power of visualization. Imagine the success you wish to achieve. Envision your dreams as if they are already reality, and let that vision guide your actions.

4. **Skilful Action is Key**: Dreams need a solid foundation of action. It's not enough to dream; we must take steps to bring those dreams to life. This includes planning, designing, and being open to feedback.

5. **Celebrate Community**: Great creations are often the result of collective effort. By embracing collaboration and community

input, we can build something that reflects the shared values and aspirations of many.

Conclusion: The Mind Architect's Legacy

Nandini's story is a powerful reminder that true architects, like **Lord Vishwakarma**, don't simply build structures; they build **dreams** and **possibilities**. They know that even the most broken situations can be transformed into great creations through **mind power**, **empathy**, and **skillful action.**

In the end, Nandini didn't just create a community centre; she ignited a movement. A movement where individuals began to see the potential in themselves and in each other, inspired to explore the **unlimited possibilities** around them.

Just as she transformed a community's broken dreams into a beautiful reality, we all have the power to turn our challenges into **great creations**. With the right mindset, anything is possible. Let us embrace our inner architects and shape a world that reflects the beauty of our collective dreams.

The real life story of **Raj**, a young man from a modest background. He grew up in a small town with limited opportunities but always had big dreams of building a successful career and creating a better future for himself and his family. Despite facing financial constraints and societal pressures, Raj believed that his **mindpower**—his ability to think positively, take conscious action, and stay committed—would be the key to transforming his life.

The Early Struggles

Raj faced many challenges throughout his journey. His family could barely afford his education, and he had to take up part-time jobs while studying to support his expenses. He saw others with more resources, connections, and privileges succeed while he had to constantly fight against the odds. It would have been easy to give in to despair, but Raj understood that external circumstances could only control so much. He believed in the power of his **mindset**, and this belief became his guiding light.

Step 1: Mindset Shift

Raj's first step toward sustainable growth was his realization that **everything begins in the mind**. He began practicing **mindfulness** to become aware of his thoughts and emotions. He learned that negative thinking—self-doubt, fear, and frustration—would block his path to success. So, he reprogrammed his mind using **affirmations** and **visualization**.

- **Daily affirmations**: Every morning, Raj would start his day with affirmations such as:

    - "I am capable of achieving great things."

    - "I am resilient, focused, and determined to succeed."

    - "The challenges I face are opportunities for growth."

- **Visualization**: Raj would spend time visualizing his future self—a confident, successful leader in his chosen field. He would imagine himself walking into his dream office, contributing to a project, and being recognized for his hard work. Visualization helped him feel as though his goals were already within reach, allowing him to act with **confidence and purpose**.

Step 2: Learning and Growth Mindset

Raj knew that to become the best, he needed to continuously grow. He embraced a **growth mindset**, understanding that failures were part of the journey and not something to be feared. Every setback became a learning opportunity.

- **Learning from failure**: When Raj didn't get a job offer after a series of interviews, he didn't see it as a sign of his inadequacy. Instead, he analyzed what went wrong and where he could improve. He took feedback constructively, working on his communication skills and improving his technical knowledge. Over time, his resilience grew, and his ability to handle rejection strengthened.

- **Investing in self-education**: Raj made a habit of reading self-development books, listening to podcasts by successful leaders, and taking online courses in his field. He understood that **knowledge and skills** were his best investment for the future. His mind was like a garden, and he continuously planted seeds of learning that would bear fruit in the years to come.

Step 3: Harnessing the Law of Attraction

Raj used the **Law of Attraction** to bring his dreams closer to reality. He believed that by focusing on **positive outcomes** and radiating the right energy, he could attract opportunities that aligned with his vision.

- **Gratitude practice**: Raj kept a **gratitude journal** where he wrote down three things he was grateful for every day. This practice kept his mindset positive, making him more open to opportunities and possibilities.

- **Visualization for job opportunities**: When Raj applied for jobs, he didn't just send in his resume and hope for the best. He would sit quietly and **visualize himself getting the offer**, seeing the congratulatory emails, and imagining his excitement. This mental rehearsal helped him stay optimistic and prepared.

Step 4: Creating Opportunities Through Action

Raj understood that **mindpower alone** isn't enough without taking action. His **daily habits** were geared toward making progress on his goals. He maintained discipline, often working late nights after his part-time job to develop skills that would make him stand out.

- **Networking and relationships**: Raj was proactive about building relationships with mentors, colleagues, and industry professionals. He understood that success wasn't a solo journey and that **collaborating** with others would open doors.

- **Consistency and resilience**: Raj stayed consistent with his efforts, even when progress seemed slow. His **persistence** helped him stay the course, and he knew that every small action contributed to the larger goal of a brighter future.

Step 5: The Breakthrough Moment

After years of hard work, self-discipline, and using the power of his mind, Raj landed a job at a top multinational company. Not only did he break free from the financial challenges of his past, but his **positive mindset and resilience** also made him a top performer within the company.

- **Promotions and recognition**: His unique approach to challenges, optimism, and growth mindset helped him rise through the ranks quickly. He was recognized not just for his technical skills but also for his ability to **stay calm under pressure** and solve complex problems with creativity and innovation.

- **Sustaining growth**: Raj continued to practice mindfulness, visualization, and self-reflection, ensuring that he stayed grounded as his success grew. He recognized that **sustainable growth** isn't about short-term wins but about consistent **self-improvement** and a clear vision of the future.

Step 6: Giving Back

Now in a leadership role, Raj became a mentor to others who were in situations similar to his earlier life. He taught them how to leverage their mindpower to achieve success, emphasizing that growth starts from within. Raj's **mindset tools**—gratitude, visualization, mindfulness, and the law of attraction—became a foundation for others to learn from.

The Key Life Lessons for Sustainable Growth

1. **Master Your Mind**: The external world is a reflection of your internal state. By mastering your thoughts, you can shape your reality. Positive thinking, visualization, and affirmations are powerful tools for manifesting success.

2. **Growth Mindset**: Don't fear failure—it's a stepping stone to greatness. Learn from setbacks, stay persistent, and trust that every challenge builds resilience.

3. **Daily Action**: Consistent, focused action is the key to achieving long-term success. Progress may be slow at times, but it's the steady effort that creates sustainable growth.

4. **Attract What You Focus On**: The energy you put out into the world is what you'll attract. Focus on your goals, maintain gratitude, and believe in your ability to succeed.

5. **Resilience and Gratitude**: Stay resilient, and practice gratitude even during tough times. Gratitude keeps you positive and motivates you to keep moving forward.

Conclusion: Bouncing Forward, Not Just Back

Raj's story is an inspiring example of how **mindpower** can turn dreams into reality. Through his mindset, continuous learning, and commitment to daily action, he transformed from a struggling student to a thriving leader. His journey reflects that **sustainable growth** isn't a sudden leap, but the result of **consistent mental discipline, resilience**, and **a vision for the future**. No matter how difficult the circumstances, the power of the mind can help anyone create a **bright future** and become the best version of themselves.

Happy Reading and Good Luck for your true-Life transformation!

9 798896 103554